Prai

All the Women

"These perfectly chosen Woman Words are a healing s   om new sistahs, now my family, for whom I will fight, with whom I will stand and because of whom, I will build."
—Alfre Woodard, Actor, Activist

"In this beautifully composed chorus of sixty-nine voices, Deborah Santana has given us a fascinating and compelling anthology of essays by women of color. Each of these brief, poignant pieces illuminates one woman's negotiation between her aspirations and the forces that would constrict her dreams. The contributors write prophetically of their struggles and triumphs in the early years of the twenty-first century, challenging the reader with their revelations. *All the Women in My Family Sing* is essential reading."
—Henry Louis Gates, Jr., Alphonse Fletcher University Professor, Harvard University

"This mosaic of women's voices inspires, heals, and offers hope in dark times. A memorable collection that will make your heart sing."
—Ruth Behar, author of *Lucky Broken Girl*

"Santana has compiled a truly beautiful array of voices here, with hope being the common note they all hit and sustain. This is an accessible, teachable and cherishable collection."
—Dave Eggers, author of *The Circle* and founder of ScholarMatch and Voice of Witness

"Whether the words pour forth like jazz or salsa, indie rock or R&B, indigenous drums, kotos, maracas, or the sheng, they all ring out in stories of ancestry, forgiveness, struggle and victory. It is an eclectic collection where you may hear both new and familiar songs which seem to reflect Lucille Clifton's request that we 'celebrate' with her the fact that each woman writer has survived, indeed flourished through rivers bridged, mountains climbed or oceans navigated despite hurricane storms."
—devorah major, poet/novelist/essayist, San Francisco's 3rd Poet Laureate

"In all these fierce and anthemic pieces we see the true face of womanhood, in all its colors."
—Farai Chidea, Author of *The Color of Our Future* and *The Episodic Career*

"*All The Women in My Family Sing* is a bold, evocative anthology that cannot be read without engaging your full heart. The essays about identity, family, love, acceptance and fear are a testament to the times, unrelenting in their examination of personal and global pain. There's triumph here and the resilience specific to the female spirit."
—Nichelle Tramble Spellman, Author of *The Dying Ground* and *The Last King*, Writer/Producer of *The Good Wife* and *Justified*

"A revolutionary primer for all us well-meaning white folks who haven't a clue about what it's like to be a woman of color."
—Susan Gabriel, Author of *Trueluck Summer*

"The voices of women leading and stirring and instigating lasting magic toward a more just, peaceful and sustainable world remind us that there is hope even when we feel most disheartened…a symphony for troubled times!"
—Kavita N. Ramdas, Feminist philanthropist activist, Principal at KNR Sisters and Strategy Advisor, MADRE

"The voices in *All the Women in My Family Sing* intermingle to produce a harmony of moving experiences that taps into the rhythm of our collective desires for a more compassionate world."
—Nancy Wilson, an American singer with more than seventy albums, and three Grammy Awards

"*All the Women in My Family Sing* encompasses everything that is important about women of color—our diversity, sacrifice, crusade for equality, and the impact we have made on the lives of others."
—Jenny Bach, California Democratic Party Secretary

"This moving anthology of essays by women of color illuminates the struggles, traditions, and life views of women at the dawn of the 21st century. The 69 authors grapple with identity, belonging, self-esteem, and sexuality, among other topics."
—*Publishers Weekly*

"*All the Women in my Family Sing* is a very thoughtful, well-curated collection of personal essays written by women of color, spanning a variety of themes and experiences. It shares

stories that spark a conversation about the human experience, rather than just bringing tales about what it's like to struggle as a woman of color."
—Reviewed by Lenna Stites, City Book Review (for San Francisco, Manhattan and Seattle)

"Impassioned writers bearing witness to survival, creativity, and hope."
—Kirkus

All the Women in
My Family Sing

All the Women in My Family Sing

Women Write the World—
Essays on Equality, Justice, and Freedom

EDITED BY
DEBORAH SANTANA

NOTHING
BUT THE
TRUTH,
LLC

SAN FRANCISCO

Published in 2018 by Nothing But The Truth Publishing, LLC
NothingButtheTruth.com
Nothing But The Truth name and logo are trademarks of Nothing But The Truth Publishing, LLC.

LIBRARY OF CONGRESS CATALOGING-IN-PUBLICATION DATA
All the Women in My Family Sing:
Women Write the World—Essays on Equality, Justice, and Freedom
Edited by Deborah Santana

Library of Congress Control Number: 2017909810

ISBN: 9780997296211 (Paperback)
ISBN: 9780997296228 (E-Book)

Printed in the United States of America
2018
Cover design by Grace Jang
First Edition

Contents

Trailblazers, Hell-Raisers, and Stargazers: Careers, Work, and Worth

With Liberty and Justice for All: The Struggle for Social Justice and Equality

In a Family Way:
Family and Friendship

But Beautiful...
The Beauty Myth

The Cure for What Ails You:
Transcending Illness and Trauma

A Woman's Journey Is Never Done:
Traveling Far, Wide, and Deep

Foreword

by Deborah Santana

My mother was a fiery Irish-English feminist born in Texas. She met my African American father performing in a jazz club in Chicago in the 1940s and they married shortly after. My sister and I bounded into this world as biracial brown babies madly adored by both sides of our family and were taught that people of gentleness and faith can change the world.

DNA, the hereditary material in all humans and organisms, is made of more than three million chemical bases. More than 99 percent of these bases are the same in all people.* Through genetics, our mother and father determine the traits that determine eye color, hair texture, and the characteristics that connect us to our nuclear family. But our universal need for food and water, the search for happiness, love and prosperity belong to everyone. Yet, we often only regard and respect the people and communities within our simplified definition of family and ethnic heritage, alienating ourselves from our sisters and brothers on this planet we call home.

All the Women in My Family Sing is a tribute to the many voices of women in a chorus of cultural refrains. Each essay is a personal story about the victories and challenges women face every day as innovators, artists, CEOs, teachers and

---

* U.S. National Library of Medicine, https://ghr.nlm.nih.gov/primer/basics/dna

adventurers. All of the essays reveal how glorious it is to live authentically in our identities.

ᕬ

In the seminal anthology *this bridge we call home*, Gloria Anzaldúa writes: "Bridges are thresholds to other realities, archetypal, primal symbols of shifting consciousness. They are passageways, conduits and connectors that connote transitioning, crossing borders, and changing perspectives."*

To change inequality and heal the wounds of those who have been marginalized or not seen, we must use our heads to understand, our hearts to embrace and our hands to connect with those whose paths we have not walked. The essays in *All the Women in My Family Sing* give readers a clear view into different life views, practices, languages and traditions. The writers create a bridge between worlds we know very well and those we do not, encouraging us to open our hearts and minds to dismantle any barriers keeping us from unanimity.

These essays are a conversation to educate and illumine as well as to give hope, strength, power and joy. Marian Wright Edelman writes in her essay: Women "are anchor reminders of a great heritage of strength, courage, faith and belief in the equality of women and people of every color. And they are role models for the tireless and indispensable behind-the-scenes and frontline leaders whose strength and determination are desperately needed in every generation—especially right now."

In the three years I have worked on this anthology, since reading the first narratives that were hummed from hearts and written down, I have grown exponentially. The essays have

---

* *this bridge we call home: radical visions for transformation*, ed. Gloria E. Anzaldua and Analouise Keating (New York, NY: Routledge, 2002)

added beauty, abundance, humility and grace to my life. To read them is to travel each woman's journey and to sense what they have experienced as they summon us to sit within their awakenings.

We are each unique in our exploration of identity. We may not agree on others' definitions of our ethnicities, our genders or our beliefs because we rightfully own a personal standpoint from which we derive our value. Want Chyi writes: "I decide what it is to be Asian. An American. A punk. A writer of color, I embody the road less traveled..."

Whether we swelter in the heat of a Baghdad sun or freeze at the edge of an Arctic glacier, reading these essays offers us a chance to commune with others as we "becom[e] fluent in each other's histories."*

It is my sincere hope that the sonorous melodies of these women transport each reader to a world of inclusion and understanding.

---

* *Feminism Without Borders,* Chandra Talpade Mohanty, Duke University Press, Feb 28, 2003

Editing Identity

Cultural Identity, Gender, and Sexuality

Home Going

NATALIE BASZILE

As a boy growing up in south Louisiana, my father had an after-school job pumping gas at the local station. This was in the early 1950s. He was a poor Black boy in a small Southern town, and on hot summer days it was nothing for him to work barefoot. On his lunch breaks, he dragged a folding chair inside the station where it was cool, and for twenty minutes or half an hour, he'd take a nap, his body reclined in the folding chair, his bare feet propped up on a stack of tires or a toolbox. It should have been a restful time. Instead, the white boys who worked in the shop with him liked to play a game: They slathered liquid rubber on his bare soles and lit them on fire, then fell over themselves laughing as my dad, shocked out of sleep, scrambled to extinguish the flames. The white boys called the game "Hot Foot."

My father left Louisiana for good in 1957. The night of his high school graduation, he packed his bags and caught a ride to California with a woman from his town who needed someone to help pay for gas and take turns covering the long miles— through Texas, New Mexico, Arizona. The woman dropped my dad off at his aunt's house in Los Angeles before continuing up the coast to Oakland, where her husband worked in the shipyards. The moment my dad loaded his cardboard suitcase in the woman's trunk, he thought he would never return. He was free. He'd survived. California, he'd come to believe since he was a child watching the westbound Missouri Pacific barrel through his town, was the land of promise and opportunity. And in the decades that followed, until the year before he died, he only returned to Louisiana once a year, every spring in April or May, before it got too humid, to visit his mother and his siblings, who'd somehow forged an uneasy peace with the place and decided to stay. He always took his mother, my grandmother, Miss Rose, on a road trip—New Orleans; Grand Isle; Little Rock, Arkansas—wherever they could drive to and get back from in three days, four days tops, because that's how long he could stand to be home before the ghosts of his boyhood started to haunt him. The clock started ticking as soon as his plane touched down. There were simply too many things he hated about Louisiana: He hated the poverty and the constant threat of violence; hated the weeds and grass that grew up through cracks in the sidewalk, and the fact that practically every man in his family was a minister in a storefront church. He hated the sight of old Black men pedaling down the side of the road on bicycles when he thought they should have been driving cars. Even after he married my mother and had my sister and me, when he brought us down for the occasional holiday visit, he packed a bottle of Chivas Regal in his suitcase to self-medicate in the event our flight out of Lake Charles was delayed or, God forbid, canceled.

Yes, my father had fond childhood memories of hunting birds and small animals and fishing off the dam in the woods behind his house. Yes, he told the hilarious story about a harrowing bareback horse ride across a narrow bridge and exaggerated tales about battling with alligators. But that's where the dream of "home" ended. For my dad, going home was complicated. There was nothing nostalgic or romantic about the south Louisiana he left behind, and aside from the annual road trips he took with his mother, and later with me, he never fantasized about moving back. "Bury me someplace where I can see the Pacific Ocean," he liked to say.

Indeed, reverse migration for Black people of my father's generation wasn't as simple as picking up and going backward. The future for Black folks like my dad lay ahead of them: in Los Angeles, Oakland or Chicago, Detroit, Philadelphia or New York. The best days for Black people have always been ahead of us—tomorrow, not today, and certainly not yesterday. My father loved the people and the food of his home state—the cracklins, red beans and dried shrimp—which he carefully gathered and lovingly packed in insulated food bags to bring back to California. He wanted to carry the taste of Louisiana with him, even as he despised the place. "I knew I had to get out of the South the day they killed Emmett Till," he often said. If you were young and Black and male seeing the mangled body of Emmett Till in a magazine, I can understand why there was not enough sweet tea in the world to make you go back.

So it's no surprise that I didn't grow up knowing much about my father's Louisiana. Painful truths don't make good bedtime stories. It's no surprise that my father never sent me "home" for the summers or even for brief, unchaperoned holiday visits. Instead, I grew up in a Los Angeles suburb. I went to the mall on weekends and the beach on summer afternoons. Louisiana, for me, was Miss Rose's voice on the end of the line during the Friday afternoon phone calls my dad made from his office, the occasional letter, and the bulging box of homemade pralines, smoked sausage, dried shrimp and spicy boudin that she sent every Christmas. Louisiana was long distance. Someplace unfamiliar and almost unimaginable. So it shouldn't come as a surprise that I didn't know the place. How could I, with a father for whom the memory was so emotionally fraught? For a father who grew up in the belly of segregation and in the storm of intolerance and bigotry? Nor should it come as a surprise then, that my dad was curious and deeply troubled when I started making trips to Louisiana on my own.

I discovered Louisiana as a young adult; first when I began tagging along on my dad and grandmother's road trips, through the stories they told as we drove over backcountry roads and the things they spoke of in hushed whispers. I discovered Louisiana when I started researching my novel, a book that took more than a decade to write. I discovered Louisiana, and for the most part, I loved it. I loved the heat and the light and the music and the food. I loved that my family down there is clannish in the best sense of the word; that they welcome me whenever I appear on their doorstep, no matter how long I've been away. Home going is complicated for Black folks my dad's age, but I wonder if for younger people like me—people who grew up after Jim Crow's back was broken—it's different.

I wonder.

But I won't lie. I've witnessed Louisiana's beauty, but I've also glimpsed her ugly side. I can't forget the picture of President Obama's face someone glued to the cartoon body of Steve Urkel, the dorky '80s sitcom character, and pinned to the wall of a boat repair shop. My ears will always ring with the voice of the Cajun security guard who flagged me down on a service road outside Henderson, stuck his head through my open window and berated me, spittle and flecks of his sandwich landing on my shoulder, for driving too fast and told me I was a "long way from home" after I explained I was driving to the New Orleans airport and had only stopped to take a picture of the bayou. He threatened to arrest me, relenting only after I called him "Sir." I've met some lovely people who have opened their homes and their hearts, but I have also met some people who are invested in the myth of their white supremacy; people who will say *anything*, do *anything* if it means reminding me of what they believe should be my place.

So in the end, I suppose I have a divided heart. I love south Louisiana, but the shadow that is my dad's south Louisiana boyhood hangs over my Southern California identity. I love that I have Louisiana roots and Louisiana blood in my veins, but I love California a little bit more. And yet, unlike my father, I can entertain the fantasy of going back home. I even bought the smallest postage stamp of house in New Orleans so I'll have a place to crash. I'll visit, I'm sure of it. I'm just not sure how long I'll stay.

❧

NATALIE BASZILE, whose best-selling novel *Queen Sugar* was adapted for Oprah's TV channel by award-winning director Ava DuVernay, has an M.A. in African American Studies from UCLA and is a graduate of Warren Wilson College's MFA Program for Writers, where she was a Holden Minority Scholar. *Queen Sugar* was named one of the *San Francisco Chronicle's* Best [Books] of 2014, was long-listed for the Crook's Corner Southern Book Prize and was nominated for an NAACP Image Award. She has had residencies at the Ragdale Foundation, where she was awarded the Sylvia Clare Brown fellowship; Virginia Center for the Creative Arts; and Hedgebrook. Her nonfiction work has appeared in *Lenny Letter*; *O, The Oprah Magazine*; *The Rumpus.net*; and *The Best Women's Travel Writing, Volume 9*. She is a member of the San Francisco Writers' Grotto. Natalie lives in San Francisco.

Look Where You're Living

Maria Ramos-Chertok

I have my second child at age forty-two and already know I'll never join another moms' group again. I am unqualified to discuss the topics that seem to get the most airtime: Tahoe and skiing, home decorating, Charles Schwab, marketing as a career choice, how to make a good margarita and fashion trends. I feel like a freak.

This decision begins six weeks after my first son is born, when I move from San Francisco to Mill Valley—a town located twelve miles north of the Golden Gate Bridge. I try not to think about it too much as I hold my newborn and watch movers pack my life into boxes, pulling clear tape across the tops to shut the cardboard panels tight. It is late in December, that time of year when the sun sets early and darkness moves in for a good stretch. I am forty and a half.

Days later, sitting in the new house alone on a long white couch, breastfeeding an insatiable creature that seems determined to suck every shred of independence out of my body through the nipple, I realize I am both alone and lonely. My quandary is not a new one—no family nearby and a husband gone all day at work. Prior to that moment, I'd spent hours of time alone willingly and had known loneliness in the company of large groups. This feeling is different, because when I consider the largely white, upper-class suburb surrounding me, I thirst to find people I can relate to as a bicultural, bilingual woman who grew up in a working-class home with a racially diverse family and community. My mother worked as a waitress, the daughter of a Jewish immigrant mother from Russia and a German Jewish father. My father, a printer, emigrated from Cuba before the revolution.

Everyone told me to join a moms' group. I joined three.

The first one was with moms whose children's birthdays were around the same date. I wanted to talk about the issues I assumed only a new mother could relate to: how unappealing sex felt, how hard it was to be in a routine of newborn demands, how life as an independent woman seemed over, how the hemorrhoids from childbearing seemed more painful than the act of giving birth.

But the moms never cracked. They smiled. They were fine, their babies were sleeping like bears in hibernation, they touted recipes for making organic carrot puree baby food and mostly all had decorated their children's rooms with Pottery Barn accessories. I started to feel shame about not buying anything new for my baby—I found a used crib on Craigslist, got hand-me-downs from several friends whose kids were older and never even thought about a fresh coat of paint.

The group got worse when one mom decided she hated another mom and started excluding her from outings. I became a confidante to the ousted mother, who was astounded at the meanness and talked about leaving Marin County as soon as she could—not having experienced anything like this since junior high school. She eventually did move away.

I figured this is the way white women behave, so I decided I'd join a newly formed Latina moms' group. I was raising my son with Spanish as his first language even though my father hadn't spoken a word of Spanish to me or my siblings. I was committed to taking back my heritage and passing it along to my son. I fantasized that this group would become my lifeline. I showed up for the first group and was met with a polite hello. No *besos*, no *abrazos*, no belly laughter. I was not sure how to act in this technically Latina group that seemed as unfamiliar to me as the first one.

We continued to meet, interspersing our conversations in English with phrases to our children in Spanish. Yet, the conversations remained largely focused on the children—with mothers often appearing as attachés, there for the purpose of expounding on the finer points of their children's amazing skill and development. That group fizzled when I hosted a baby shower for one of the members who was expecting again and during the shower another member ran into the bathroom sobbing. Several whispered conversations later, we learned that she had recently had a miscarriage and was in profound emotional pain, yet she had told no one in our *madres* group.

She was lonely. She was alone.

The last group was for women over forty. I concluded that due to having a baby later on in life, my real problem was that I was not among peers. I needed mature women—women who had lived, who had wisdom; women who could talk about more than just their children. That group lasted a total of one gathering. By the time you reach forty, you're pretty much over having to act like you care about people you don't care about. Unless you fall madly in love with one of the women, you'd rather spend your limited time trying to figure out how to see the real friends you had before you had kids, who don't live close by.

When I speak to my longtime friends about the dilemma, they have one of two responses. The more hopeful of them tell me that "it will all change once [your] kids get into public school" because then I'll "become friends with the families of your sons' friends."

It happens for some that way, I concede.

The second response is from the realists.

"What do you expect? Look where you're living!"

They name what I've been trying to deny. I wanted my children to attend a "high performing" public school with rambling forests and big, green playing fields and I chose that at the expense of racial and class diversity. I feel like I'm living in some kind of lush and well-manicured, self-imposed hell.

And then my son asks me a question a few days after I read him a children's book about Rosa Parks and the Civil Rights Movement.

"Mama, if we were alive during that time, which water fountain would we have to drink from?"

I listen to his question and I feel my insides skid to a halt, like rubber burning on asphalt.

It hits me like a bolt of truth. Would his father's European Jewish heritage and my maternal Jewish heritage mean we'd enter the door for whites only? White enough to pass? Or would my dark, thick curly hair, coffee-and-cream skin and Spanish mark us as "Colored"? His question holds up a cracked mirror to my face—showing me what it looks like to be divided and broken all in one piece.

I know I must tell him that we will stand with the people who go to the river and drink from the earth, not from the construct of hatred, and that if we can't find a river we will travel far and wide, risking it all in hopes that we will meet up with others seeking a river. I want him to understand that even though we may get very, very thirsty, we must wait until we find those who want to take that journey with us. And, as I look into his thoughtful eyes, I realize I am no longer lonely and I am no longer alone. My people are out there. I will find them.

◌

MARIA RAMOS-CHERTOK grew up in Hackensack, New Jersey, in a purple house that her mother opened as a shelter for battered women and children in the 1970s. Her early life was filled with political activism and exposure to social justice issues.

An avid writer, she published her first article for teens on dating violence in 1993 and continues to write and publish in a variety of genres, including fiction, nonfiction and poetry. She leads The Butterfly Series, a writing and creative arts workshop for women who want to explore what's next in their lives.

Indian Territory

ELIANA RAMAGE

The town we come from, where I've never been and will never go, is called Dahlonega. It's from the Cherokee for yellow, yellow which means gold, gold which means "why they took our mountains when they took everything else." *Dahlonega: It's Pure Gold!* 4th Best Summer Weekend Escape. 10th Best Historic Small Town. Best Wine Town Runner-Up. Southern Dream Town.

In a box in a cabinet at my parents' house is a great-great birth certificate from the state of Georgia. And then a death certificate from Indian Territory. It's the in-between I'm angry about. I always have been.

❧

They say our history isn't in the past. A Maidu boy said that to us Native first-years in college, the first time I left home. He said our tribes weren't static, that we were part of where they went next. "If any of you become an astronaut," he said, "that's part of the story of your nation."

I didn't become an astronaut. I left for New Hampshire, Tel Aviv, Iowa. Avram left for DC, Noah for New York City. People, non-Native people, sometimes ask, "What kinds of Indian things do you do?" They're hoping for proof of something they don't understand. I don't answer because where do I start? How do I write my life into a set of images they'll recognize, make us look like the Indians they imagine?

Avram walks my parents through the American Indian Museum, over and over and over again, every time they come to see him and ask to go. Noah sprawls out on the couch with a tall glass of milk gripped between his feet, typing out an Instagram post on settler colonialism. I write fiction about a Cherokee geologist on Mars. We know where we came from, and where we left. Where we'll spend our lives going to and from and to.

∽

My cousin left home to teach English in Namibia. I was young—young enough to assume that his *Cherokee Phoenix* subscription went with him. *How fantastic,* I used to think, *our newspaper in Africa.*

He was tall. He used to sit us on his shoulders and carry us long distances on his back. The last time we ever saw him, he stood out in the yard and grabbed us by the arms. He swung us around him, faster and faster, our feet flying up into the air.

Several years after his suicide, my mother told me that her sister told her that a girl in Namibia had sent a letter to my cousin in Tennessee. She had been his student as a little girl, and waited to contact him till she turned sixteen. She wanted to know if he would marry her. She wanted him to know she could leave her family, leave her country, be a good wife.

I don't know if my aunt wrote back, if she tried to explain in one letter the life I still wonder about. I wonder if he ever carried his students, or swung them around. If their feet ever lifted off the ground.

∽

We left Georgia at gunpoint for Indian Territory. Stayed to see that taken, too, and made into Oklahoma. A generation ago we left for jobs with the VA: Texas, Georgia, Tennessee.

Being right back where you started, it's both home and not-home. Driving through the mountains in east Tennessee and western North Carolina, even as a child I felt they were beautiful, and mine.

And then: My school orchestra was asked to play at the home of Andrew Jackson, the president who slaughtered us. Field trips to the old Indian exhibits at the Tennessee State Museum, looking through the glass at Andrew Jackson's piano, Andrew Jackson's top hat. An American Hero, it says still. Everywhere its own small-town myth about a Cherokee princess throwing herself off a mountain. Everywhere.

～

When my older brother left for college, we all left with him. The five of us drove him up to school, postponing our return home with each new task. We measured the unscreened window in his dorm room and counted the floors below. We visited his mailbox. We bought him five packs of floss and a tub of peanut-butter pretzels.

Avram said he didn't need any of this.

My father said, "We forgot stain remover."

We followed him through the city. We made his bed and unwrapped his new toothbrush, said overly loud hellos to the students on his floor. He was leaving us.

We didn't drop him off until we had to, minutes before orientation. We left him on the sidewalk, the first of three children to move up north. The whole drive home, my mother said, "I hate that window. It isn't safe. I hate that window."

～

My second trip to Standing Rock ended the night before the election of a man who would, later, push a pipeline across treaty lands and lay a wreath at Jackson's tomb. I didn't know that then.

I knew Navajo tea in thick paper cups and mittened fists in the air. Pressing my weight down on the flat edge of a chef's knife like a Cree woman taught me, crushing garlic into soup for two hundred. A cold wind tearing at my forehead but my shoulders wrapped in a thick blanket, my legs stepping slow to the side, laughing in circles with Meskwaki girls at the round dance.

It was something like family. My brothers and I are grown and living far apart, none of us yet gone back to the region my family seems to always be leaving and going back to.

What I think of most, though, when I think of that camp, is leaving it. I was in the back seat of a car full of women I loved. We were Colombian, Sugpiaq, Omaha, Chickahominy, Cherokee Nation. It was all night-black around us, so many stars blocked by the roof of the car, and we were singing pop songs at the top of our lungs. We turned up the radio as loud as we could stand and we danced, sharp edges of seat belts cutting against our chests. I was not alone. I never have been.

∾

ELIANA RAMAGE is a writer, teacher and Cherokee Nation citizen. She is completing an MFA in fiction at the University of Iowa, and her stories have appeared in the *Baltimore Review,* the *Beloit Fiction Journal* and the YA anthology *(RE)Sisters.*

Klansville, USA

CAMILLE HAYES

When I was six years old, my white parents and I moved to North Carolina. If there were one thing in the whole of my life story I could change, it would be that. Considering what befell me subsequently—abuse, addiction and depression, just to name the top three—that's really saying something. But bad habits of living, even deadly ones, can be broken. They leave traces, of course. I am bruised, but the healing of those kinds of wounds can leave you stronger than you would have been if you'd not been injured. Some scar tissue knits so tight that it shores you up like bone. Some catastrophes you can learn to love.

On the other hand, if in fourth grade a boy tells you, without malice and for your edification, that you'll grow up to be ugly because *nigger women aren't pretty*—well, you'd be surprised at how much staying power a comment like that can have. Surprised that its potency seems immune to ameliorating forces like maturity and reason, the passage of time. You'll be surprised in your forties to find that you have never stopped being eight years old, devastated and ashamed.

At least, I am surprised. I don't think it's overstating it to say that I'm still in a mild state of shock from my encounter with the South, my whole life spent gently reeling from that early blow. Or maybe it was more like a bite (the Carolina woods are full of pit vipers) administering a slow-acting poison I could never quite flush from my system. It lingers in my blood to this day, corroding all my bones, breaking down my skeletal self-regard. I'm still toxic from it.

Here was my family's introduction to the South: When I was around three, on a family road trip, we were kicked out of a swimming pool in Virginia because I was, as the employee who ejected us put it, *very brown*. It was the 1970s, and while segregation wasn't technically legal, it was still the de facto organizing principle of Southern life. My parents didn't understand any of that—all they knew was that laws had been passed so things like this shouldn't be happening. They were white hippie kids from San Diego; how *could* they understand?

The official end of my parents' innocence sounded like high heels on pavement: the coarse staccato *click-clack* of the modest working-girl pumps worn by the young woman sent to kick me out of that pool. I try to picture my parents that day, sitting poolside in all their counterculture glory, beads dangling and paisley aswirl. The most pressing thing on my mother's mind was probably how she'd survive an East Coast summer. Humidity, like state-sponsored racism, was new to her. Until the very moment the high-heeled girl appeared, I doubt they'd fully thought through the move to the South; I don't think they'd considered all the implications for me. They were optimistic and young; they cleaved to the belief that ideals and right intentions could somehow accomplish what the National Guard had not. They, after all, had only the one little girl to protect. That couldn't be so hard. Surely that was not impossible.

For me, what happened at the pool is mostly anecdote—I remember it secondhand, from my parents' retelling. I can't imagine it affected me much. In my catalog of racial traumas, the pool incident doesn't really rate. But here is a parallel fact: I didn't learn to swim until I was forty. How related are these things? I resist yoking them together, the segregated pool and my failure to swim. The symmetry is too exact; it strikes me as improbable, too literary for real life. Still, it bears mentioning. At three I'm kicked out of a segregated pool, and at forty I could count on my two brown hands the number of times I'd entered a public pool since then.

It's interesting, is all I mean. Those two facts look interesting together.

Here's another interesting, almost too-cinematic reality: The state where we eventually settled, North Carolina, where my father had gotten his first job and where I would live, on and off, until I was twenty-one, was in the '70s affectionately known as "Klansville, USA," because it proudly reported the highest per-capita KKK membership of any state in the South. We didn't know this at the time, of course, although we did notice that the Klan was very *visible*, holding rallies and adopting highways, but we assumed it was like that everywhere. I didn't discover this factoid until decades later, and when I first read it, I put down the book and said aloud, "No wonder I was such a neurotic little kid." The very state was menacing me.

No wonder I couldn't sleep.

∾

Race is like that, in America: It can impact you invisibly, a contagion spreading unseen from mouth to hand, hand to mouth. You know when you're infected, but by then it's too late, and it's impossible to prove where the sickness came from. It could have been anywhere, so it might as well be nowhere.

The whole body of our nation is infected, so why name

names? But for me, at least, it's possible to locate a point of origin. Charlottesville, Virginia, by a swimming pool. Greensboro, North Carolina, at a bus stop. And it's fitting that I learned my lessons there, since the South is the original wound, left too long untreated, the place where the fester began and where the rot is most pervasive. It's the poor injured foot, empurpled, necrotic, at which the doctor looks askance: *Can we save it?*

I always knew the South was bad, and for me in particular: a biracial, mongrel girl, an eluder of categories. I always knew I'd have to leave. And when I did I was gone like a shot, never to return, never even able to visit again for more than a few days at a time. I left at a run. One way to map the irregular path of my life since then is that of flight—first north, then west, then west again—fleeing the site of my first infection.

I now cling to the edge of the continent, still wary, still giving the air an occasional sniff for that whiff of disease—the sign that it's time to move on farther still. I'm as safe now as I've ever been; as confident I won't hear racial slurs uttered in public as one can be in this country.

But the smell of contamination lingers, and the land has run out under my running feet. Hawaii would be fine, I guess. I like the beach just fine.

∽

CAMILLE HAYES is a communications professional, social change advocate, author and blogger, covering politics and women's issues at her blog, Lady Troubles (www.ladytroubles. com). Her writing has been featured by The Good Men Project,

Bitch magazine and the *Ms.* magazine blog, and she's a former columnist for the *Sacramento Bee*. Camille holds a bachelor of science in psychology and a master of arts in English. When she's not busy complaining about injustice, she likes to cook, make jam, hike and kayak near her home in San Francisco.

The Bad Black

Randi Bryant-Agenbroad

I'm not a good Black. But I used to be.

In elementary school, I was always dressed just a bit too properly, face and legs heavily lotioned, donning two pigtails, using perfect diction and grammar, never missing a day of school—even when I had a 102-degree fever.

I worked hard for good grades because I wasn't just representing me, I was representing my entire race. My mother walked me to school every day before she went to work, her hand holding mine. Every night, she sat on the edge of my bed, doing supplementary work with me as I ate sliced apples and drank cold milk. "Molding" in our house went on around the clock and throughout the year.

One summer night, when the sun had disappeared but her heat hadn't, my cousins, aunts and I sat outside of my grandparents' yellow wooden Texas rancher. Crickets provided background vocals to my aunts' tales of growing up and my cousins jumped rope and played "Go Fish." I sat between my Aunt Lena's legs—she on a higher step—as she parted my hair, greased my scalp and braided sections of hair into a beautiful woven pattern. Each tug on my hair hurt, yet being cocooned between her legs and the ritualistic movements of her hands made me feel a part of the night's haze.

Early the next morning, after a breakfast of biscuits with homemade apricot preserves, I flew home to Virginia feeling positively regal. I felt like the beautiful women from Africa I had seen in *National Geographic;* however, when I got off the plane and saw my mom's face, I was stripped of any pride I had enjoyed. Suddenly I was a different woman in *National Geographic*—breasts exposed, dusty skin, flies on my lips, eyes dead. My mom's eyes let me know immediately what her lecture told me later: Braids would not get me far in life. I never got braids again.

Instead, I was given a relaxer to turn my kinky hair straight. I started wearing my hair in a poorly feathered imitation of Farrah Fawcett's, wearing Izod shirts and blue eye shadow, and coating my lips in Bonne Bell strawberry lip gloss. I bopped along to songs by Duran Duran and The Police. I bopped along at Pat Benatar concerts and bopped through school with my white classmates. Every now and then I'd hear comments such as, "But, you aren't *really* Black," or "But you're *different.*" I never knew what I was supposed to say.

"*Thank you?*"

So I never said a word.

One night when I was thirteen years old, I went to a friend's slumber party. The five of us became a human pretzel—our bodies intertwined in one queen-sized bed. We were talking about boys and bands and gossiping about rumors from school when one of my friends, a slender, sweet-faced girl whose mother eventually became one of my teachers in high school, suggested, "Let's tell nigger jokes." I lay in my position, in the middle of the pretzel. My stomach began to roil, my breathing ceased. I didn't say a word.

I didn't say a word when I was the only one in the eighth grade *not* invited to the big skating party hosted by one of my good friends because her dad "hates Black people," nor when a group of girls told me that I absolutely could *not* try out for one of the lead roles in the school play because "princesses are white." I sat on the edge of the circle and made silly commentary during the countless games of spin the bottle because there was an unspoken understanding that I, as a Black girl, wasn't included.

For the longest time, I continued to play my role. Part of being accepted is being compliant. Good Blacks don't see or speak about racism. It makes everyone (meaning whites) uncomfortable. I didn't challenge these many slights because I knew that I would be accused of either being the angry Black girl or of playing the "race card." Honestly, I didn't want to lose my friends, either. I didn't want to call attention to the difference I had worked so hard to hide. Instead, I was the funniest, most articulate, least controversial Black friend, student and employee anyone could want.

And I was rewarded: friends, scholarships, great jobs, promotions.

A "good Black" is one who is acceptable to white America. Essentially, white people like the idea of hiring or befriending an ethnic person, as long as she is not "too ethnic," "too different" or, in my case, "too Black." The more like them you are, the more comfortable they are. The more acceptable you are, the greater your chances of success. The molding process for most minority children begins in elementary school and continues throughout life.

❧

But somewhere along the way, I got assimilation fatigue. It's exhausting being in any closet, denying who you are, genuinely and fully. I asked myself, *Why am I changing my radio station before you get into my car when I'm giving you a ride?* Or I said, *No, it's not okay to touch my hair like I'm a zoo animal.*

Yes, I love where I live, but it's tough sometimes. Would you live somewhere that was 99 percent Black? Send your kids to a school that was 97 percent Black?

My fake smile is retired.

My real smile, real self is here: kinky-haired, rock- and rap-loving, sushi- and soul-food-craving, Black Lives Matter-supporting, crazy, unedited me. I won't compromise who I am to make you comfortable. And I have learned that with the right people, I don't have to.

Somewhere along the way I fell in love with myself: my womanhood, my Blackness, the complete me. I have taken ownership of the skin I am in—melanin and all. I'm no longer willing to change to make anyone comfortable or to be "acceptable" because I have finally accepted me.

∼

RANDI BRYANT-AGENBROAD, a graduate of Tuskegee University and The College of William & Mary, has spent her adult life writing training manuals for Fortune 500 companies and denying her dream of writing fiction. Age forty hit and so did her determination to finally go after her dreams. Since that point, she has started a popular blog, Beatnik24.com, writes every day and is in the process of completing a nonfiction book titled *Neversays: Things That You Should Never Say,* as well as a currently untitled work of fiction. She lives in Marin County, California, with her husband, two sons, two cats and huge black Lab.

The Color
of Transparency

Shyla Margaret Machanda

Raised in Toronto, Canada—touted as one of the most multicultural cities in the world—I was a blessed child because, as my mother says of herself, she grew up color blind and I followed suit. My mother was born in Toronto, raised by her father, whose family came to Toronto from Barbados in the 1800s, and her Irish-French Canadian mother, whose early adoption and mysterious origins shrouded much of my mother's knowledge of her heritage. My mother was the quiet, unseen middle child of seven girls. Her mother didn't know how to care for her kind of hair, and her short afro misguided people to call her "son" and "young lad." They were the only biracial family in her neighborhood during the '60s and '70s—a peaceful suburb and ancient farmland in the Durham area just outside of Toronto.

My father was born and raised in Mumbai, India, by his Indian father and Indian-Portuguese mother. Their family came to Canada when he was ten years old. He often told us how long and hard he stared at the first snow, how he ate his lunch in the washroom and endured the ridicule of his peers whenever he mispronounced his v's and w's. Today, he has no hint of an accent, cannot speak Hindi and is often mistaken for a man of Spanish origin. He hasn't been to India since his father's funeral when he was twenty years old. It is the history of those who raised me that bends my understanding of my own ethnicity, not just a color or country or origin.

To my young mind, I wasn't mixed. I was me. And yes, me happened to be a certain shade. But my warm and sun-kissed hue of brown was like my mother's and I didn't think much about it. I knew my mother looked the same as my Indian father, so I concluded that my mother must be Indian, too. The minor fact that my gran was a pale white lady with blue eyes and white-blond hair incited no questions or confusion on my part. I also never wondered where my grandpa was from. He was a jazz drummer who sang to my brother and me, and his skin was the shade of dark wood after the rain. But it was his booming laugh and gruff commands to change the TV that imprinted themselves on my childhood memories of him. The color of my grandparents' skin was ever-present, but it was their words, laughter and music that formed their identity.

We ate Canadian food: pot roast with steamed broccoli and plain rice with butter. Insert my father's jokes regarding the horror of butter on rice. We did eat curry on occasion, but only at restaurants or while visiting my Chocolate Grandma (who got that nickname because she always gave us chocolates, not because she was brown).

I was also raised in a Christian household. From an early age, I knew that my identity was rooted in my relationship with Christ and not in a certain gender, ethnicity, social class or religion. When I tell people that I am Canadian, they refuse to believe me. "No—what are you really?" I reiterate that yes, I am Canadian. The origins of my ancestors are important, but it is the least of what defines me. I yearn for more knowledge of my history, but I am truly a free person in a country blessed with great liberty.

I am also mixed-race, but this isn't a life-altering concern of mine. It is a simple fact, just as valid as it is to those who hold their mixed-race heritage high, front and center to their identity.

One summer's day, I stood in the art gallery where I gave tours. A gentleman approached me and asked, "What are you?" Poking and prodding further, he asked where I was really from. I held back mixed feelings of amusement and irritation as he tried to place me, as if I could be placed like a doll in a box. He had no questions about the art, the gallery or my work. I was just a curious thing he wanted to categorize. I longed to tell him—I defy categorization.

That question is posed solely for the benefit of the asker, not for the one being asked. I know who I am. But it continues to baffle me that others need to secure the cultural ethnicity of someone before conversing with them. If the question isn't anthropological in nature—if you aren't asking because you wish to know more of the culture and traditions of my people— then I don't understand the need for the inquiry.

It is my mother, my father, my grandmother, my grandfather and the sum of their impact on my life that stick to me like tiny pieces of a mosaic, making up bits of me and reflecting bits of them. These are the people who made me—not the color of what the eyes see but the sum of our experiences.

I am a human. I am a woman. I am a Canadian. I am equal to all people as they are equal to me. I am not exotic because you are unable to place my background. I am not an other, or an alien. It is not your job to find out where I am from. You should be more concerned with how I treat my family, whether or not I pay my taxes, whether I have ever been in love, if I have experienced great loss or if I am currently in a state of deep sorrow or joy.

Be concerned with the color of transparency instead of the color of one's skin. Be concerned with who we all are—really, truly, deep within. Search for honesty in the answers given, in action and deed. See my heart on my sleeve and the love and joy within me that strengthen me each day. My color is not how you will know me. Instead, look further and you will see. Look deeper.

That is how you will know me.

~

SHYLA MARGARET MACHANDA is a musician and writer from Toronto, Ontario, Canada. She divides her time among writing and performing music, working in the nonprofit sector and reading as many books as possible during her daily commute. Shyla graduated from Trinity College, University of Toronto, with an HBA in English and fine art history, and attended the Independent Music Production program at Seneca College at York University in Toronto. Sometime in the next five to seven years, she hopes to prove to all the naysayers that unicorns really do exist.

From Negro to Black

LA RHONDA CROSBY-JOHNSON

Colored was coming to an end. I'd be a Negro, they told me, like the young preacher who led a bus boycott, the woman who sat down and made America stand up, the Harlem minister with a single letter for a last name. "Colored" and "Whites Only" signs over water fountains and public facility entrances were coming down all over the American South. The front of the bus was all ours! The next-door neighbors might even one day be white. My grandparents, parents, aunts and uncles stood a little taller, held their heads a little higher. They had been Colored a long time and had been called worse even longer.

Since this Negro thing was new to all of us, we wanted to make sure we got it right. We stopped talking too loudly in public places, made sure never to wear our house shoes outside. On Sunday mornings, we placed neatly pressed and folded handkerchiefs in our patent leather pocketbooks. On Monday mornings at school, the new Negro children stood tall in straight Negro lines while we waited for our Negro teachers to retrieve us from the playground. The new Negro adults wondered where this thing would take us. Would we be able to vote without guessing the number of jelly beans in a jar or the number of bubbles in a bar of Ivory soap? The Negro men all hoped for better jobs with pay equal to their new white "brothers," or at least something a little more than they made when they were Colored.

I was just about getting the Negro thing down when the world turned Black. Huey Newton. Angela Davis. The old schoolyard adage "If you're white, you're all right; if you're Black, get back" was quickly replaced with "Black is beautiful, brown is hip, yellow is mellow and white ain't s*#t." Negro History Week expanded into Black History Month. The slow and way-too-patient Civil Rights Movement began to make us frustrated, as our sons were forced to fight a war against a people who had never done them any wrong. These now Black people recognized that the removal of "Colored" and "Whites Only" signs didn't grant the access they had dreamed about and marched for, and that the right to vote meant nothing without something for which to vote.

I watched my parents, who had once been Colored, struggle to decide if being Black might be an improvement over Negro. Did these loud, bold, proud, fearless, gun-carrying, Constitution-quoting young people have the answer? Had the marchers, bus boycotters and We-Shall-Overcomers missed something?

I certainly felt more at home in my new Black skin than I did during my brief time as Negro. No more burned necks and ears from a scorching hot comb. The afro meant no more Saturday mornings hoisted onto two telephone books while Mama "worked with my kitchen." Now my kinks were beautiful. Afro Sheen said so every Saturday morning as I attempted to imitate the dancers on *Soul Train*.

It soon became evident that the end of Negro was going to be difficult. For our once-Colored-then-Negro-now-Black selves, change meant that the man who had declared "I have a dream" would be shot dead on the balcony of a Memphis hotel, while revolutionaries were spied on and killed in their sleep.

The chant "Burn, baby, burn" was accompanied by Molotov cocktail fire that left our neighborhoods in ashes. The government that prided itself in touting "We the People" certainly didn't have us in mind. Black was definitely beautiful: We had a Miss Black America contest, after all, but it looked like this change was going to take a lot more than a new hairstyle and a dashiki.

I wanted to get this Black thing down in a way that would make my people not only proud, but strong. I began to study "Black"—searching out Maya Angelou, Richard Wright and Langston Hughes in my junior high school library. It meant Mama signing the permission slip necessary to check out *The Souls of Black Folk* and *I Know Why the Caged Bird Sings*. I had never needed a permission slip to check out *Little House on the Prairie* or a Hardy Boys book. My parents nurtured my new Blackness, challenging me to challenge everything. So, when Mama signed her third permission slip, she included a note telling the librarian, "Let La Rhonda read what she wants to read!" My mother and father somehow knew it would be my Blackness that would raise the next generation, long after hairstyles changed and fists once held high in solidarity and defiance were lowered.

We've moved on from Black to African American. While I like the geographical connection to Africa, a continent I have yet to visit, Black always felt like home. I raised an African American son who was compelled to learn to navigate the world without an entire movement behind him, since we were done with Black by the time he arrived.

I watched the pride we felt "back in the day" dissolve as our race desired better jobs and bigger houses in "better" neighborhoods—code for No Black Neighbors, Please. We whispered our "Blackness" and hid as much of it as possible in a multiracial, multiethnic, multicultural stew that had no flavor. We hungered for acceptance to white schools and the chance to wear $200 basketball shoes named after athletes who hoped they could somehow make their Blackness invisible by jumping higher and staying in the air longer. It seemed our favorite color had gone from Black to green.

The journey from Negro to Black was quite a ride. Now, here I am, African American in a time overflowing with achievements that were marked "First"—America's First Black President. There were sorrows that made us weep and wail, as we donned wristbands with the hashtag #BlackLivesMatter. We marched and protested and stood before tanks to convince those who would shoot us and leave us dying in the streets, those who would use the power of their badges to imprison and rape us, that we are here to stay. We still need the courage to stand when others run away and to develop tools to fight enemies more cunning and violent than the KKK of my Colored grandparents. We still need to hope, to dream, this time with our eyes wide open and grounded in the realities of continued division. There will be better days for my people. There will also be days when we wring our hands and wonder if we weren't going backward instead of forward.

It doesn't matter if you proudly check the box next to "Black/ African American" or make a list of your genealogy next to the "Other" box. What matters is where we go from here. What is the responsibility of those who traveled from Negro to Black to African American? How do we make this entire trip mean something long after we're gone? We stand.

❧

LA RHONDA CROSBY-JOHNSON is an educator, writer, certified Integral Coach and founder and CEO of BARUTI Enterprises. She is dedicated to creating and supporting environments for transformation. She was born in Oakland, California, and was a product of Oakland public schools before entering San Francisco State University. She received a bachelor's degree in social work in the winter of 1984. La Rhonda, a much-sought-after speaker and facilitator, is proud of her nearly thirty-five-year career, which has focused on women's wellness, providing access to health care, reproductive rights, community development and education. She is currently working on a novel and establishing a publishing company.

AWOL WOC

Janine Shiota

I always wondered—if I were living in Japan, would I be a woman of color? Ethnically speaking, I'm Japanese, but really, I am what other Asians call a "banana"—yellow on the outside, white on the inside.

Even living in San Francisco, a city where one-third of the population is Asian, do I really qualify as "a woman of color"? The label "woman of color" always made me cringe. It felt too explicit, too heavy, too limiting—maybe even militant. I experienced it as separatist, a catty group who leaned toward tribalism. I strived not to see color or gender in others, so why did I want to draw a line in the sand in front of myself? If I heard someone lead with that self-descriptor, I would think to myself, *Oh, she's that girl. Always going to be about gender and race. Run away!*

My first-generation grandparents were born in Tokyo and Fukuoka but settled in Hawaii after having had an old-world, traditional arranged marriage. My second-generation mother was born in Hawaii, raised strictly and rebelled completely. She moved to San Francisco by the time I was born. Post-divorce, she defied convention: Instead of baking pies and cleaning house, she got a new life and went straight to hippie-landia during the Summer of Love. She was riding motorcycles and nude body-painting—on Thanksgiving, no less! I adored and idolized her. She brought my brother and me to each outing. I joyfully played happy-go-lucky child

33

prankster at every gathering held in those large communal Haight Street flats. I watched, eyes full of wonder, as people played guitars and smoked grass. We all danced, giving peace a chance.

We hung out with Vietnam vets who worked out their PTSD camping, dropping acid and blowing things up with barrel bombs and gasoline. I loved running wild in nature, gum stuck in my unbrushed hair, blissfully wearing my brother's old hand-me-down plaid pants with a clashing handmade tie-dyed shirt. Howling with dogs, hiking, shooting guns and riding motorcycles, I grew into a scruffy tomboy; I wanted nothing to do with being a girl. Girls definitely didn't get to do anything fun. "Girls don't run outside; boys do that!" my grandmother would say during summer vacations in Hawaii. "You stay inside and make dinner with me."

I was jealous of my brother—free—outside in the sunny yard and humid air. And I certainly wanted nothing to do with being of color. "A good Japanese girl doesn't do *that*!" my grandmother would say with utter disgust. *That* being whatever I happened to be doing, saying, wearing, thinking or getting into at that moment. The limitations were endless, my aversion therapy complete.

Once back on the mainland, I dove deep into my cowboy-hat-, boots- and plaid-shirt-wearing sullen teenage-hood. I wanted to be an individual with an identity forged outside of my race and gender moniker of "Japanese Girl."

I became friends with boys. So much easier than girls. There was less protocol, no fussiness and none of the same rules. I shied away from girls; my disdain for the unwritten codes of conduct ran deep. I hated the extreme drama and swift psych-warfare punishments. I traded summers in Hawaiian family prison for Alaska—shooting guns, riding motorcycles, fishing and helping build a house. Heaven.

When we moved to Marin, I was one of three Asians in my school and I was always addressed by the name of the other two by confused teachers. The Asians (yes, I grouped them together in my mind like that, too!) had stifling rules. All Asians were my grandmother, demanding that I conform, be "good," "do the right thing," "focus in school" and "wear something that doesn't make you stick out!"

During young adulthood, hanging out with guys became problematic. Sooner or later, sexual tension crept in, sometimes in the form of lurking objectification or fetishized creepiness wrapped in a too-long hug or awkward comment. Sometimes buddy comfort was ruined by sexual rejection. I couldn't just hang out with guys anymore. Bummer. Girls and I were mutually uncomfortable with each other. Their judgmental daggers didn't pierce me. I didn't care what they cared about, had no use for the self-imposed fence of their puritanical ideas of body and sex. I felt drained by the "hurt feelings" ("get ooooover it!"). I found solace with gay men. Finally, relief! I could say what I wanted, wear what I wanted and hang out without weird sexual tension. I was just a person again, not confined by expectations of gender or race.

I had no identity ties to my gender. At best, it was a place of resigned constraint. At worst, a defensive stance where I threw on the persona of a distant object of desire to be used as a sharp tool. A 2-D construct of aloofness, nothing to live in. Nor did I feel deep pride or connection with my ethnic heritage. I was no WOC.

It is only now, squarely in middle age, that I have learned to slowly embrace my "woman" status. It has been a gradual

softening. Like trickling water: the fluid, seeping acknowledgment of the quiet, reserved, graceful strength of my
grandmother living within me. To accept her not as a lim-
itation or barrier but a place of solace and strength. And to
admit and dip my toes into feelings with the loving mentor-
ship of other women I have been lucky enough to meet. As
time goes by, I realize that my closest friends are women of
color. It is only lately that I have fully embraced the support
and nurturing from women of amazing depth, breadth and
balance. Stunningly wise women. Infinitely kind women. I am
swimming downstream for once. There is an unspoken understanding, a conversation that doesn't need to happen. We have
a shared experience of coping; their Hawaii was a boardroom,
or their grandmother was a college professor. There is an ease.
And I am just a person again.

And about that "of color" thing. Now I am experimenting.
I can't say that I feel at home among a pack of Asians. My reference points aren't the same. I don't feel relief in the pod or
ethnic pride at markers like Asian Heritage Month. I feel inau-
thentic, a fraud, sure to be found out at any moment. And yet...
and yet...I find a new appreciation and understanding of the
immigrant experience of my grandparents. I find comfort
in the shared community of our larger clan and its tether to
history and larger cultural traditions.

I've come to the conclusion that I am, in fact, a Woman of
Color. I do have color, but my color isn't a history, ethnicity,
badge of honor, flag to wave, trump card or anchor point. I am
just a person, whose color comes from my collective life experiences. It is the unique shades of me, my internal prism worn on
my sleeve and lived out loud.

◠

JANINE SHIOTA has a varied background in theater arts, production, fundraising, community outreach, real estate and hospitality. She currently serves as a commissioner for the San Francisco Arts Commission and is a founding board member of ArtCare. She lives in San Francisco with her handsome hubby, continues to work on a script called *Legacy* and hopes to finish it...one day...soon...really. After she gets home from work, she picks up her four-legged child from doggy day care and does another load of laundry. She is beyond thrilled to be included in this anthology.

Home:
A Transgender Journey

MILA JAM

Like most girls, I wanted a fairytale life; I wanted to be a princess who was rescued by a prince. But I was a girl born in a male body, and I learned to rescue myself. Instead of conforming, I made a choice to own the woman I knew I was meant to be, and to guide my family along the way.

❧

Early on, I didn't have the vocabulary to understand my destiny. I just listened to my heart. The charismatic little Black girl in my head yearned for answers and understanding, yet was stifled by the physical presence of the well-behaved little Black boy others viewed me to be. That boy was raised by a community who told him to be an upstanding Black man, not a respectable Black woman. I would look in the mirror and see *him*, while remaining completely aware of the female spirit within *her*.

I wanted to fit in. I wanted to be accepted, and to make everyone around me happy. I didn't want to disappoint anyone or be a disgrace to my family. I was the overachiever—the child who was not only smart and driven, but respectful and nonthreatening. I made sure to get excellent grades and follow all the rules. As if revealing who I was would make me seem less worthy. I was friends with my friends' parents and impressed my teachers.

The performing arts were my refuge. Acting and entertaining kept me busy. I was always on a clock, like the white rabbit: school in the day, theater rehearsals at night, a show almost every weekend and out-of-town events every other month. I was hardly around long enough to get bullied, even though I felt peers talking about me. I stayed out of trouble by running from situations. Learning to keep to myself. The busyness allowed me to escape the reality of marginalization I would continue to face in life.

❧

I believed my exterior would magically shift over time, that I would somehow shed my male form and develop female attributes. That the internal compass grounding me was working right.

One cannot know what the future looks like when transitioning; it is imperative to walk in faith. The search for peace and an understanding of my own identity involved an immense journey. I felt a massive disconnect. A consistent concern that never went away. A yearning to feel at home, and not like an estranged visitor in my own experience.

I grew up in the Black church, and while it taught me strength, the lessons were often condescending. Opposing all of my internal beliefs. I was taught that *I was a sin*. I learned that *what I am makes me bad*. Being myself shouldn't make me wrong, or a bad person. Being told I'm not a child of God challenged my mental stability. In fact, the church helped me understand why I did not want to be an oppressor. I was oppressed.

I felt shame because I was taught to feel shame. I never interpreted my desire to love men as homosexual, but that was the narrative I was given. When authorities told me I was going to hell if I felt like this or that, it ate at me.

My oppression in the church helped me discover my passion for travel and experiencing different cultures. I started traveling internationally when I was fifteen, visiting South Africa, the Netherlands and countries in Asia. Living abroad was transformative in a positive way.

The doctrine that is anti-LGBT and anti-trans—and that the Black church supports—is unhealthy. I know how possible it is to be loved beyond my gender identity, beyond genitalia.

Being trans made sense to me way before it made sense to anyone else. The journey includes helping other people understand. I remember realizing my perception of self was different than others' perception of me. As a child, I experienced myself as a girl; I just didn't understand how to manifest the truth.

Fortunately, I had a very supportive aunt. She has always been like my fairy godmother. When I wanted to grow my hair out, she said, "It's just hair...It isn't harming anyone." That meant the world to me.

My aunt understood me better than anyone. She had friends in the LGBTQI+ community and seemed to always love me unconditionally. It helped my mother and other family members to understand, and finally accept me.

It takes a tremendous amount of discovery, strength and self-love to embrace myself as a transgender woman of color.

I grew up calculating the strikes against me. I had to learn how to live life with conviction and confidence. To create feelings of self-worth, regardless of anyone else's opinion of me. I got tired of masquerading and found a way to escape.

After I began transitioning, it took three or four years for my mother to acclimate. There was a year of her looking at me as if to ask, *What is happening? Why can't you just entertain this as a little something to do for fun?* She wanted to know why I couldn't just "put it on and take it off when you go to bed."

"Because when I go to bed, I'm still a woman. I can't 'take it off.'"

One day my mother finally "got it," and understood it wasn't a game and I wasn't "trying" to be anything—I was just being.

When she got it, I could see in her face that she understood, as though she were saying, *You're relearning your identity, your presentation to the world.*

For the past ten years, my mother has become well aware of the need for equal rights and has proven to be, above all else, someone who simply cares about her daughter.

∽

After acting school, I toured with the musical *Rent*. In a Black family, success gives you a pass. They might disapprove of your behavior, but ultimately they'll approve of the outcome if you're a success: You might be kissing a man on TV...but you're on TV!

Success always made everything better in my family.

In *Rent*, I'd been selected as the understudy for the character Angel. I was discussing my acting with my friends and family when a cousin suddenly announced that I was going to make "an ugly woman."

I was far from transitioning, but I was so discouraged by what he said! I got jabs from people who didn't even know they were affecting me. Still, I've learned that I've got to give people a grace period to transition with me.

In a similar vein, I remember a New Year's Eve party, early in my transition, when someone asked, "Are you wearing a bra underneath that outfit?"

Even though I felt comfortable exploring all the feelings that accompanied wearing a bra, her question made me feel like I had to validate someone else's opinion, and I—being super-sensitive at the time—didn't know how to react. Eventually I said, "Yeah, I am."

That's why I love *The Wiz*; I love the whole idea that we know all along who we are, but we've got to go through all these changes and stages to allow ourselves to meet our true self.

As a trans person, I didn't know what was going to happen, but I went into it hoping for the best. I wonder how caterpillars know they will become butterflies. Perhaps they don't. But a caterpillar pays attention to the signals in its body, and allows change to happen. It cocoons and becomes a reincarnation of itself.

 ❧

In the beginning, my life was like a movie script, with my family as the casting directors, and myself like an actor in their feature film. Everyone had a role to play, and there were no exceptions made for me. I would only be loved, it seemed, if I stayed committed to the part I was given. I didn't fully understand my role, but it was required that I participate. I challenged everything I was raised to believe and discovered true self-love. As I've blossomed, I've learned that I have to stand in my truth no matter what others think of me. That jumping into the light of uncertainty is better than remaining in darkness.

I now carry the pride and support of the amazing women who raised me. I carry self-discovery, vulnerability, purpose and truth. Beginning in one reality and butterflying into another. Waking up with grace because my life is a success— and I'm simply doing it from home.

 ❧

MILA JAM is an award-winning NYC nightlife recording artist, entertainer and CEO of artist collective THEJAMFAM (@thejamfam6). From touring internationally with the hit Broadway musical *Rent* to performing alongside Grammy Award-winning producer Mark Ronson (The Lilly Allen Show), she's danced for Jody Watley, Lady Miss Kier (Deee-Lite) and the late James Brown and has opened for Natasha Bedingfield. Mila has made candid appearances on MTV News, MTV. com and Perezhilton.com. Mila Jam won Best Music Video (2013) for her single "Masters of the Universe" and Best Dance Entertainer of the Year for the New York City Nightlife GLAM Awards.

At Home in the World

Immigration, Migration, and the Idea of Home

Reclaiming Indigenous Space

Blaire Topash-Caldwell

Indigenous peoples do not have the same concept of space that the Western world does. We don't take for granted that time and space are related. It took quite awhile and a lot of National Science Fund funding for the Western world to discover that time does not exist independent of space.

For Indigenous peoples, our oral stories make this evident. Our ancestors don't pass on and revisit us. They are always here. Always existing and affecting the world. Their spheres of influence extend far beyond their actions in history.

I was once told that our actions and how we treat each other reverberate throughout history, and to therefore always be conscious of what we do. While I don't disagree with this, I want to add that the entanglements of our actions also affect history—things seemingly in the past and irreversible. That is how I see things. The entanglements of our consciousness and love for each other are realized in our prayers, our blood memory and our relationships with each other.

In processes of reclaiming our space, Indigenous peoples are retelling our own stories. Projects of reclaiming space are diverse and abounding. However, one common thread they share is that they seek to disrupt common misconceptions about us—the types of misconceptions that have historically perpetuated violence against us and compromised our cultural integrity.

Rhonda Purcell (Pokégnek Bodéwadmik), the language coordinator for the Pokagon Band of Potawatomi Indians, speaks to reclaiming cultural integrity when she explains:

> *Indigenous space encompasses the mental, physical, emotional and spiritual areas of our physical existence. For a long time, our ancestors' indigenous space was denied. Mentally, they were forced to stop seeing the world from an indigenous view, through suppression of language and ceremony, and would eventually assimilate into a western view. Physically, our ancestors began to consume different foods, hair was being cut at this time, and they would wear westernized clothing. Emotionally, children were being stripped from their families and cultural identity, which impaled generations of people that are still suffering from the effects today (personal communication, December 2015).*

Purcell further explains how historical trauma of boarding schools, the criminalization of our traditional religions, the stealing of Indian children and other structural violence alienates Indigenous communities from the traditional foods and healthy sociality that "nourish our spirits with ceremonies and language." For her, reclaiming Indigenous space means having "the right to live the way the Creator intended."

I was the only person of color at a barbecue and I was eavesdropping on some graduate students who were griping about how they wished their grandparents had taught them Italian, Greek, etc. They were second-, third- and fourth-generation

Americans. I got angry. Should I have told them that grand-parents in my community and other Native communities were beaten and made to eat soap for speaking Bodewadmimwen and other Indigenous languages?

Should I have told them it was illegal to speak our language, practice our ceremonies and, ostensibly, to be Indian until the American Indian Religious Freedom Act of 1978? Should I have told them there is no Rosetta Stone for me to buy to learn my language? *If I learn Bodewadmimwen on the internet, will my ancestors still be able to understand me?*

Purcell also spoke about the "impaled generations." The historical trauma that Indigenous peoples have always been privy to and that is now being proven by Western science. Scientists call it "epigenetics." We just call it life. Louise Erdrich reminds us of this in *Love Medicine*:

> *We chewed sweet grass tips and stared up and were lost...At times the whole sky was ringed in shooting points and puckers of light gathering and falling, pulsing, fading, rhythmical as breathing. All of a piece. As if the sky were a pattern of nerves and our thought and memories traveled across it. As if the sky were one gigantic memory for us all. Or a dance hall. And all the world's wandering souls were dancing there.*

Indigenous women, especially, have the ability to heal. We have our own love medicine. In my Great Lakes Indigenous culture, we have a Midewiwin Society and Medicine Lodge. We also have a healing dance called the jingle dress dance. When we dance, the curled tobacco can lids sewn onto our dresses jingle with the memory of the medicinal plant and our customs. The result is the sound of rain washing away trauma. Our feet swish across the ground, activating the bond between Mother Earth and her medicine and our steps.

All of my ancestors still sing to me in my DNA.

∿

BLAIRE TOPASH-CALDWELL is a Ph.D. student in the Department of Anthropology at the University of New Mexico and an enrolled member of the Pokagon Band of Potawatomi Indians (Pokégnek Bodéwadmik). She is working on her dissertation about how natural resource management policy affects tribes in the Great Lakes area. Blaire is also a jingle dress dancer (a traditional healing dance originating from the Great Lakes area) and artist—making all of her own regalia, from sewing to beadwork. She is passionate about raising consciousness regarding Indigenous issues within and outside of academia.

Proof of Blood

SARA MARCHANT

Using the turn signal on my husband's truck caused the headlights to shut off, so we took it back to the dealership. Two of the mechanics were taking a break near the vending machines in the rubber-smelling waiting room where I sat watching my husband pace. I enjoyed listening to the men speak Spanish, because the language reminds me of my childhood. The smaller mechanic had recently returned from a deep-sea fishing trip and recommended that his friend go with him the next time.

The second, taller man demurred; he couldn't go. He shot a glance at me, sitting so near, as if to gauge my attention or intention. I smiled blankly. They smiled back politely and kept talking, as if I were deaf or a well-behaved dog. Their language was their cloak of protection; my physical appearance was mine.

—"I can't go deep-sea fishing, because I don't have any fucking papers," the larger man said. By his accent, I knew he was from Tabasco.

—*Why didn't he have any fucking papers?* The smaller man demanded to know, and his accent was similar to if not the same as the one I grew up listening to in Southern California's Imperial Valley.

—He didn't have any fucking papers because he was in the country illegally. What did his friend fucking think?

—But fuck, man, how did he get the fucking job?

—Never mind, none of his fucking business.

—Fuck!

The overwhelming number of fucks in the tire-scented air turned me into my proper eldest sister, who always threatened to wash my mouth out with soap when I used "swears," and I laughed in judgment. The conversation stopped and they stared at me. My husband quit pacing. In Spanish, I asked the larger mechanic, "Do you kiss your mother with that mouth?"

The man blushed. Both mechanics glanced around hurriedly, muttered what might have been an apology, but probably wasn't, and walked out. My husband finally sat down and asked, "What was all *that* about?"

I translated the conversation into English for my husband, who pretended to be shocked once he stopped laughing. Then he called me a hypocrite for calling them out on their use of the f-bomb (I have been known to drop a few) and rude for eavesdropping. Never mind that it's rude to speak in front of someone as if they aren't there, or assume that someone doesn't understand you just because she does not *look* like she might understand your Spanish-language potty talk. I've been claimed as a landsman by Puerto Ricans, Chinese, Russians and Portuguese. The Jews recognize me as a member of the tribe, and occasionally so do fellow Mexicans, but not as often as you'd think. I feel like part of no people and every people. I've never looked like or fit in with my own family.

My mother was not married to my biological father. My mother was married to someone else. When I was six weeks old, my Jewish mother left me with my Mexican/Portuguese paternal grandmother while she went to the doctor. That evening, when she undressed me for a bath, my mother discovered a tattoo on my left shoulder. It looked sore, but I wasn't crying. She cleaned it, covered it and didn't say anything about it for fifteen years. She had never seen a tattoo like the one marking me except for the matching one on my father's shoulder.

My mother was afraid to talk about the tattoo, or even to ask my father about it, because she didn't want to draw any attention to it, me or my origins. She was afraid of repercussions from her abusive husband. Most of my mother's decisions during my early years, she told me when I grew up, were based upon concern for my safety. She kept my background secret because she didn't want either of us hurt or killed. My generic physical appearance was a cloak upon which I was taught early to rely.

When I was six years old, I asked about the tattoo for the first time. My mother gently sidestepped my questions until both my biological father and his mother were dead. She told me when I was fifteen what she knew of my heritage, about her discovery of the tattoo and her reasons for keeping it a secret. My paternal grandmother marked me with the family tattoo, my mother told me, because she knew it was the only acknowledgment of my father's family I would ever know. It is the only acknowledgment of my father's family I will ever carry, it turns out, because I cannot have children of my own.

As far as I know, I am the only child of my father. His genes will die with me. My mother used to point this out regularly in her quest to make me continue fertility treatments once I'd decided I'd had enough. She doesn't do this anymore—argue with me. She no longer uses my secret heritage as a weapon after so many years of insisting I keep it cloaked. Not since I told her to mind her own business. Not since I told her that this is my body, my life, and I couldn't take any more. I am living in plain sight, on my own terms. I am no one's fucking secret.

And yes, I kiss my mother with this mouth.

∽

SARA MARCHANT received her master of fine arts in creative writing and writing for the performing arts from the University of California, Riverside/Palm Desert and her bachelor of arts in history from the University of California, San Diego. Her work has been published on the *Manifest-Station, Every Writer's Resource* and the blog *Excuse Me, I'm Writing*. She lives with her husband in the high desert of Southern California.

The Perfect Life

FABIANA MONTEIRO

I used to wake up every day in the village to the delicious smell of coffee, freshly baked bread, scrambled eggs and tasty *cachupa*—a kind of corn and vegetable stew. I remember the whole family eating in my grandmother's room every morning. It was a spacious room with one large bed and another tiny bed; the room was also breezy, perhaps because it was covered with straw. It was the time we told each other about what had happened the day before. I remember the first time I made rice by myself—I mixed the rice with potatoes because I thought it was the best thing to do, but nobody could eat it because it was hard and uncooked. The next day during breakfast, everyone made fun of me. Now that I know how to make decent rice, there is nobody here to tell me that it's good.

Now in America, I have no time to buy fresh bread; I wake up every day in a hurry. I take five-day-old bread from the freezer and toast it, drink milk and have *cachupa* maybe once a year. I have no family meeting every day during breakfast, because everyone else is still sleeping when I wake up early in the morning. My mother used to make *cachupa* almost every day, cooking it on an open fire outside. My grandmother, mother and the siblings I grew up with are still in the village. In this American life, I am with my father. My father knows how to make *cachupa*, but does not take the time to cook it. I miss the laughter, the sound of waves breaking, my chores and the calmness of the village. I miss my family!

I had a perfect life in the village, but I was the only one who didn't know it. The perfect life is not the one we dream about but the one we have and don't realize. Not everyone is lucky enough to come from the place I lived and to have the family I have. I complained about everything before I knew how hard this American life could be. Every day, we had to get water from a tunnel that was built over an underground spring. I didn't like to go there because the water was heavy to carry home. If I had the choice between being a cashier at Marshalls and carrying that water, I'd carry the water. To carry the water was the most important job we had to do; after that we could play.

My life was simple and we were poor, but I was happy. Here I get up, go to school and after school go to work as a cashier. In my life in Cape Verde, I had a family. The love is there, and I am here. It is funny how I long for everything that was routine and I am homesick. What I've learned is that you only understand the importance of family members and places when both are far away from you.

∾

FABIANA MONTEIRO, age twenty, is passionate about knowing people's stories. Her greatest motivation is her family. She dreams about going to university and becoming a writer in the future.

Swimming in
the New Normal

SHIZUE SEIGEL

During the Civil Rights era, my dad and I grew obsessed with the news. He'd come home from the Presidio in San Francisco, peel off his uniform and flip on the TV. He chain-smoked Camels and folded origami while I did my homework. Together, we watched the Little Rock Nine clutching their books as they ran past a gauntlet of jeering schoolmates. I wondered if Dad had seen the same hate as he got on a train that took him to a Japanese American concentration camp in 1942. He didn't like to talk about it.

As we watched protesters being dragged by the hair at a Woolworth's lunch counter, Dad said Negroes should be more patient. *Like the model minority?* I wanted to ask. But I kept my mouth shut. Dad would have said, "Who do you think you are? You don't know what you're talking about!"

And what *did* I know? I was a fourteen-year-old kid born after the internment camps closed. Dad was serving in military intelligence to prove that Japanese Americans were loyal. His buddies had earned Purple Hearts in the 442nd Infantry Regiment to prove we were not yellowbellies. They didn't want the incarceration to happen again. But did they extend that hope to all people, or just people like them?

As we watched fire hoses wash House Un-American

Activities Committee demonstrators down the steps of
City Hall, Dad grumbled that I was being brainwashed by
Communist-sympathizing teachers. I didn't say I thought *he*
was being brainwashed.

I didn't believe in the Cold War, or any kind of war. My
touchstone was Dad's mom, my immigrant *Baachan*, who had
raised ten kids in a skid row hotel. She'd suffered through immigration laws, alien land laws and mass incarceration. She'd lost
children to pneumonia and a husband to heart disease. Through
it all, she developed a deep Buddhist faith. She lived in the here
and now, in gratitude, without bitterness or fear.

She didn't need to prove anything to anyone. To her, nobody
was "better than" or "less than"; we were all imperfect *ningen*,
human beings. Her perceptive smile lit up dark corners in
everyone's hearts.

Still, I didn't want to get my dad in trouble by getting arrested
at a demonstration, so what could I do to support equal rights?
Every morning on the way to school, I wriggled past the blond-
ies in preppy tweeds and parochial-school plaids who clogged
the front of the bus. Sometimes I snagged a seat on the long
bench in the middle of the bus. One day, a large, round girl
planted herself in front of me. Her skin gleamed like chocolate
frosting, and her unprocessed pigtails waved as she hollered,
"Girl, git up off yo ass an' gimme that seat." As she towered over
me, I flipped through thoughts as fast as a cop in a potentially
dangerous situation. If I gave up my seat, I'd be tagged as an
easy mark. If I showed outrage, I might be lighting a match to
a cherry bomb. How could I stand up for my Asian American
rights without making her feel bad?

The girl looked like she got teased for being fat; she looked
like she took out her frustrations on the volleyball court. She

looked like her mom had already yelled at her that morning. I felt sorry for her.

I smiled up at her, keeping any trace of my dad's self-righteousness out of my voice. "I was here first, but I can hold your books." I waved at her armload of binders, Pee-Chees and textbooks.

The girl jumped back as if she'd been stung by a yellowjacket. I pointed to my lap. "Just put your books on top of mine." She rolled her eyes and shoved her way further back in the bus, shaking her head and saying to no one in particular, "Did you hear that? Girl be crazy!"

I never saw the girl again, but I remembered her thirty years later when I got a job in public housing.

By that time, the social experiment known as urban renewal had eradicated the Fillmore/Japantown neighborhood in the middle of the city. The laundries and pool halls, rib joints and teriyaki houses, curbside car repair outfits and barbershops had been pushed together underneath shabby Victorians that weren't up to code. They were eradicated in the 1960s and 1970s, along with affordable housing for the stoop-sitting grandmas, the kids playing double-dutch, the youngbloods sucking beers at the corner and black-clad *obasans* bowing to each other on the way to the Japanese bookstore. The Geary Expressway drove a chasm through the community. Japantown was transformed into a sterile showcase for Japanese corporations, and African Americans were bulldozed to the edge of town, out of sight and out of mind. If they were in the news at all, the focus was on drugs, violence or AIDS.

It was because AIDS skyrocketed among Black women in the 1990s that I got a job in the projects at the far end of town. I was surprised that this was where some folks from the Fillmore had ended up. They seemed worse off than before the Civil Rights Act. The glass-littered, trash-strewn neighborhood was dotted with stripped cars. People squinted suspiciously, "You a social worker or what? You from Child Protective Services?" Why else would a middle-aged, middle-class Asian American woman be there? To show I was not there to take away their kids, I wore African trade beads with my shabbiest clothes. I even left my denture at home to show off my missing tooth.

My job was to help a group of peer volunteers write stories about safer sex. We needed to educate the girls who hollered because their moms hollered at them, who were reading at a third-grade level because the school was so inferior, and who had babies at fifteen because they were not given access to healthcare and protection.

At first the community was as wary of me as the girl on the bus, but I must have channeled my Baachan because eventually they opened up and talked about STDs and two-timing partners and unexpected pregnancies. "I'm telling my story so the young girls won't make the same mistakes I made," they said. I realized it wasn't just drugs and AIDS and violence that killed, but a soul-rotting sense of worthlessness. The project helped the volunteers know they were making the world a better place, one condom at a time.

The program ran out of funding after eighteen months. I lived off my savings for another eighteen months writing and rewriting proposals until the authorities decided to put the money toward more police patrols.

I was broke, but I didn't want to return to the cold canyons of the Financial District, where corporate clones in power suits scrambled to keep up with a new normal of escalating mortgages, SUV payments and wine-country getaways. They were like frogs boiling to death in a slowly heating soup pot. They didn't seem to notice they were in pain, any more than my dad.

I decided to do what Baachan did: entrust myself to the Buddha, one day and one job at a time. For the past twenty years, I've worked at what I believe in—mapping trails in state parks and preserving stories of ordinary heroes— people like Rui, who ran away from Meiji Japan to seek freedom in America; Doc Joe, a Quaker who quit his job to teach at a Japanese American concentration camp; and Rufus Cox, a sharecropper's son whose nightly geometry lessons helped kids get into college.

My dad never quite said he was proud of me, but I know my Baachan would have been proud of us both. We each did what we could in response to racism

◆

SHIZUE SEIGEL is a San Francisco writer and visual artist who explores marginalization, displacement and cross-cultural social justice through memoir, poetry and essay, as well as photography, painting, mixed media and cartography. Her books include *In Good Conscience: Supporting Japanese Americans during the Internment*, *A Century of Change: The Memoirs of Nellie Nakamura* and *Distillations: Meditations on the Japanese American Experience*. She is finishing her memoir, *Miss Goody-Good Grows Up*, with support from a San Francisco Arts Commission grant. As a largely self-taught writer, she leads community-based freewrites and her work has been published in several anthologies.

Escape from the Cambodian Killing Fields

Tammy Thea

In the killing fields of Cambodia, I lost both of my parents. I lost two of my children. I lost my sister, my niece and nephew, my brother and sister-in-law and my dog. In total, I lost thirty-seven immediate family members during the Khmer Rouge's rule. When I shower, I see the scars all over my middle section from a stomach infection that nearly killed me, too. When I see the scars, I remember that I am so strong.

I spent an entire year in the Khao-I-Dang refugee camp in Thailand. Three hundred and sixty-five stuck days. The camp held crowds of escapees with thousands of questions and no answers, with disfiguring war and landmine injuries, with broken hearts. It held those whose desperation drove them to be violent to their own, and the hopeless many who'd been rejected for resettlement altogether...anywhere. Khao-I-Dang was along the Thai–Cambodian border, where I'd crossed, running barefoot with hundreds of thousands of other scared, confused Cambodians, escaping the true hell of our home outside Phnom Penh, once a verdant land known for its cultural heritage and architecture. The Khmer Rouge, the communist party of Cambodia, was responsible for our displacement and one of the largest genocides in human history.

❧

When the wheels of my plane touched down on U.S. soil at San Francisco International Airport in the winter of 1980, I remember looking out my window, letting out a lungful of breath I'd been holding in for five years, and thinking it was the most beautiful sight I'd ever seen. I knew I had to forget my overwhelming past to move forward. America—new and hopeful—would distract me while I tried. To me, America meant freedom; it meant opportunity; it was a nice person saving me from a life of certain sadness.

The Khmer Rouge had wanted agricultural reform, but that led to famine. They wanted absolute self-sufficiency, and, with the lack of medicine sent to the country, caused thousands of preventable deaths from treatable diseases like malaria. Almost a quarter of the population of Cambodia was forcibly relocated, tortured, commanded to labor twelve months a year, killed by mass executions, malnourished or starved. Arbitrary executions and torture were carried out against any forces perceived as being even subtly subversive—including professionals, teachers, intellectuals and anyone suspected of being connected with the former government or foreign governments. My auntie made me shave my head so that I would not be beautiful anymore. Beauty threatened the Khmer Rouge, she told me. I didn't cry when, at twenty-five years of age, the knife grazed my scalp bald and my raven hair fell into the dirty water of Phumi Talon Lake, where I bathed each night, and floated away.

For four months, I had lived at the Bataan refugee camp in the Philippines. The Red Cross had brought me there. For many weary refugees, it was the final of many stops on the way to permanent resettlement.

I was able to come to America because my cousin Billy

sponsored me. Through his sponsorship, I received refugee welfare to begin my new life. I didn't know how to read or write in English and I didn't know a single soul besides Billy. Through the refugee welfare program, I was hired at Manning Cafeteria on Geary Boulevard. I kept to myself as much as I could—still unable to see a version of my life where I had love or friendship or felt warmth. And I was okay with that.

Everything was so new in this new country that I didn't have much time to think about what I was missing or about all the holes inside me or about whether or not they'd ever be filled again. In retrospect, I realize that this first distraction America provided carried me safely through a time when, had I been left to acknowledge my reality, I may not have made it.

One of the first interactions I had with another person in America was with an African American dishwasher who worked alongside me at the Manning Cafeteria. She was very mean to me and yelled at me because I couldn't speak English or understand fast-talking directions. I remember crying about her treatment of me every day after work, once I was in private.

After three years in America, the small Cambodian community in San Francisco that had adopted me put me into an arranged relationship with Lee Thach. He was from Vietnam: a refugee from the same war as me. He, too, escaped through the Philippines. It turned out we were at the Bataan refugee camp at the same time. How we could have met in the chaos of countless faces—anguished and broken as our own—I don't know. But we liked to think we could have.

Lee was a kind man and one of the first people in America who really understood me. When you are a small Asian woman in America, some people think you are like any other small Asian woman. When you can't speak English in America, some people think you are like any other person who can't speak English. Countless people looked past me and over me and through me. I was just another person in a sea of people. But Lee *saw* me—he saw what made me different and what made me Tammy. He understood that for me, it wasn't enough just to survive in America. I'd been surviving for years. What I wanted was to *grow*. We were engaged after two weeks.

Manning Cafeteria closed in 1984 and I decided to go to a two-year school program to learn English as a second language at City College of San Francisco…a college education. This was the first of many firsts I never thought possible before I stepped foot in the United States. While at school, I got pregnant and had our first child, baby Navi, in 1985.

Navi was autistic. We didn't have money for his special needs, but we didn't have any choice but to make it work. Privately, I wondered if what my body had been through in Cambodia had done this to Navi. It was very difficult, seeing him—innocent and well-meaning—struggle to communicate. The fact is I knew what he felt: speaking no English when I got to America, I'd also struggled to communicate and felt the frustration of being unable to make my feelings known when it seemed like everything depended upon doing just that. When I got pregnant again the next year, I prayed to God for a healthy baby. Baby Danny was born. God knew better than we did, because Danny was autistic too.

A year after Danny was born, I saw a mother with two kids who were more severely disabled than my boys. These kids could not walk or talk at all—they were in wheelchairs and unable to control their movements or volume of their voices. I realized then how very lucky I was. Having two autistic children was very difficult and there were times I was very sad—there still are, when I think of how my boys will get along once I am too old to care for them. But I never once thought that because I'd been through hell and lost everything and everyone that I didn't deserve to give birth to two autistic children. They are mine and I am theirs. Lee and I love Navi and Danny very, very much. Like my past, they teach me. And like me, they have bright futures here in this bright land of possibilities.

In 1987, with two infants and very little money, I could speak enough English to enroll in Marinello Schools of Beauty in San Francisco. That trade would lead to a career that would help me support my family. Lee worked to put me through to graduation. By 1989, we'd saved just enough to rent a small storefront in Mill Valley and named it Tammy's Nails. It was a beautiful winter day, not unlike the one a decade earlier when I'd landed at SFO to begin my new life. As we opened the doors of Tammy's Nails for service, I remember wondering what my parents would have thought of me now. Their little girl from a foreign land who beat incredible odds, escaping literal and then emotional death, now an American businesswoman— hardworking and free. I was very, very proud of myself in that moment. I still am. I was willing to speak up and unwilling to be a victim. I was growing. I still am.

I am very grateful that my sons won't see the horrors I saw in the killing fields. I am grateful they've gotten to start their lives in America and have the ability to make their own dreams come true here. I want to teach my kids to work hard, never complain and, above all else, to take care of themselves. I want to teach them to be happy with whatever God gives them, the way I am happy with whatever God gives me.

I cannot think of my peaceful childhood home in Ta Khmau or the fruit trees I used to run through there, laughing. I cannot think of the people or parts of me I have lost. I cannot think of the ways I don't belong: how my broken English might make me seem stupid and how people sometimes look at me funny or how I have to commute an hour and a half to work to afford housing for my family. I can only think of what I can do now and what I can be grateful for now. I think of the people I know now and maybe they feel my strength and maybe that makes them stronger and maybe that is my purpose.

～

I have felt tremendous sadness in my life, but my story is up to me and I will not let it be a sad one. That is because of America. America gave me support from the beginning. Some time ago it occurred to me: The African American dishwasher at Manning Cafeteria who was mean to me — she also had a safe place to work for her dreams because of America. In that way, she and I were the same. America gave both of us a chance.

I don't need a fancy life and I don't need a big house. I don't need to be the smartest person and I don't need to speak perfect English. I don't need a happy past or an unscarred body. I don't need to be recognized here in America. Because here is where I recognized myself, and I am happy.

～

TAMMY THEA is a sixty-five-year-old Cambodian woman. She survived the Cambodian killing fields in the 1970s and escaped through multiple refugee camps to San Francisco, where she became a cosmetologist and eventually a business owner in Marin County (now Tam Valley Salon in Mill Valley, California). Tammy lives with her husband, Lee, and their younger son, Danny, in Hercules, California. Her older son, Navi, is a systems administrator living in Oakland. Tammy hopes to go back to school to study writing and literature. Her pride for her sons and her desire to never stop learning are what keep Tammy motivated.

This Is How You Do

PHIROOZEH PETIGARA

When I asked to come from California to Karachi to research my novel, my aunt and uncle welcomed me with open arms. My cousin moved into the spare room and gave me his spacious one, applied a fresh coat of paint and set up a desk overlooking the garden—"so you can write," he said. When I wanted to extend my five-week trip to seven, I agonized over how to approach my family. They'd already been so generous; how could I ask for more? When I finally got up the nerve, their response was simply, "It's your house. Why are you asking?" My North American mind could not grasp this South Asian model of hospitality. But this is how you do in Karachi.

Born in Pakistan, I had spent most of my life in Canada and America, yet my writing always drew me back to the country of my birth, an endless source of fascination. During my stay in Karachi, I met writers and publishers, professors and activists at the Karachi Literature Festival. I researched my novel at local archives, poring over hundred-year-old documents amid academics and grad students. I held in my hands the very first newspaper to be published the day after Pakistan split from India to become an independent nation. I saw an Urdu play at the Arts Council. A theater company put on the musical *Grease* and I found myself in tears—to see the youth of this conservative Muslim country in Western attire, singing and dancing on stage, to see that despite Karachi's reputation, despite its very real problems, there were people here who were living life to the fullest, touched me deeply. This person connected me to that person, as you do in Karachi, and I got a gig at a gym teaching the Bollywood fitness program that I taught in California. Who knew they had gyms in Karachi? I was constantly surprised: This was not the Pakistan I had grown up in. The Pakistan I had grown up in had been under martial law, ruled by the military dictatorship of Zia-ul-Haq in the 1980s. For the first time, I got to engage with my country in a way that was meaningful, that aligned with my values. This Pakistan, this more liberal, more creative Pakistan, began to quell the great East–West clash that had lived inside me for a long time.

But while I marveled at all the things I was getting to do, the people in the tiny Parsi community to which I belong were appalled at all the things I was not doing. It took time for the subtext to sink in. "So, where is your husband?" actually meant, "Why aren't you home feeding him?" "When are you going to have children?" meant, "Writing is not an appropriate use of time for a young woman with viable ovaries." My claim that I was child-free by choice was ignored: "Don't worry, there's time!"

It's not that I didn't pick up on any of this. There were times I felt incredibly frustrated. It had been this very opposition between my beliefs and those of my country, my community— this predetermined fate of all women, so rigid, so stifling—that had made me pull away from my own people a long time ago. Perhaps it was my North American entitlement that told me I could be an independent woman, a carefree writer, in a place whose every value—of gender, procreation, patriarchy—clearly stated the opposite. Perhaps I just allowed the excitement of my trip to overpower these rumblings of oppression. It was feeling so good, so healing to create this little nook for myself in this complicated city of my birth; I told myself I would focus on the positive, so I continued on. I watched Bollywood movies with my uncle, went for coffee with my cousin, did yoga with my aunt. I had practically grown up in their house, and being with them in this way, I cherished both the nostalgia of my childhood and the new, adult bond we formed.

Two days before I was to go back to California, my aunt approached me. She put a hand on my shoulder and I saw worry in her eyes. "Jaan," she said, "I am your aunt; I helped raise you. Don't mind if I give you some advice." I had seen how close she still was to her sons, how they sought her advice in a way I never had with my parents. I happily waited, eager for a mother-daughter connection. "I want to tell you, all this writing and all is okay, but for the sake of your marriage, you must make the time, every morning, to make your poor husband an egg."

I would have laughed, had she not sounded so sincere. At the same time, another, deeper part of me crumbled. Her words, said with so much love, so much tenderness, landed a double blow: Not only did they push me back into the gender role I actively rejected, but there was a strong sense of dismissal in her request. Writing didn't count, being a good wife did. How stupid I felt. All those mornings at the breakfast table when I had giddily told my aunt and uncle about my research, the archives, the literature festivals—had this been their only thought, that I wasn't home making an egg for my husband? That he was perishing in California without me? That I was a shitty wife?

That same night, after a big dinner party, I joined my aunt, uncle and cousin in the sitting room. This was the room where, once upon a time, my aunt had laid out her miniature tea set for us kids to play with, where my uncle had performed magic tricks, where my cousins and I had acted out scenes from Bollywood movies we'd seen the night before.

My uncle swirled his whiskey. "You know what I would tell your husband if he was here right now?" We used to call him Baloo, my uncle, because he loved *The Jungle Book*, because he had a big belly and a low baritone, because he truly lived by the bare necessities of life. I imagined he would want to tell my husband how cute I'd been as a kid, about the play I'd been in, in this very apartment complex. Maybe he'd tell my husband to come with me next time. It's how you do in Karachi, express devastation that a spouse didn't come along.

He drained his drink. "If your husband was here right now, I'd tell him, 'What is this, *yaar*? You let your wife run around like this? What are you even getting from this marriage? You may as well have an affair on the side—at least you'll get something out of it.'" I sat frozen, not fully taking in the words coming from his mouth, my gentle Uncle Baloo. He fumbled for his phone. "I'm going to call him right now, tell him to..." My aunt jumped up to distract him, as women do, my cousin reassured me with a nod that my uncle was just in a mood.

I woke up in the middle of the night gasping for breath. There were tears on my cheeks—had they begun in my sleep? It had taken time for my aunt's and uncle's words to sink in, to make their way into my skin and cut tiny gashes onto my heart. I sat shaking in the darkened room that my cousin had painted just for me. It didn't matter that Karachi had fed my soul. I had not stayed home in California to feed my husband, and in their eyes that's what mattered. What I chose to do with my life, the things that were dear to my heart, were not how you do in Karachi.

I returned to California the next night, convinced that my aunt and uncle saw me as a deplorable wife, an embarrassment to the family name.

A year later, my husband and I split up. This is definitely not how you do when you're from Karachi. At first, I did not tell any of my family what was happening. Eventually, I told my parents, and later still, my grandparents. But the people I most dreaded telling were my aunt and uncle back in Pakistan. They'd thought I was a bad wife because I didn't make my husband eggs; what would they say knowing I had left my marriage entirely?

I saw my aunt and uncle several months later, this time in Canada where my family lived. I feared a confrontation, questions, pleas to go back to my husband. But they greeted me warmly, as though nothing had changed. There were big family gatherings in my grandparents' small apartment, and for a while, it was like the old days again, the whole extended family under one roof.

"Did you see the new Salman Khan movie?" my uncle asked me in his deep Baloo voice. I relaxed as we slipped into our common tongue, Bollywood.

One evening, I stepped onto the balcony, the crowd inside my grandparents' home too overwhelming, and came face-to-face with my uncle nursing a drink and watching the sunset. After a while, he said, "I wanted to talk to you about your husband. I waited till we were alone." I took a deep breath, waited. "You should try a Pakistani-style divorce. You live apart for a year, see what you miss about each other, and you will want to get back together again."

I had been living alone for ten months and it had only convinced me that leaving my marriage was absolutely the right decision. He continued, "I was so happy that you had him because he was well-off, he took care of you."

Inside me, an intense collision of feelings: relief that my uncle still loved me, touched that he cared about my well-being and fiercely intense anger that he thought I needed someone to "take care of me." I clutched the balcony railing at the implication that I couldn't take care of myself. Deep down, I'd always known that I couldn't tell my family the reasons for my divorce, and my uncle's comment confirmed my intuition. I couldn't tell them that what I wanted in a partnership was not to be taken care of, financially or otherwise. That what I wanted was to connect with my partner soul to soul, to learn with him, grow with him, experience all the beauty of the world with him. My family would have laughed at this, then worried about where they had gone wrong in raising me. I had kept all this tightly locked away.

"Or," my uncle continued, "you can also live together as companions. You do what you want, he does what he wants, and then you come home at the end of the day!"

I squeezed the railing hard. He was describing exactly what my marriage had become, near the end. Why my soul had wilted away without my knowing it. "That's all I wanted to say." He hugged me, his Baloo belly pressing into my chest.

∾

This time, it took a whole week for the impact of this exchange to hit me. Same gasps for breath, same uncontrollable tears as that night in Karachi. Yet this time, my uncle's words hadn't been an attack. It was clear he had put a lot of thought into this speech, had genuinely wanted to help me solve my marital woes. I imagined him planning his speaking points somewhere over Abu Dhabi as he flew thirty hours to meet us on this side of the world. It was a sweet gesture. And yet.

Even as I acknowledged that my uncle's heart had been in the right place, there was still intense anger. Deep rage. No one in my family ever asked. They told. Told me how to be married. Told me how to be divorced. Talked at me, not to me.

Time passed. Anger gave way to sadness. A deep and thorough heartbreak. Because I knew that even if my family had asked, I couldn't have told them the reasons for my divorce. Many in my family could not understand why I had walked away from a "perfectly good" marriage, from a husband who "provided" a house, who "gave me" the "freedom" to write. This was absolutely not how you do when you're from Karachi.

But I am from Karachi. And I do these things. So where does that leave me? Who does that make me?

It makes me many things. In some circles, I'm a writer and teacher and healer who facilitates social justice workshops and teaches trauma informed movement. In some circles, I'm an outcast, a failure, the subject of many a dinner party conversation. Doing what I do makes me immensely liberated and, at times, deeply isolated, especially from my own people.

At the same time that I grieved my divorce, I also grieved my relationship with my family. As desperately as I wanted to claim my Pakistani roots, write about my homeland, maintain a connection with my family, the reality was that I was much more North American than Pakistani. The way I lived my life, the things I chose to do, were not how you do when you are from Karachi.

Two years after my divorce, my mother still wonders if I'll get back together with my ex. My grandmother asks if I've met anyone to marry yet. The sadness in my heart has turned into a weary acceptance. This is the only world they know, the only way of being. I love my family, and I have learned to keep a self-protective distance.

The events of that trip to Karachi cracked my core. But these cracks opened space. Space for healing, for release and acceptance, space to choose anew, choose for myself, choose myself. I chose to put myself in a certain place in the world, and in order to do so, I had to remove myself from other places, places I once inhabited, places that had been a deep part of me for a long time—a lifetime—but places that no longer served me. One day, I may return to these places, but when I do, I will inhabit them differently.

Because from now on, this is how I do.

❧

PHIROOZEH PETIGARA is a writer and educator based in Oakland. Her work appears in *Good Girls Marry Doctors: South Asian American Daughters on Obedience and Rebellion,* Yoga International and VIDA: Women in Literary Arts. She teaches a variety of classes to older adults, including creative nonfiction, Bollywood dance, yoga and meditation. She is currently working on her memoir. Read more at bharosa.co.

Truth Be Told

SRIDEVI RAMANATHAN

They look at me incredulously. I have just detailed my summer vacation, and my elementary school friends ask, "They have TV in India?" I'm surprised by their question.

"These 'Amrikans' think India is all poverty and sickness," my mother, clearly exasperated, explains to me at the dinner table. She speaks with an Indian accent. "Everything they know about India is from the UNICEF commercial on TV. It gives a wrong impression," she sighs, shaking her head and furrowing her brow.

"There is poverty in India," my father joins the conversation, "but there is also so much wealth."

"Yeah, why don't they show that?" my mother barks. The "they" she refers to are the people who decide what's shown on TV. "India is best when it comes to philosophy. Hinduism, Buddhism, Jainism and Sikhism are all religions started in India. Gandhi's philosophy of nonviolence: In what country did he use it to end two hundred years of British rule? India. This was big global news. Why don't they show that?"

"Everybody knows about the Taj Mahal, too," my father states. "Isn't it one of the seven manmade wonders of the world?"

"Yeah, why don't they show that?" my mother snaps again. "Indian architecture is best. How many beautiful temples and palaces!" She speaks louder and more rapidly. "Art is best in

India—sculpture, carving, painting...and dance! So much dance in India! Classical dance, folk dance, Bharatanatyam, bhangra...and mythology! Endless mythology! Why don't they show any of that?" She pauses to serve herself more rice. "And food—culinary arts. India is world famous for its curry!"

"Not only food for eating but food for medicine," my father picks up the discussion while my mother eats some of her meal. "Ayurveda is the ancient Indian art of medicine where all remedies are made from nature. Those Ayurvedic doctors are amazing. They do two things. They take your pulse by putting their fingers on your inner wrist. They also ask you to stick out your tongue so they can look at it. From just these two things they know exactly what is wrong with you! Isn't it amazing? And treatment depends on the particular person. Even if two people are suffering the same illness, the treatment may be totally different."

"Not to mention yoga," my mother swallows her last bite and throws in.

My father then sums up and concludes the conversation with, "Mother India has it all!"

Yeah, why don't they show that? I wonder.

The town I grew up in was rich with ethnic and cultural diversity. Indians and Hindus, however, were a minority among minorities. Unexpectedly, my family found ourselves needing to be on guard about perceptions of Indians—a guard that remains hoisted despite the passing of years, a relocation of place and a change in surrounding individuals. Perhaps it was all the countless comments and situations with the persistence that the statements and beliefs were "true"—despite logical arguments—that impelled me at an early age to think critically about the concept of "truth."

One poignant memory from my high school years is of an incident that occurred far from the school campus. I had been selected to take part in a special multiday training camp for high school students on entrepreneurship. Two students from every school in the entire state, both public and private, were chosen to attend. I was delighted to be picked.

One of the guest speakers was the president of a large international corporation. He was an excellent role model of a successful businessperson. He took the microphone and began his presentation. He was a white American man facing a field of assorted teenagers from many ethnic groups. As the only Indian present, I was probably noticeable. He certainly noticed me.

He singled me out and asked, "Are you from India?"

"My parents are. I'm Indian," I responded, answering the question he asked and telling him what he really wanted to know.

"I've been to India," he said, eyes fixed on me. "It's a dirty country." He shook his head, "I'd never go back. Lots of dirt and poverty."

Though my brown skin hid it, I flushed with embarrassment. He had directed the spotlight and uncountable eyes on me, shamed me for my cultural roots and taught the rest of the audience (a sampling of students from across the state, no less) about India—a lesson reinforcing the limited "truth" about India that they learned from the UNICEF commercials. Some role model! How was I supposed to respond to that?

The guest speaker either did not understand or did not care about the impact of his statement. If such an incident happened now, I would have a very informative response. I'd also tell him that if he took the time to venture out of his own neighborhood, he'd see that there was dirt and poverty in America, too. But as a teenage girl in a large crowd of peers (including cute guys), I wasn't going to bring further focus on myself by being confrontational and risk getting kicked out. As a result, despite knowing his statement was not wholly true, I played along and did what I knew would get the attention off me: I nodded my head.

Another time, when I was in college, a Japanese American classmate insisted, "Indians eat monkey brains! Even my boss says so!" She had learned that from the movie *Indiana Jones and the Temple of Doom*. "Do they?" she asked me somewhat curiously and somewhat accusingly. People actually believe this stuff, I realize...again. Never mind that a significant number of Indians are vegetarians, including me and my family.

Not all the episodes were irksome. Once my mother and I went to listen to a visiting swami-in-training give a talk on Hinduism. He was a white American, and he recounted his visit to India beginning with, "There was so much food everywhere!" My mother's eyebrows sprung up, pulling her eyelids along and causing her eyes to widen. Her lips remained closed, but they stretched out into a smile.

"Finally!" she exclaimed afterward. "Finally someone acknowledges the truth! And an 'Amrikan' at that!" Her eyes remained lit up and her lips smiling for the rest of the evening. She must have worn that smile to bed with her.

Mainstream media broadcasts the narrative that immigrants desperately hustle to the U.S. to escape their dire homelands. They are impatient to "modernize"—in other words, "westernize"—and "move ahead." People believe all immigrants are eager to hack off their roots and dispose of anything "ethnic" about themselves. They assume immigrants' goal is total assimilation: to be as American as they can be.

For some immigrants, this is true. For others, not at all. Some are in this country because circumstances brought them here; if they could, they'd leave. Some immigrants take things in stride, doling out compliments and criticisms of both past and present localities as appropriate.

As immigrants in the U.S., my parents had no intention or desire to cast off their ethnic, cultural and spiritual roots. I can say with complete conviction that if that had been the price to pay for entrance into this country, they would have simply walked away. Without a doubt, my parents were not going to jump into the "American melting pot." Their strict rules on curfews, limitations on my outings and close surveillance of my friends and activities made sure I didn't slip into it, either. Our family home had a dedicated prayer room where we performed sacred ceremonies based on the Hindu calendar. We also organized Indian cultural programs and attended those of other cultures. My parents have no problems with plurality, so they favor the salad bowl metaphor: While cohabiting in the same nation, all people maintain and are appreciated for their own heritage. No one need melt away.

I continue to think critically about the idea of "truth," particularly when it comes to people, culture and context. It's quite fitting that today I facilitate diversity circles. These are gatherings of people to explore, understand and celebrate our community's multiculturalism. Though activities, movies and speakers are organized to stimulate conversation, the deepest learning comes through our personal stories. The discussions reveal a plethora of shared and differing experiences and viewpoints. A participant shares expecting to receive nods of agreement, which are often received. That said, what another shares afterward may drastically contrast with what the previous person stated. Others in the room may underscore the differing opinions by sharing their stories. Some are surprised by the lack of conformity; after all, we live in the same country. Some learn that the assumptions forming their reality are just that—assumptions based on their unique life circumstances. Some are shocked to discover that other people experience the world differently. Participants occasionally leave feeling triggered, validated or both—but always with much to think about.

So what have I learned about "truth"? I recall an old Indian parable my parents told me as a child. The story is about several blind men describing an elephant. Because each man touched a different part of the elephant (the belly, the ear, the trunk, the tail), each had an altogether different idea of what the elephant was like (a wall, a handheld fan, a tree, a rope). They had different ideas concerning the "truth" of an elephant, and each was convinced that he was correct. Likewise, when it comes to people and culture, "truth" is complex and has infinite angles. Truth be told, there is no one truth. There are many truths, and they lurk within our questions and reflections.

∽

SRIDEVI RAMANATHAN is devoted to empowering girls and women through relevant and revealing education that speaks to the mind and the soul. She founded Story Digs (www.storydigs.com), through which she conducts talks and workshops based on her scholarly research on mythology and folklore. She holds a master's in teaching and is currently pursuing a doctorate in philosophy and religion with a concentration in women's spirituality. For years, she has actively participated in programs and events that empower girls and women, including One Billion Rising and Take Back the Night. She is a writer, dancer and artist. She is profiled in the book *Birthing God: Women's Experiences of the Divine.*

Home

POROCHISTA KHAKPOUR

This week I managed four plane flights and have two more to go. Ever since the Muslim travel ban, I worry about travel in a way I never before have.

I tell myself, *I am getting better again, the antibiotics are working again; how can I not be well?* No one around me understands how I can balance so many things: teaching classes and flying off to events.

And all the mess I have to carry with me: my multiple bags and my cane—and sometimes a bottle of water. And there are all sorts of food people like me who have Lyme disease aren't supposed to eat, and so in my bags I have more bags of food I label in my head as *just in case.*

At the airport, a man wants to help and I don't let him. He asks me how I handle all those things in my hands and I say, "I've worked in restaurants and I was a yoga teacher once." He looks very interested, so I say, "I'm a writer now, a teacher of writing, too," and I walk away.

In the TSA line, a white woman cuts in front of me—it's her first time getting a pat-down, she tells me, and I tell her it must be my one hundredth-somethingth time. I'm next, I tell her.

She tries to cut in front of me several times more, frantic that her bags will be gone, but I remind her firmly and politely that I will not allow her to cut in front of me in line, that I am not going to let her do such a terrible thing. Don't be that person, I tell her, and she sighs. I go ahead and the TSA worker who saw it all shakes her head, and we have a laugh about her antics. In the bathroom, that same white woman knocks into me and I pretend I don't notice.

The flight out to Bangor is delayed, and in the waiting area, everyone is fairly old and white and I try to find the group I think is most "liberal-looking" (like certain people from Vermont, I tell myself—maybe colorful sweaters, wacky jewelry, something like that).

In my memoir, I write a lot about how having Lyme allows me to bond with white Americans of the Northeast more, and, here in Bangor, while waiting for my plane, it again proves true: Everyone has someone they know with Lyme—and it's always bad.

I shake my head along with them. In a matter of minutes, the woman who I think of as looking the most liberal out of the bunch, it turns out, also has some chronic illness. She tells us that she was finally diagnosed in a hospital in Florida. "A doctor—a Muslim doctor, actually—" she says, and the word actually freezes me up. I hear myself blurt out, "My people are great doctors!"

Silence. I smile, they smile. Hard smiles.

A minute later the airline agent, a young Latina woman, announces more delays. The man next to my supposedly liberal older lady makes a big show of not understanding her. Hands in the air, eyes rolling, looking to others who nod along. He's saying something, asking himself, *Who the hell can understand her?*

"I can understand it," I tell him, "and she's doing a great job. Let me tell you all about how hard her job is," I find myself saying to this man, "and let me tell you all about LaGuardia

Airport and New York City, because clearly, Sir, you are not from here..."

I hear myself go on and on; he looks away and I decide to move on.

An older South Asian woman who sees me leaning on a column to balance all my belongings asks me to take a seat, then begs me to, but I tell her it's my illness, I can't stand up and sit down as easily as I used to, so I just want to make sure I'm up. She looks confused. It's easier to pace, I tell her. She asks me to explain and I try to explain my disease, which she's never heard of, that it was a bug that bit me, but she moves a few seats away and looks to the ceiling.

Eventually I get there, finally, and I do my thing in Maine, and it all goes well, as it often does in universities—partially because I think they think one thing of me and then they see another. I surprise everyone, sometimes myself.

I sleep better in hotels than anywhere on earth these days, and while in my hotel bed I think about the comfort of universities and the false comforts, too, and I wonder: How do I manage balancing it all? When I read for that hour I'm slated, I read—hard angry bits about identity and ethnicity and Iran— and I can swear they hear me.

After my event, several young women of color had come up to me to thank me—and I can't think what for, but I remember that feeling: that feeling that someone, anyone, close enough, might voice a reality somewhere even remotely close to your own. I think about being better for them. I think about my students, suspended in all sorts of chaos this term—all because of this stupid Muslim travel ban—and how I have no more answers for them. Did I ever have any?

On the way back, the flight is so delayed, so many times, so many hours. Bangor Airport is tiny and silent in a way I love, and yet in another way that scares me.

I try to joke with TSA as I often do and one agent tells me it's not the weather he thinks that's delaying us but the no-fly zone around Trump Tower. We laugh and then he sees my name and does his thing and I am on to my pat-down and I ramble on about Lyme and the TSA agent tells me her mother is dying of Lyme. There it is: the bonding. But there also: the anger at the government, at healthcare. The expense, the pain.

When we finally get on yet another plane, yet again, I notice (as I have many times in my life) how I am the only non-white person around, and I watch how white people are acting with each other. I look at how "okay" they all seem with everything.

During the flight, I end up dropping things. I drop things so often and the flight attendant helps me so many times that she finally tells me she's from Atlanta, as if that is supposed to mean something to me. The man next to me, an older man, looks at my ID and with a big smile asks me where I'm from. I say Iran. I try to say it with an even bigger smile.

He asks when I left. He's very open about his calculating the years, and when he finally determines that I was one of the ones who left "back then," he approves.

One of the good ones. By the time I get home, I think what I always think: When will home ever get to be home?

∾

POROCHISTA KHAKPOUR is the author of the forthcoming memoir *Sick* (Harper Perennial, May 2018) and the novels *The Last Illusion* (Bloomsbury, 2014)—a 2014 best book of the year according to NPR, Kirkus, BuzzFeed, PopMatters, Electric Literature and more—and *Sons and Other Flammable Objects* (Grove, 2007)—the 2007 California Book Award winner in "First Fiction," a *Chicago Tribune* "Fall's Best" and a *New York Times* "Editor's Choice." Her writing has appeared in the *New York Times*, the *Los Angeles Times*, the *Wall Street Journal*, *Bookforum* and *Elle*, on Al Jazeera America, Slate, Salon, Spin, CNN, and The Daily Beast, and in many other publications around the world. She's had fellowships from the National Endowment for the Arts, the University of Leipzig (Picador Guest Professorship), Yaddo, Ucross and Northwestern University's Academy for Alternative Journalism, among others. She was last writer-in-residence at Bard College, adjunct faculty at Columbia University and visiting faculty at Vermont College of Fine Arts's MFA program. Born in Tehran and raised in the Los Angeles area, she lives in New York City's Harlem.

stay

MICHELLE MUSH LEE

You were born in a pool of blood / steps from platform / Oscar Grant was slain / stay / my midwife whispers in the 18th hour of labor / my belly is fire & stick of dynamite / my arms are two white flags & hang over the edge of the birth tub in surrender / stay / my darling, i wish we could have met someplace less bloody but your father & i made you here / & that night you were born / steel train that witnessed Oscar take his last breath belted / joyous blackhoodie howl announcing your birth / in the 21 hours it took to unearth your name from crux of my flesh / i petitioned Most Holy Theotokos: save me / rescue me from this death / i begged her to hurl me into the comforts of Oakland Kaiser's manicured halls & picketfence white walls where / rooms overflow w/ epidural & pitocin / your appa whispers: stay, you were made for this / stay is the shortest prayer / offered at an altar built on the back of a new lover's head / stay is an answer / omas might give sons if caught between redblue lights on blueblack night / in a city / that's made sport of extinguishing black, brown & yellow life / stay / fighting to stay (when everything says run) is love / is gripping to promises we make after rice hits carpet in dead of night during blueflame fights / after i've outfitted appa in small & shame & everything in us wants to run / stay / he says: let's give it 30 more minutes & if you aren't ready to push we'll leave / on craigslist / apricot & fig trees line Alameda's prime real estate / tease me with tastes of sweet suburban afternoons & clean air & California distinguished schools / outside our bedroom window / guns bark & snap (always at somebody's son) / never stop to wonder why / black eyes on other side of barrel / look like his / my city is holy, holy, holy / Oakland / be city of lovers / be me & my beloved clinging to each other in the dark / our bodies curved like gold question marks / my city is looming change / is priuses & spritegreen low riders gliding down Tele & 23rd / be white & asian hipsters in boutique-bought eyewear / Oakland is / top travel destination in the world & 4th most dangerous city in America / (most dangerous for who?) / be roses in concrete / be sweet poem between gold teeth / be city that sprays its prayers across miles & miles of burners along the amtrak line / be old school & new school / 4th generation child of Southern migrants & new wave transplants of jerry brown's 10k / is sunnyside & trestle glen / is rich folk & working class / acorn & the ville / artsy youth & tech professionals / Oakland be / Adams Point & Temescal / be murder dubs to 8duece & Mac where broken thieves steal childhood dreams / stay / my love, when you're older i'll tell you about survival / when your little rescuebot-mind wonders / why / we live in a place of more cigarettes than stars / cornerstores & bars / why / men in blue be so mean / why / they so slow to show but so fast to pull when families need them most / seeds don't always choose their homes, they are sown / stay / & the loveliest thing i've seen was your father pruning a persimmon tree / he turned around, smiled & said: we have to teach it to grow

MICHELLE MUSH LEE, Ed.M., is a poet, educator and arts and culture advocate who uses poetry to preserve the water of her story in this American desert. She moves from the intersection of mind, heart and spirit, and is propelled by what learners *do know*. Mush's presentations and storytelling have been featured on HBO, PBS and AfroPop, and at the National Asian American Theater Festival, the New Works Theater Festival and the Brave New Voices Festival. She holds a B.A. from the University of California, Berkeley, and an Ed.M. from San Francisco State University with a focus on equity and social justice. Mush is a former Compasspoint Next Generation Leaders of Color Fellow and is frequently a featured speaker on racial literacy, spoken word pedagogies and contemporary youth poetry movements. Mush currently serves as an advisory board member for the Alameda County Department of Education's Integrated Learning Specialist Program and as a senior advisor of pedagogy at Youth Speaks, Inc. She is the founding CEO of Whole Story Group, Inc., a creative consulting firm specializing in story-rich strategies for social change. www.wholestorygroup.com

Trailblazers, Hell-Raisers, and Stargazers

Careers, Work, and Worth

The Tireless Indispensable

Marian Wright Edelman

Every day I wear a pair of medallions around my neck with portraits of two of my role models: Harriet Tubman and Sojourner Truth. As a child, I read books about Harriet Tubman and the Underground Railroad. She and the indomitable and eloquent slave woman Sojourner Truth represent countless thousands of anonymous slave women whose bodies and minds were abused and whose voices were muted by slavery, Jim Crow, segregation and confining gender roles throughout our nation's history. Although Harriet Tubman could not read books, she could read the stars to navigate treacherous terrain and find her way north to freedom. And she not only freed herself from slavery but returned to slave country again and again through forests and streams and across mountains to lead other slaves to freedom at great personal danger. She was tough. She was determined. She was fearless. She was shrewd and she trusted God completely to deliver her, and other fleeing slaves, from pursuing captors who had placed a bounty on her life.

"'Twa'nt me. 'Twas the Lord. I always told Him, I trust You. I don't know where to go or what to do, but I expect You to lead me. And He always did...On my underground railroad, I never ran my train off the track and I never lost a passenger," she was quoted as saying. No train, bus or airline company can match this former slave woman's safety record. And few of us could match her faithful partnership with God, determination to be free and willingness to help others to be free without thought about self-sacrifice.

Frederick Douglass wrote to Harriet Tubman on August 28, 1868, eloquently summing up her life and that of so many Black women throughout American history: "The difference between us is very marked. Most that I have done and suffered in the service of our cause has been in public, and I have received much encouragement at every step of the way. You, on the other hand, have labored in a private way. I have wrought in the day—you the night. I have had the applause of the crowd and the satisfaction that comes of being approved by the multitude, while the most that you have done has been witnessed by a few trembling, scared, and foot-sore bondmen and women, whom you have led out of the house of bondage, and whose heartfelt 'God bless you' has been your only reward. The midnight sky and the silent stars have been the witness of your devotion to freedom."

In every major American social reform movement, women—including women of color—have always played a critical role. Women at the forefront, acting as catalysts for progress when it needs to happen, make the front pages and the history books. But women have also always been the invisible backbone, unseen but strong, of transforming social movements and of all anchor institutions in society—our families, congregations, schools and communities—employing behind-the-scenes, quiet, essential leadership and organizational, communication and fundraising skills to get things done.

Many people know Dr. Martin Luther King Jr. first rose to national prominence as a civil rights leader by serving as a spokesperson during the Montgomery Bus Boycott. Not enough of us recognize that there would not have been a bus

boycott that needed a leader without a vigilant community catalyst working behind the scenes looking for the right spark to
challenge hated bus segregation. Jo Ann Robinson had been
pushing for change in Montgomery buses and putting the
community infrastructure in place for a boycott long before
December of 1955. Mrs. Rosa Parks' arrest was not the first
such arrest in Montgomery, but she was the right public face
that could mobilize the entire Black community—and Jo Ann
Robinson was vigilant and ready to spring into action when the
opportunity arose.

Or consider Ella Baker, a transforming but too-little-known
woman and overpowering justice warrior for my generation
of civil rights activists. She was a staff member of the NAACP
and the Southern Christian Leadership Conference and often
a powerful behind-the-scenes advisor to close colleagues like
Dr. Martin Luther King Jr. She was an institution builder and
stressed the importance of servant leadership and strong institutions that could last over time rather than reliance on a single
charismatic leader.

Ella Baker was also fully aware of—but unintimidated
by—the men she worked with who devalued the advice of
women and sometimes resented her forcefulness, prodding
and "mothering." She made no special effort to be ingratiat-
ing. More than fifty years ago she said, "Until the killing of
Black men, Black mothers' sons, becomes as important to the
rest of the country as the killing of a white mother's son—we
who believe in freedom cannot rest until this happens." Her
words continue to be a rallying cry for all of us who believe
our nation still does not see and value Black, brown and white
children's lives the same way.

Women like these remind us of who we are, whose shoulders

we stand on and who we can be. They are anchor reminders of a great heritage of strength, courage, faith and belief in the equality of women and people of every color. And they are role models for the tireless and indispensable behind-the-scenes and frontline leaders whose strength and determination are desperately needed in every generation—especially right now.

∾

MARIAN WRIGHT EDELMAN, founder and president of the Children's Defense Fund, has been an advocate for disadvantaged Americans for her entire professional life. A graduate of Spelman College and Yale Law School, Edelman was the first Black woman admitted to the Mississippi Bar and directed the NAACP Legal Defense and Educational Fund office in Jackson, Mississippi. She has received more than a hundred honorary degrees and many awards, including the Albert Schweitzer Humanitarian Prize, the Heinz Award, a MacArthur Foundation Fellowship, the Presidential Medal of Freedom (the nation's highest civilian award) and the Robert F. Kennedy Lifetime Achievement Award, for her writings, which include: *Families in Peril: An Agenda for Social Change; The Measure of Our Success: A Letter to My Children and Yours; Lanterns: A Memoir of Mentors; I'm Your Child, God: Prayers for Our Children; I Can Make a Difference: A Treasury to Inspire Our Children;* and *The Sea Is So Wide and My Boat Is So Small: Charting a Course for the Next Generation.* She is married to Peter Edelman, a professor at Georgetown University Law Center. They have three sons and four grandchildren.

What It Takes: A Letter to My Granddaughter

BELVA DAVIS

Dear Sterling,

For a half-century, I have made my living as a journalist, telling other people's stories. Sometimes, they were stories of joy and success, but too often they were accounts of struggles, and many times they were accounts of tragedies.

Sterling, you are more than your skin color, your hair texture, the shape of your body or the sway of your walk. You are a one-of-a-kind creature who has great power to create. It is your mind and where you let it direct your heart that will tell your story.

To be a true Black woman in America today, I have to live with confidence that you will see the silliness of judgment made on the basis of the image God has created in you. The first step to freedom is learning to love yourself. Once you believe in yourself, no amount of name-calling or slights will hold you back.

There is no way my mother could have imagined my life. I was born at home in a shotgun house on D Solomon's Alley in Monroe, Louisiana. Her idea of success was that I would learn to read and write. There were no laws then that demanded she send me to school. So many Southern children were relegated to work as soon as their help was needed to support the family's basic daily subsistence.

I was lucky. My parents sent me to Miss Bessie's private school. It was a one-room schoolhouse with children from kindergarten to sixth grade.

You, my dear, are expected to learn whatever it takes to make the world a better place. As for me, I've done what I could as a "rolling stone." Dylan's lyrics to that song are a lament of sadness and disappointment. I take another view. I stepped off a mountain with caution, but not fear. I wasn't afraid to take risks, to be alone in my pursuit of intangibles or knowledge received wherever I could find it.

A stone that rolls down a mountain is bound to hit hard earth from time to time and even a surface as hard as the stone itself. My most fervent wish for you is that you not fear the collisions or the empty spaces of your dreams. The spaces and the dreams belong to you. You are the rock and in command, as long as you truly believe in yourself…as long as you forgive yourself when the occasional failure touches your life. In fact, those may be the most important teaching moments in your life.

Learn from the stamina of tennis great Serena Williams and learn from Misty Copeland, the first Black principal ballerina with the seventy-five-year-old American Ballet Theatre. Believe that if Oprah Winfrey can become a billionaire, so can you. Know that if Ursula Burns can handle being the first Black woman to run a Fortune 500 company, Xerox, so can you. If Condoleezza Rice can be successful as the first Black woman secretary of state in these United States, so can you. If Maya Angelou could master languages, write dozens of bestsellers, sing, dance and inspire people around the globe, so can you. If inspiration from afar is not enough, look no further than your own mother, Darolyn.

Against all odds, she started her own company and now oversees a large government program that gives hundreds of troubled youth a second chance.

All of these women represent what it means to be a woman of color in America today. They teach others to move through life with no barriers. You must go beyond where your grand-mother has traveled, for your own future, as well as for all souls who inhabit this planet. You must care and add to the grandeur of what it means to be a woman of color in the world today.

I remember seeing your strength from the time you started to walk at seven months old, to the time you were five years old and pulled at the bandleader's jacket on our family's holiday cruise to ask if you could sing with the band, which you did, singing the lyric of Adele, though rather off key. There was also the day you were looking through some old photographs, saw a picture of me and in all innocence asked, rather seriously, "Nana, what happened to your boobs, are they all gone?" I knew then that you would never have trouble asking anybody any-thing. I'm counting on that spirit to keep you curious, to keep you testing yourself and using your knowledge to make the world a better place.

∼

BELVA DAVIS is the first Black woman to work as a television news reporter in the western United States.

During her impressive career of nearly four decades, Belva

has been honored with eight local Emmys, a number of lifetime achievement awards including the International Women's Media Foundation's, and honorary membership in Alpha Kappa Alpha sorority. She is profiled in the Newseum, the world's first interactive museum of news, and in the HistoryMakers Library of Congress collection, both in Washington, D.C.

She was one of the founding directors of the Museum of the African Diaspora in San Francisco. Belva Davis has also received four honorary doctorates, and archives have been named for her at San Francisco State University and the Indiana University Bloomington Black Film Center. Her memoir, *Never in My Wildest Dreams: A Black Woman's Life in Journalism,* was published in 2011.

Forever, for Always, for Luther

Deborah J. McDuffie

Brand new to advertising, new to the industry, and with my boss across the water in England, I began composing and producing music. Talk about being thrown into the fire. I made a few BIG mistakes, but I quickly caught on. I was young and naive, the only African American female music producer/composer in the industry at twenty-one. I felt very privileged and oh-so "special."

When I was twenty years old and a senior in college, we were required to write three letters of application to firms that specialized in our area of expertise. My friend's uncle was a heavyweight art director at BBDO, Pepsi-Cola's New York advertising agency. He gave me the names of two African Americans who were music directors at ad agencies in New York. This was the time of "equal opportunity" and firms were frantically looking for qualified people of color to hire. Both men expressed an interest in hiring me, and after an interview at McCann Erickson—then the world's number-one ad agency, home to Coca-Cola and Miller Brewing Company accounts—I was offered a position as production assistant trainee in the music department.

I doubled up on credits and finished college early, beginning what would be a whirlwind music career in April 1971. I stuck to my decision and joined McCann, and overnight I was working for one of the most incredible singer/songwriters in the music industry, Billy Davis, who wrote the most popular jingle in advertising history, "I'd Like to Buy the World a Coke." He took my formal music education and transformed me into a "hitmaker." Billy wrote "Higher and Higher," "Lonely Teardrops" and "Rescue Me."

Jingles are a lost art today, but when I was in advertising, they were the driving force in marketing. One of the first television commercials I produced was Smokin' Joe Frazier's "Tastes Great, Less Filling" Miller Lite television commercial in 1972. That's when I met Fonzi Thornton, an incredible singer who eventually became the cornerstone of my "A Team." It was Fonzi who introduced me to Luther Vandross, and, since that day, both singers were integral to the sessions I produced. I rarely used one without the other. We became fast friends.

∾

It seems like only yesterday Luther and I were standing on the corner of 56th and Broadway in Manhattan. He put his headphones on my head and said, "You gotta hear this, Debbie. I want to know what you think."

> *Oh my love, a thousand kisses from you*
> *Is never too much, I just don't wanna stop*
> *Oh my love, a million days in your arms*
> *Is never too much, I just don't wanna stop*
> *Never too much, never too much*
> *Never too much, never too much*

The rhythm was infectious, the orchestration larger than life, with his lead vocals floating effortlessly over it all. I instinctively knew this cut would make it. The key was getting it on the radio and getting Luther a record deal. The motto in the record industry is, "I want whatever sound is selling records!" The motto in advertising was, "We want *whoever's* selling records to endorse our product."

Luther's solo voice captivated me. He sang effortlessly. Other singers joked that he didn't know how to sing a bad note. I personally don't think he could have, even if he'd tried.

Luther's signature "woo" was the result of a bad cold and my desire to have a "sizzling hot" sound in a Gino's Pizza commercial. We were recording three different commercials at the session that day, with Patti LaBelle and a very young bassist, Marcus Miller, and the other soloists. Because of his cold, Luther had a wonderful raspy sound, which he hated. He did not want to sing the solo, but Patti was one of his diva idols, and he sang with the rasp and smoothness and created a perfect sound.

I booked Luther on every session after that. Not only was his voice amazing, but he could sing "first girl" as well as bass, and I loved having that flexibility.

I told him I would do what I could to persuade the powers at Epic Records, a division of Columbia specifically geared to Black music, to at least give him a singles deal. That night at dinner with the A&R director at Epic Records I said, "If you never listen to anything else I say to you, you gotta sign this guy. He's going to be BIG." It took months of pushing before the label head agreed to give Luther a shot. To this day, the A&R director who pushed so hard to get him signed gets no credit for bringing Luther to the label.

Sun is shinin' there's plenty of light, new day is dawning,
sunny and bright
But after I've been crying all night
The sun is cold and the new day seems old
Since I lost my baby

All Luther wanted to do was sing and write. He didn't care about anything else. The "business of music" swept him up into a world where he felt he didn't belong. He wasn't comfortable. When he moved to L.A., he changed. He became distant. His scope of friendships narrowed considerably. Eventually I had to go through Fonzi to get to him. I think it was easier for him to cut everyone off than to take the time to constantly choose whom to keep in his world. It hurt, after we had been so close, but I believe it's the only way he could survive.

Many years passed. In early 2003 I felt the urge to reach out to him. I had not spoken to Luther since I left New York in 1994 and moved to Florida. Electronic music had changed the music industry and my expertise was no longer a commodity. I decided to follow my original college path and teach. With teaching, I fell in love with music all over again. Some of my students were as talented as the superstars I had produced. I was thankful to be able to use my composing skills and my live event skills once again. Working with young people is the greatest reward. All of my years in the advertising/record industry paid off in the classroom. My students were fascinated with my background. They would Google me because they didn't believe me. Then they saw my name in movie credits, or online on various music websites, and they were even more eager to show me they were just as good as the folks I had produced in the past.

One of my students sounded so much like Luther when he sang "So Amazing" that I began thinking about the fact that few folks knew Luther's musical background was the church. Why hadn't he ever recorded a gospel album? I taught a wonderful all-city youth choir in Jacksonville, Florida, and my spirit kept hearing Luther singing with the choir. I wanted to produce that album. I called Fonzi, and asked him to reconnect me with Luther, which he did. Luther agreed to the project.

A few weeks later, he experienced a stroke.

Our relationship moved to a spiritual level. The first time he reached out to me in a dream he grabbed me in one of his big bear hugs and said, "I'm okay, Deb, I'm okay. Don't worry about me." Six months after that, in another dream, I was rounding the corner in my house and we "bumped into each other." He said to me, "Deb, I can walk but I'm having trouble talking and I can't sing at all." I knew in "real life" he was in a wheelchair and am still puzzled by his statements in that dream.

The last dream I had was the week before he made his transition. I didn't "see" him as in the earlier dreams, but his voice was crystal clear and really excited as he said, "Deb, my voice is back and I'm sounding better than ever."

I woke up the next morning and promised myself I would call Fonzi right away to let him know that Luther would be singing again soon. Days passed and I never made the call. Perhaps if I had talked to Fonzi, I would have understood what Luther was trying to tell me. On Thursday one of my students asked me how Luther was. I told him I had this wonderful dream and that I was sure Luther would be singing again soon.

He left us the next day.

He was trying to tell me he was getting ready to leave. He didn't know how to say it without freaking me out, so he painted a picture that should have let me know he was going home. Where he could sing again. I didn't realize how deeply he is embedded in my heart until his spirit was no longer on the earth plane. The void is immeasurable.

Musicians live in a world that cannot be described in human words. Others can sometimes catch a glimpse of it, but musicians are like twins who have a special language. We understand each other. Often, we don't even have to verbalize our thoughts. Music is energy, music is vibration, music is God in action. Everything artistic already exists. It is just a matter of who pulls it out of the ether and brings it into manifestation. Even though I haven't written a jingle in many years, I create them in the classroom spontaneously. I can't explain how I do it. It's in my DNA. I hear the harmonies for vocal arrangements in my mind. Sometimes the music comes so fast, I must sing it into my phone. You can take every music course known to humans, but it's making it alive that creates unique musical moments. Luther and I were kindred souls who found peace with the music and with each other.

Luther took a piece of me with him when he transitioned. But I still have a piece of him in my heart.

And when I'm very quiet, I can hear him singing.

My brother, you sound better than ever.

I love you.

❧

DEBORAH J. MCDUFFIE is a multi-award winner with an impressive forty-five-year career combining talents in production, composing, teaching and artist development.

She is credited with being the first female jingle composer/ producer in the music industry. A "behind the scenes" legend, so to speak.

McDuffie has composed and produced music for a wide variety of advertising agencies and record companies. She also received critical acclaim for restructuring and producing Apollo Theater's Amateur Night. McDuffie currently teaches chorus, musical theater and dance techniques at Atlantic Coast High School, privately trains new artists and heads the music department at Unity Church of Jacksonville.

You're Hired!
Being African American
in Education

Dr. K E Garland

Excitement and anxiety intertwined and settled in the center of my belly. My future as an educator rode on my performance at the Duval County Job Fair. I opened the door. Rows and rows of tables and folding chairs lined the hotel's conference room. Principals and assistant principals sat ready to hire enthusiastic teachers, such as myself.

That day, I spoke to one person, Mr. C.

As a white male, Mr. C stood at no more than 5' 6". His wiry glasses sat upon his small face. He did that thing that spectacle wearers sometimes do when their glasses are sliding down and they don't want to exert the effort to push them back up. He twitched his nose slightly. This was a habit that I noticed from this day on, including when I taught under his administration. He sat at the short end of the table; the white table tent stood behind him. It read: *Black English Teacher.*

"Are you hiring?" I asked.

"I need a Black English teacher," he responded.

"Well, I'm Black. And I'm an English teacher," I said as wittily as possible.

"Good. Where are you from?"

"I just moved from Michigan."

"The school is forty-five minutes from Jacksonville," he said while peering over his glasses.

"That's fine."

"Good. Fill out this paper and we'll get you processed."

It couldn't be this easy, I thought to myself. I reached into my brown messenger bag.

"Do you want to see my portfolio?" I asked. And I wanted to add, the one that was worth my final grade during my internship; the one that shows my transcript, past lesson plans, Michigan certificate and proof of my ability to teach?

"No. No. I don't need to see any of that."

Just like that, I was hired.

It took little time for me to understand why there was one African American science teacher, one African American middle-school teacher, one African American math teacher and me, the Black English teacher. Apparently, this school district was slow to desegregate under Brown v. Board of Education. Achieving unitary status was difficult. Subsequently, there was a district-sanctioned mandate to hire more minorities at this and other area schools. The *Black English Teacher* sign made sense now.

The school was interestingly rural and white. During hunting season, the student parking lot was littered with trucks that housed gun racks. When reading *The Crucible*, a student created a collage that had a noose with "the correct amount of rings around it." She knew because her uncle was a Klan member and had helped her with the project. This school's implicit cultural practices were so deep that I found myself in the principal's office many times for supporting student-led discussions about sociocultural issues centered on race and gender. Whether it was the Confederate flag or pregnant girls attending public schools, every Friday my students and I conversed about relevant news article topics. To say this was frowned upon would be an understatement.

"Mrs. Garland," Mr. C began, "you do realize that you're in the 'Bible Belt,' right? You're not in Wisconsin anymore."

"It's Michigan," I corrected.

"Or wherever," he added.

Still, teaching at this school was rewarding in its own way. I was able to reach students who didn't look like me. And I introduced them to literature intended to broaden their understanding of people who didn't look like them—but maybe felt disenfranchised just the same. Twenty years later, a former student reflected on the value that reading *A Raisin in the Sun* held for her. She also shared her joy in teaching it to her current students. Though appreciative for these experiences, I will never forget how it felt for my credentials to be dismissed simply because the school needed a *Black English Teacher*. And quite honestly, I never intended to feel that way again.

Three years later, I resigned from that position. Instead, I taught English at an urban high school filled with African Americans, Bosnian and Sudanese refugees and lower-middle-class white students. Each day brought fulfillment. Many of the students and I had similar life experiences, and teaching there felt like home. I wanted to spread this joy. I'd intended to do so by cultivating my own culturally relevant message as professor of education. By 2004, I was admitted into a prestigious doctoral program.

The next six years, I taught part time during the day and drove 140 miles, round trip, to attend classes and meetings. Sometimes, my then five- and three-year-old daughters would ride with me. They'd sit outside my major professor's door completing worksheets, while she and I conversed about next steps. Reading, studying and writing occurred at night or on the weekends. Marital activities took place when time allowed. Stress manifested into gray hairs, weight gain and sleep paralysis.

But I made it. I graduated in 2010 as Dr. Garland.

A couple of years after walking across the stage, I secured a tenure-track assistant professor position at a major research institution in the same state.

My initial position was clinical, and thus temporary. But my colleagues were so impressed with my work and work ethic that they scrambled to find a way to permanently hire me. However, in 2012, academia's budgetary restrictions meant there was no such position to offer. Until, suddenly, the only African American tenured professor in our department suffered a heart attack and died. Once the department had mourned the loss, the chair, a white male figurehead, had a seamless solution. They wouldn't have to pay for a search. They wouldn't have to interview me. This was perfect. *Serendipitous*, he said.

"She was in what's called an Affirmative Action line. The only person that can fill that line is a minority," he said with delight, "and if we don't use it now, then we'll lose it."

Suddenly, I felt as if I were sitting at the short end of that table with Mr. C again. I wondered if the department chair could recall my research interests. I wanted to ask him if he knew the title of my last publication or presentation. Because, even though I worked in an impermanent position, my scholarship remained current.

My silence and blank stare served as a response instead.

"Surely, I don't believe in tokenism. But this is perfect!" he continued.

"A win-win," I added with a weak smile.

He looked directly in my eyes and returned a far-stretching, toothy grin.

I accepted the offer. Now *I* was the only tenure-track African American professor in that department.

And just like that, just like sixteen years prior, I was hired.

That's how I attained my tenure-track job at a research university. There's nothing else to the story. Ph.D. confirmed from a credible institution. Research conducted and publications under my belt. And my tenure-track position was offered as a result of my work ethic, in addition to identifying as Black. The department chair never introduced me to the faculty. He never explained where I came from. He never described my work, my background or how I would contribute to the college. Consequently, I can count on one hand how many faculty members actually spoke to me while I worked there.

These minor details contributed to my perceived academic worthiness, or lack thereof.

I never felt as if the department, college or university chose me because of my academic skills or research background. Like my colleagues, I was qualified. But I felt less than competent every time I arrived on campus and unlocked my office door. I had come full circle. From Mr. C's need for a *Black English Teacher* to the department chair's need for a minority professor. Neither really knew my academic background and what I had to offer. They both knew my skin color. And that made me a great hire.

❧

DR. K E GARLAND is native to the West Side of Chicago but has lived in Jacksonville, Florida, for the past twenty years. Her professional background is based in education. She holds a Ph.D. in curriculum and instruction from the University of Florida, an M.A.T. in English from Jacksonville University and a B.A. in English education from Western Michigan University. Personally, she aims to motivate through writing. For example, her self-published book, *Kwoted*, includes original and motivational quotes. Her creative nonfiction has also appeared in *For Harriet*. She can be followed on Twitter @kwotedkegarland and on Wordpress at https://kwoted. wordpress.com.

Finding Home

KELLY WOOLFOLK

Growing up as a young girl in the San Francisco of the 1970s, I learned to find my way. I was an only child being raised primarily by my divorced mom, who took her breaks during summers and occasional Christmas vacations when I would travel to Washington, D.C., to spend time with my dad and his family. We lived in the Richmond district of the city in a series of apartments that were always comfortable, some of which had the added benefit of being across the street from a playground or walking distance to school or the beach. I had friends in the Sunset district, along Divisadero Street, in the Haight and Noe Valley, all of which provided a vivid backdrop to my nascent development. San Francisco was still enjoying the afterglow of all that '60s love, and people were easygoing and open about most things. I took the bus around town by myself. I interacted with gay and straight, young and old, able-bodied and twisted figures of many backgrounds, all of whom influenced my perspective of what life was. I felt safe and carefree about my place in the world.

I attended one of the finest schools in San Francisco: an elite, all-girls private school in Pacific Heights, an exclusive neighborhood overlooking the glistening bay and Golden Gate. In school, I excelled and discovered my affinity for foreign languages, becoming advanced in French. My third-grade teacher enchanted us by revealing details of life around the world and my young mind drifted to thoughts of Indian women in beautifully colored saris and luscious chocolate factories in Switzerland. I was one of only two (or, in good years, three) Black girls in my class. But I was popular, smart, a great athlete and pretty—a combination that made me fit for just about anything preteen girls might decide to get into.

Summers were good, too. I usually stayed with my paternal grandparents, who were of the sweet, loving variety and lived on a hospitable, lively street—always a cake baked, quarters given freely at the sound of the ice cream truck, block parties, Hula-Hoop contests and catching fireflies on balmy evenings. Life was interesting, challenging and as normal as I knew. On only a handful of occasions do I recall feeling the first inklings of being assigned a separate identity, an outsider within my world. It happened in both places: in San Francisco, among my classmates, and during summers in D.C., with neighborhood kids. At home I was called different from those "other" kids who gathered in the back of the city bus as we rode home in the afternoon. I didn't sound like them when I spoke and I was less animated than they when goofing with my friends. As the familiar faces from my insular world stepped off the bus at stops not far from school, I remained for the longer ride to my home, listening to and watching, peripherally, the "others." Their joking and cadence was not altogether unfamiliar to me. I recognized it, but was not of it. In D.C., the opposite occurred. I remember alternately having girls clamor to brush and braid my "good" hair and being derided about being "piss-colored" or "talking white." I was accepted but not entirely acceptable.

I continued to build upon my foundations from both coasts, pulling threads from the skeins of my experiences, weaving them into the fabric of my life. I became a chameleon, able to blend seamlessly between cultures, linguistically fluent not only in French and English but also the dialects, Black and white, East and West, that dotted my lifescape. In high school, I added Spanish to the mix and ultimately completed my B.A. with that major. At the time, I didn't have an answer to the oft-asked question "What are you gonna do with *that* degree?"—as if I'd chosen something that might as well involve embalming the dead. I just knew I liked languages and I was willing to withstand the skepticism evidently inherent in my choice.

By the time I graduated from college, I had spent several summers outside of the U.S. on educational or cultural pursuits. The die had been cast, an international life and career were all but assured; the only looming question was *How?* Later, still unsure of my trajectory, I decided to pursue a legal education and became a lawyer. I embarked upon practice as I simultaneously ran from the profession. It took a full two years for me to stop clarifying that being a lawyer was what I did, not who I was, and I still held to thoughts of international travel and culture, which more authentically represented my linguistic and geographic fantasies. The traditional practice of law had never appealed to me. I chose the path in order to acquire the skills and knowledge, to be able to do whatever it was I would eventually decide I wanted to do. The catch was figuring that out, and the journey would be long, circuitous and adventure-filled.

It is with this backdrop that now, as a divorced mother raising a young child across the bay in Oakland, I find many parallels between my experiences growing up and my son's. He attends a private school that offers an international curriculum where he is becoming bilingual via full Spanish immersion. Yet despite the school's integration of Latin American language and culture, he is one of just a handful of Brown and Black children in his class. Mercifully, at age six, he is still basking in the purity of enjoying friends for their common interests, like pizza and cartoons. He is all but oblivious to what history seeks to define as our differences, the discord that has permeated so much discussion and fuels perpetual dissension among so many.

Recently, at his school's annual book fair, while children excitedly browsed through the rows of books covering everything from pictorials of insects to chapter book mysteries, space and crafting books, I scouted those offerings with a bent toward children of color, books with brown and black faces on the covers or delving into topics that might include experiences similar to my son's. Among them I discovered a beautifully illustrated book about Rosa Parks. I believe I gasped audibly when I saw it, in equal parts delight and subconscious concern for what lay within. Here I was, confronted with having to explain all that had for so long remained unspoken in my early years, and which I would now have to determine how to navigate with my child. I felt I had to purchase the book but wondered if the time had come, so soon it seemed, to dredge up the historical ugliness of the civil rights struggle, continued policies of brutality, cultural exploitation and dehumanization worldwide. Must I intrude upon his life of wonder and optimism and draw his attention instead to hypervigilance, always being at his best to uphold the untenable burden of American Blackness and potentially saving his life? It was all just too much. The heaviness of Trayvon and Tamir saddened me and while I wanted to avoid it for a while longer, I knew I could use this book as a portal into what could become a deeper discussion as my son developed.

When the time came to read the book about Ms. Parks to him, I was ready. It was easier than I'd imagined. She had stood up for herself and fended off a bully as a child. This trait of bravery stood her in good stead as she faced greater challenges as an adult and came to challenge the very system that sought to disenfranchise and devalue her. Perfect. I'd always taught my son to protect himself against bullies, so that line of understanding was easy. And it allowed me to integrate lessons of historical bullying and standing up to that, challenging rules to make them fair for everyone, choosing friends, evaluating people by how they treat us and make us feel. But the underlying matter of *having* to have this dialogue, to brace my child for a seeming eventuality, left a lingering distaste in my psyche. As the mother of a young brown boy, my natural inclination is to celebrate him, to encourage and support him in achieving his life's best, whatever he should desire that to be. And, as the mother of a young brown boy, I am protective and alert, concerned for his well-being and safety, both physical and emotional. Many seeds have been planted in him that, with any luck, will germinate into thriving sprouts of self-confidence, fearlessness tempered with sound judgment and an appetite for adventure and curiosity about the world around him.

As he begins the journey of self-discovery and elucidating what feels right to him in this world, I have prepared another step for us to take, together. My prior efforts have led me to the precipice of what feels like a new home. Soon I will undertake my professorial debut at a university in the Dominican Republic. This culmination of language and travel and identity and inclusiveness is sure to enrich us both as we engage with others who feel the same intrinsic rhythms, feel many of the same pains and aspire to many of the same goals. It will be an opportunity to experience life from the inside out, not being misidentified by virtue of our appearance but assumed to be part of the status quo. We will be part of the norm. I expect to breathe a little easier, laugh a little more fully, sleep more peacefully. My son will one day arrive at his own conclusions about who he is in the world and what that means for him. This experience outside of the United States will be a part of that process. With any luck, I will weave these strands of experience into personal and professional opportunities here in the U.S. and back and forth through Panama, Cuba and any other place that feels like home.

ॐ

KELLY WOOLFOLK is an attorney (LL.M., Berkeley Law) with a variety of work and life experiences. After her initial foray into the entertainment industry as an actor in Spike Lee's *School Daze*, she began her career in the legal department of Virgin Records in Beverly Hills, a stint that led her to pursue her first law degree. Upon earning her J.D. from Howard Law, she worked first for the federal government and later represented private employers and clients in real estate and commercial transactions. Her favorite work as an attorney to date is as counsel for a television production company in Los Angeles, where her creative interests flourish. Kelly also consults with a community college in the San Francisco Bay Area and is looking forward to sharing her knowledge and experiences as an adjunct professor in the years ahead. Kelly lives in Oakland, California, with her son, Andrew.

The Tunnel

Veronica Kugler

"I don't want to be married anymore," my husband said after a particularly revealing therapy session. Once the love and romance were scraped away, our underlying reasons for coming together were no longer valid. His spontaneity and caprice had been just what I needed when we first met and I was at the doorstep of a long, monotonous life. He was a recent widower with three young daughters and saw in me someone who could take charge and keep his family running smoothly. But as a responsible mother of more and more children over the years, I needed stability and predictability and as his grief became easier for him to manage he no longer wanted me making all the decisions.

"I don't want to go to therapy anymore." He continued. "I'm done with this marriage."

The finality in his voice and the flash of relief in his eyes said it all. He looked as if the long-coveted freedom was finally within his grasp. There was no point in arguing. I was too stunned to cry, as he detailed his elaborate plan of how we'd split everything from the house, to the cars, to our children.

Nine years earlier when I met my husband, I had been in Paris living out my childhood dream. For a young Black girl, it had been a hard-won dream, fraught with naysayers by the mile. But I crafted the impossible into reality through years and years of French classes, study abroad programs in Paris and a general obsession with anything French. Even though being with him made no sense to my family and friends, it was the first time that I felt I was in the presence of my future. Stepping on that plane to leave my old dream was both the saddest and most exciting thing I had ever done.

I moved into their cluttered house in California and quickly carved out a redecorated path of kids' crafts, elaborate birthday cakes and backyard family fun. The ache of Paris faded with each hug and kiss from our sweet little girls. "The more the merrier" became our motto and soon we were a family of eight.

Homework, karate, piano, meals and bills made it easier to keep away the tears, but the moment my kids stepped out of the car and ran off to class, the floodgates broke. Our home became a minefield of pain. At every step, the sight of something else that I had added or changed while the blank space of my resume grew larger threatened to bring me to tears.

The cohesive family life that I had put all of my heart and energy into creating was about to vanish from our kids' lives. Were they going to survive our broken family? My husband hadn't even moved out yet and I already felt like this ending was killing me. How would I be able to bear it when our family was actually split in half?

One afternoon, my best friend watched me curl up into a fetal position while we talked about my future as a divorced mother.

"You know," she started off slowly, "that dark fear that you feel engulfed in is not a coffin. It's actually a tunnel. Eventually one day you will get to the end of this tunnel and see the light again."

I continued sobbing. I couldn't see even the tiniest pinpoint of light.

"But you've got to continue on," she urged while rubbing my back. "Your life is about to change drastically, whether you want it to or not." I cringed at my feeling of helplessness.

"You might as well change it the way you want it to be. If you could snap your fingers and wish for the absolute best life in the world, what would you choose? What do you want to see when you step out of this tunnel?"

Suddenly a tiny, bursting feeling of excitement deep down inside made me stop crying and sit up.

I didn't want to say it. For years, it had been my own special secret—my guilty pleasure. But every time my husband and I had gotten into a big argument, I'd secretly wished that I could leave my life and walk around with my kids in the Louvre museum in Paris. Many a time, my husband's scowl had been blurred into Mona Lisa's enigmatic smile. Sometimes I'd even have to bite down on my lip to hide my own growing smile.

"I want to move to Paris with my kids."

I looked at my friend tentatively, expecting lightning bolts to strike me down for speaking craziness. My kids were only four, six and eight, and packing up to move to another country was not going to be easy for others to understand. But she was looking at me with recognition, seeing who I truly was underneath all the layers of life's circumstances.

In that moment, I saw my old self reflected in my dear friend's eyes. Hope grew strong and flowed through my body, revitalizing melancholic muscles. I jumped up and paced excitedly around the room.

"If we lived in Paris, we could have such amazing experiences together: the museums, the people, the language, the food. There is something about Paris that makes me happy beyond anything else in the world."

A fire had been lit. I felt my energy growing, as I thought of all the things we'd do in France. "In Paris, I would not feel devastated by the divorce. I could still be a good mother and not have my kids suffer because I was too depressed to take care of them properly."

"So what's the first step you need to take to make this happen?" she asked.

"I've got to go to the French Consulate and find out how to get visas for my kids and me to move there!" I dried my tears and for the first time in weeks, I felt giddy.

Married life and motherhood had moved my wants and needs from first place to last place. But surviving the divorce and even thriving afterward would have to begin with me at my best. I was a homing pigeon fighting through the storm to make my way back home. Just like my husband cherished his own need to be free, he understood my need to be in Paris. Visas, an apartment and school enrollment were obtained through lots of effort and unrelenting determination. Skype, phones and plane tickets would become the glue that kept our kids together.

A year later, I picked my kids up from school and we took the bus to the local museum. From the moment we arrived, we enjoyed exploring our new city and discovering beautifully manicured parks, chocolate stores and monuments on every other corner; every time we stepped foot out of our front door, there was a new adventure to be had. As the only Americans in their schools, my kids were quickly embraced by new friends.

We went back to our other half for Halloween and they came to us for Christmas. Birthdays brought Daddy and summers were Californian.

The bus passed by the famous Opera House and a glimpse of

the Eiffel Tower brought tears to my eyes. This was the second
time in my life that I had made my dream come true. Being
at peace in Paris gave me the space I needed for my stories to
emerge. I began writing essays about those moments in my life
that reveal who I am. My next dream is finishing my book of
these stories.

As we strolled among the paintings in the Louvre, I basked
in the joy that felt better than I had ever imagined. We stopped
in front of the Mona Lisa and I smiled back at her. If only I
had known that she was waiting for us at the other side of that
tunnel, I would have saved so many tears.

ᘒ

VERONICA KUGLER was born and raised in California, where
she studied French despite everyone trying to convince her
that Spanish was a wiser choice. She attended the University of
California, Santa Cruz, and then graduated from the University
of California, Berkeley, with a degree in political economy of
industrial societies. She worked in strategic marketing for tele-
communication companies in France before heeding the call
of motherhood in California, and returned to Paris when her
husband set her free. She's on the board of directors of WICE
(an Anglophone educational organization for expats in France)
and has written for their blog. She's currently writing her first
book and is grateful for every moment she lives in Paris with
her children.

Willie Dee

LALITA TADEMY

When I interviewed for jobs after receiving my B.A., the first question was always "How fast can you type?"—a question never asked of the men I sat next to in my classes, who were often offered the management trainee positions I wanted. Needless to say, this was unacceptable to me.

I was the first in my family to graduate from college, with a degree in psychology and statistics from UCLA. As early as elementary school, I remember my teacher sending a note home to my parents saying that I was being rerouted into special honors classes. The assumption of college began right then: My mother and my father both made it clear that their expectations for me were high and nonnegotiable. I was excused from most chores to concentrate on bringing home more of "those As." First would come As, then would come college.

I won a scholarship to UCLA and worked summers as an accountant/salesperson in a furniture store. My parents stretched themselves financially to support my education, my mother taking on as much overtime at Alameda Naval Air Station as she could get and my father doing small carpentry side jobs evenings and weekends in addition to his full days in construction. Thanks to my parents, I graduated debt-free. But my mother hadn't worked nonstop to help me pay for college to type someone else's memos. I wouldn't tolerate that.

I went back to school for an advanced degree—this time for

an MBA to prepare myself for the world of business—throwing down the gauntlet that I was both serious and ambitious about supporting myself.

Those two extra years paying for business school came as a surprise for all of us. Especially my mother, my unconditional champion. While I pedaled my bicycle madly back and forth between campus classes, the library, my upstairs rented room and my part-time teller job at Bank of America, she worked yet more overtime at Alameda Naval Air Station, as we supplemented my assortment of scholarships and grants. She was proud of me in the way only a mother can be proud, and after I graduated again and got my first job with Xerox as a systems analyst, she visibly relaxed, confident I'd found my way at last. "We did it," she said quietly, when I showed her my acceptance letter.

My success was her success. She might have been a supervisory clerk to the working world, but now, in her mind, she too was a systems analyst. She even declined an overtime request the following weekend and worked in her garden instead.

My mother didn't take it well when I told her I was leaving Xerox eighteen months later to move to New York for a job in brand management, more aligned with my passion for marketing. *Didn't we already have a good job as a systems analyst? Had we been fired?* I assured her, gently, that I had not been fired, that I was going for a better job, paying more money, with more opportunity. She didn't like it. She was a Depression baby, after all, and for her, a secure, stable job was the cornerstone of a good life. But she was, as always, supportive, and said no more about the move.

Each time I left one company for the next, bigger job, my mother was nervous. She understood promotions, but never understood leaving one company for another. If you managed to get a good job, you held on for dear life. But one thing was constant. When I became a product manager, my mother was a product manager. When I was a marketing manager, so was she. Along the way, I'd moved back to California. Fast-forward almost two decades. With a lot of hard work, long days, airplane time, negotiations overseas and a healthy dose of risk-taking, I had risen to the level of vice president and general manager in Silicon Valley, running small businesses with profit and loss responsibility within a Fortune 500 company. Sun Microsystems was hot, the pay was great and there were bonuses and stock options to be had.

My mother and I never had direct conversations about the content of my job, but I sometimes overheard her on the phone talking to a friend or bragging to someone in her prayer circle when they came to visit her. "My daughter just brought me back a fancy kimono from Japan. Now what am I supposed to do with that? You know she's a vice president now, right?"

But twenty years of climbing the corporate ladder took its toll, and I began to yearn for something else, something different and more personally fulfilling than launching new products and obsessing about someone else's bottom line. When I announced to my mother I was going to leave my Sun job to "find myself," she was beside herself. Her initial response was to advise me that I needed to find myself...a job. I had no intention of doing any such thing for at least a year, and maybe never again.

To add insult to her injury, I became completely consumed with discovering everything I could about our family tree and its roots in slavery in Louisiana. This was a double blow. No job, coupled with a reckless compulsion to put our family business in the street. "Why dig up any of that old mess?" she asked. From my mother's perspective, she had done everything in her power to move our family away from the very notion of slavery, which was not a topic for discussion, let alone willful examination.

In my genealogy search, I found the bill of sale of my great-great-great-great-grandmother, sold in 1850 for $800 in Louisiana, and began to write a novel about four generations of Colored Creole slave women, based on my mother's ancestors. For my mother, this was a hurtful story, and she wanted no part of it. When she would call me on the phone, she'd ask what I was doing. If I said I was writing and couldn't talk right then, she would sigh loudly, letting her disgust manifest in the ensuing silence. "All right then," she'd finally say, and hang up. Other than an occasional remark about "that mess," she didn't usually verbalize her disapproval, but I always felt it. This went on for the years it took me to write my first novel, *Cane River.*

After three years of uncertainty, working on multiple drafts of a story I was unsure anyone wanted to read, and another harrowing eighteen months being rejected time after time by a succession of thirteen agents, I found an agent who believed in my novel, and then a publisher, Warner Books, which decided to make the title its lead book for spring 2001. Despite her lack of enthusiasm for the subject matter, my mother continued her role as my biggest fan and supporter, even though she hadn't (and didn't want to) read the book. And finally launch day came.

My publisher flew me to New York, and my first national interview was with Bryant Gumbel on *The Early Show.* My brother Lee told me about my mother's reaction to the broadcast back in California. My mother appeared puzzled, first that I was on TV, and then that Bryant Gumbel was asking questions about my book and seemed interested in the answers.

Not long after the interview ended, her phone rang. It was my mother's pastor.

"Sister Willie Dee?" he said. "I just saw your daughter on TV. Do you think you can get her to come down and speak at the church?"

As my brother tells it, my mother grew big in her chair, shoulders back, chin lifted. "That's my child. She'll do whatever I say."

Once the book tour wound down, and I got to work writing my second book, I sometimes got telephone calls from my mother.

"What are you doing?" she'd ask.

"Sorry, I'm writing," I'd say.

"Then we need to talk later. Better get back to it. I don't want to hold you up."

～

I've always been a little hurt, and a little baffled, that my mother never read my book, but that didn't stand in the way of her deep, unwavering belief and pride in me and whatever path I chose. Without her certainty, I'm not sure I would have had the strength necessary to withstand the difficult times. My mother is gone now, but in addition to her motherhood role, I also give her credit as corporate executive and *New York Times* best-selling author. She certainly earned it.

～

LALITA TADEMY is the *New York Times* best-selling author of three historical novels. Her debut, *Cane River*, was Oprah's summer Book Pick in 2001, was translated into eleven languages and became San Francisco's One City One Book selection in 2007. In 2015, Stanford University selected *Cane River* as assigned reading for all incoming freshmen. She has written two other novels, each released to critical acclaim— *Red River*, published in 2007, and *Citizens Creek*, published in 2014.

The Payat Paradox

CHARINA LUMLEY

The edges were frayed on the bamboo placemats that lay on our smallish dining room table—a table that barely fit into the white-walled, equally smallish dining room with cocoa-colored carpet. It was a place in our house that we rarely used because formality around food, and eating it, was never our family's strong suit.

Instead, we gathered in the kitchen, grabbing pan fried *lumpia* right out of the skillet, the crackling oil nearly sizzling the fingerprints off our brown hands. It's as if the mouthwatering scent had seized every rational part of our brains and we just couldn't wait. Sometimes a 7-kilo *lechón* would grace the speckled Formica countertop next to the sink. In between bites of the pig's crispy-like-potato-chips skin, we would snatch the roasted head and sneak up behind an unassuming houseguest. As they turned, we'd thrust the charred snout to meet them at eye level. Then, despite it having an apple wedged between its jowls, we'd use our best ventriloquist voices to make it say "eat me."

Eat me. This is important because Filipinos eat. Someone's birthday? You eat. Someone's had a baby? You eat. In her house. With her family. Even though she's still laid up in a hospital room recovering from a C-section. Someone's finished fifth place in a contest of six? You eat. That's the thing about Filipinos: Food is an expression of emotion—of delight, of

133

compassion, of kindness, of generosity, of family. And eating a Filipino's food simply becomes your acceptance of their affection.

My story began when I was three years old. My mother found me with the refrigerator door open, a chicken drumstick in one hand and a red-ripe tomato in another. I had just taken an adult-sized bite and the juice was dripping off my rounded chin into the rolls of my already thunderous thighs. A little piece of the chicken's skin stuck to the side of my face.

I'd say it was delicious. I'd say it was the best first snack that was ever snuck. I'd say that yes, at age three, I had already developed this preference of savory over sweet. But I was too young to have a memory of this. My mother, on the other hand, did remember. And her story of pride—in having a self-motivated, adventurous eater who loved to eat food as much as she loved cooking it—is a story that is told around dinner tables over glasses of San Miguel beer, rice and chicken adobo to whomever will listen, even to this day.

The story builds further when at five I greedily accepted her bowls of *dinuguan,* an earthy blood stew of kidneys, lungs, ears and intestines that looks more like the sticky mud that forms after a way-too-long rainstorm than a Philippine delicacy. And when at seven I did not thwart her attempts to feed me an eighteen-day-old fertilized duck embryo that makes even the most daring foodies turn their heads away faster than a roundhouse to the face.

But it was never about what we were eating. It was about why. And the why was simple: love. My beating heart was in a constant state of so-full-I'm-about-to burst, as was my widening stomach that became stained with the crinkled lines of stretch marks that wrapped down my hip bones to the backs of my thighs. I wore that love like a 50-pound suit of armor that guarded me from the awareness that my teenage body was growing far too large...until the background voices of woman-to-woman chitchat at dinner parties, barbecues and holidays—when rice cookers whistled with steam and disposable silver pans of *pancit*-lined buffet tables—began to broadcast squarely into my foreground. *Tumaba ka! Tabachoy! Taba!* The Tagalog words bounced around my head like coconuts. Big! Chubby! Fat!

Because I was a girl and a teenager, I assumed that the criticism they were hurling was about me. And yes, it was. But it wasn't only me. It was about each other. It was about themselves. You see, Filipina women live in a culture that is exceedingly image conscious, and sizing each other up happens as frequently as sizing up the right quantity of barbecued pork shoulder to feed you.

This became a mental paradox that was too hard for me to digest—a Filipino's wanton need to offer you food-as-love while synchronously admonishing that there was maybe one too many spoonfuls of white rice on your plate. Nevertheless, for the greater part of my teenage years, I lived within the confines of this juxtaposition, eating out of love and respect and joy, but with a jaw sore from taking judgment on the chin. To make matters worse, my 185-pound body rolled on a 5'8" frame, which for Filipinos, generally smaller in stature, meant that I stood out as Arnold Schwarzenegger in an army of Danny DeVitos.

It was only a matter of time until I fell under the spell of an eating disorder, and at eighteen, in between my freshman and sophomore years of college, I did. It began innocently enough with the circa-1980s Jane Fonda-esque menu of an ice cream scoop's worth of cottage cheese in a half-cantaloupe as my meal for an entire day. Sometimes, friends and I would grab slices of pizza after dollar beer night at our local bar that was less like Cheers and more like an ABC afterschool special that warned about the perils of binge drinking. When we'd get home, I'd say, "Oh, God, no, the room is spinning," then take off to the bathroom, slam the door and run the faucet. But the truth was the only thing that was spinning was my half-digested slice of cheese pizza—and pieces of my self-confidence—around the toilet bowl and down the drain.

In what felt like less time than it takes to heal a paper cut, I lost 45 pounds. I was regaled by my *titas*, applauded for being *payat*. This was cause for celebration, and heaping servings of compliments were accompanied by heaping servings of chicken adobo. "Maybe you're too *payat* now?" *Saboteurs,* I'd think, even though I knew their behavior was nothing more than a custom passed down from generation to generation.

Eventually, *taba* and *tabachoy* were swapped out for *balingkinitan* and *maganda,* though I had yet to feel either slender or beautiful. I was lucky to live in a house full of girls who were naturally thin and beautiful, because it meant hiding my bulimic secret was much harder than kicking the habit altogether. So I quit—both anorexia and bulimia. As cold as a turkey being brined days before Thanksgiving. But this is still not the end of the story. I was being eaten from the inside out by the fat girl who hid just beneath my skin.

While my body had grown leaner, my mind had yet to catch up. The silhouette of my former figure stuck unkindly to me, just like that piece of congealed chicken skin did when I was caught red-handed sneaking my first snack. Each morning I looked into the mirror to find a donut-round body staring back, when in fact it was shaped more like a cereal bar. Imagined lumps and rolls seared their way onto what would have been considered slender arms and a trim midsection. Some might have called this body dysmorphic disorder, but I never really put much of a label on good old-fashioned low self-esteem.

That is until one day, when I met a moose in Jackson, Wyoming, while on a five-day salon-and-spa getaway with a few John Muir-raised, craft-beer-drinking types who were most certainly from California. They made me trade late-night beers for early-morning hikes up granite peaks and through valleys of wildflowers. We kayaked through shallow riverbeds and across glacial lakes where, on one of those early mornings, the moose swam majestically through the water, so close to my boat that I thought he might hear my beating heart about to burst. This time with all-new feelings: adrenaline, wonder, adventure.

Shortly thereafter, I began my breakup with food, but it was hardly a walk in the park. It was more like thru-hiking the Appalachian Trail, with blisters and bear sightings and pancake cravings while deep into the bush. But with every step I took, both literal and figurative, I began to fall in love with what my body was capable of—running, paddling, hiking, cycling—and something unexpected and profound happened. When I looked into the mirror, I stopped seeing a body that was defined by *taba* or *payat*. Instead I saw juicy, muscular lines across my back and down my calves that had come from climbing an impossible mountain this entire damn time.

That was fifteen years ago. And while so much time has passed, I still wrestle with the cultural incongruence in which I was raised, like when I catch myself giving my six-year-old half-Filipino son a Frisbee-sized chocolate chip cookie to celebrate high marks from his kindergarten teacher. Or when

a win at his little league game most certainly means a chocolate salted caramel donut with a glass of milk. The difference?
There will never be a side of shame that comes with any of those
orders. Not over my athletic, confident, enduring, alive body.

ᵔ

CHARINA LUMLEY is the COO of Movemeant Foundation,
a 501(c)(3) nonprofit organization that provides life-changing
health and fitness programs to young women so that they may
learn self-esteem, self-confidence and positive body image.
Charina has been a senior-level publishing executive with
nearly two decades of successful sales, marketing and business
development experience at such titles as *Dwell; Backpacker;
Climbing; O, The Oprah Magazine; Men's Health;* and *Martha
Stewart Living.* While she spends most of her time chasing
social impact, Charina also chases the bike in front of her, the
latest food truck and her adventuresome son.

Asian American Punk

WANT CHYI

I no longer remember how I got home. But it was my parents who dropped me off, pulling into the dim parking lot of the Carmel Public Library. I'd asked if I could go the week before— just a bunch of kids playing music, I shrugged. My parents weren't fooled. They cut the engine and insisted on getting out with me. Doors slammed in the dark. The muscular chrome of an SUV gleamed silver, dwarfing our marshmallowy Geo Prizm. Boys hollered, triceps curving out of short sleeves, streetlight shadowing the pecs under Abercrombie tees. They were probably my age but seemed older: bodies hardening into men who jeered and teased; hands that grasped footballs, splintered skateboards, the hips of my blond classmates in low-rise jeans. They glanced over. I wanted to shrivel into nothing.

I was a sophomore, fifteen. Four-foot-nine and engulfed in a turquoise sweatshirt my Taiwanese relatives gave me. Pants my mom made from evergreen corduroy I chose at JOANN Fabrics. Mismatched and baggy, they reduced my height still further. The sidewalk, normally desolate at this hour, filled with chatter. Girls in black mesh, in cardigans buttoned over collared shirts, clattered toward the entrance. I wanted to disappear my parents: my father in his grey sweats and sneakers, my mom squinting through her glasses like a frightened old lady. The air was electric, dangerous. We could all sense it. Finally my parents drove away. I felt like tonight, anything could happen. I could fall in love. Break my arm. Become a different person.

Teens from every clique pushed against each other with excitement. A bunch of guys—some in my grade, some a year older—hauled in guitars, amps, drums. Like a machine gun, "Checkcheckcheckcheck, onetwothree," Troy, frontman of Mulse, spat into the mic. He kept signaling: higher, more.

The volume swelled. People chatted. I had no idea what I was in for. Someone yelled for silence. The room hushed. Jake, who'd organized the evening, stared stonily into the crowd. Dangling from his hand was a triangle. With those bulging eyes and clenched jaw, the effect was of a troll cradling Tinkerbell. I waited for someone—myself?—to giggle. The band lay in wait behind him.

One tap and a single clear note pinged out. Mulse jumped, Vans and Chuck Taylors landing in a crash of sound. And there it was. My intro to punk: huge, permanent, instant. Drumsticks hammered down, the guys' split kicks barely missing each other. Bass chugging, guitars charging; all around me, fists flailed. Joy burst through me. I had no idea how four people could create this much sound. That first clash, that first show— that was it. The music swallowed me whole, my love for it pure and immediate. I was alive, enlarged. Nothing in my world could have prepared me for it.

I never spent time with kids my age. I didn't *hang out*. I existed solely, imperfectly between two worlds: school and home. At school, I was the Short Asian Girl. Thousands of students pushing through the halls, I'd squeeze past elbows, my face turned from the bottom pockets of backpacks, my child-sized violin hugged to my chest. My white counterparts would glimpse me out of the corners of their eyes and gasp. I was a living Lego, my hair a helmet, the whole of me cutesy and yellow, a person in miniature—too small to be believed. Mom trimmed my bob according to the customs from her school days in Taiwan: girls in uniform attending same-sex high schools stripped of distractions. Had I been good enough to compete, I might have thrived in such a system. But in the U.S., where popularity curried more favor than meritocracy, everything about me fit the Asian stereotype of the overachieving, violin-playing good girl. Too small, too novel to be human. The school newspaper profiled me. No one explained their choice; the answer obvious: I was a headline, not a person.

At home, I tried to be a *guāi xiǎo hái*, a model child: obedient, excellent. "Your older sister and father pick things up so quickly," my mother would say to me. "We're not as naturally gifted. But by working hard, we get the same thing." She enrolled us in kindergarten at age four, already knowing addition, subtraction, our ABCs. Though insecure about her English, she demanded—despite her accent, despite racist administrators and their exasperation—advanced placement. She sat with us through our homework, assigning more on weekends, the driving force behind private music lessons. The third of eight, Mom raised her siblings in a shack worse than the one we visited when I was nine, the faucet a cut-off garden hose. The eldest of six, Dad emigrated for his science doctorate in 1980. He missed my sister's birth. Mom nearly died, the blood refusing to clot, her memory of it vivid enough to be my own. I never asked Dad what it felt like to miss the birth of his first baby. To be Chinese is to sacrifice for a better life. In every house we've ever lived in, his Ph.D. from Cornell University towered over me. In such a foreign country, all my parents could count on was a sure career path, a way to provide for our family.

As a minority, I didn't know how to be, my school and home selves constantly warring. Punk's enraged howls unleashed a third me: truer, somehow, than the other two. Punk meant defiance, pride in the profound *otherness* I felt. I started attending shows, my hair undyed, jeans intact, too frugal to purchase band tees to prove my belonging. I wasn't interested in looking good or fitting in; I thought punk was where you fit if you didn't fit anywhere else. When the bands played, I could forget that no one onstage or in the audience looked like me. But between sets I'd weave through the crowd, my peers eyeballing my presence.

At home I wasn't Asian enough; at school I wasn't American (i.e., white) enough; at shows, I wasn't punk enough. Carmel, Indiana, one of the most affluent suburbs in the Midwest, is still 90 percent white. At fifteen, I didn't consider the hypocrisy of white males singing about people they rarely saw.

But I still believe. No other music, no other ideology calls more to me. I decide what it is to be Asian. An American. A punk. A writer of color, I embody the road less traveled. I am as punk as they come.

I now remember how I got home. The flyer stated the show would end at nine, so at the appointed hour, I left the noise, the crowd, and the energy, the library a lighted box behind me. I missed the end. The Geo Prizm my parents would later give me—small and hardy, its locks manual, windows hand-rolled, its Japanese engine outlasting any SUV's—slowed in front of me. I crawled into the passenger seat, my dad driving me home, the heart he and my mom had made thudding to this wild beat.

∾

WANT CHYI has taught composition and creative writing across the United States and in Singapore. She has an M.F.A. in fiction from Arizona State University and was the international fiction editor of *Hayden's Ferry Review*. Originally from the Midwest, she now lives in the Bay Area and currently reads for *Zoetrope: All-Story*.

With Liberty and Justice for All

The Struggle for Social Justice and Equality

We Are America

AMERICA FERRERA

Adapted from the speech given at the
Women's March in Washington, D.C., on January 21, 2017.

It's been a heart-wrenching time to be both a woman and an immigrant in this country. Our dignity, our character and our rights have all been under attack, and a platform of hate and division assumed power yesterday. But the president is not America.

His cabinet is not America. Congress is not America. We are America. And we are here to stay. We march for our families and our neighbors, for the future, for the causes we claim and for the causes that claim us. We march for the moral core of this nation, against which our new president is raging a war. He would like us to forget the words, "Give me your tired, your poor, your huddled masses, yearning to breathe free" and instead take up a credo of hate, fear and suspicion of each other. But we are gathered here, and across the country and around the world to say: Mr. Trump, we refuse. We reject the demonization of our Muslim brothers and sisters. We demand an end to the systemic murder and incarceration of our Black brothers and sisters. We will not give up our right to safe and legal abortions. We will not ask our LGBTQ families to go backward. We

147

will not go from being a nation of immigrants to a nation of ignorance. We won't build walls and we won't see the worst in each other, and we will not turn our backs on the more than 750,000 young immigrants in this country currently protected by Deferred Action for Childhood Arrivals (DACA): They are hardworking, upstanding, courageous individuals who refuse to live in the shadow of fear and isolation. They bravely took to the streets to declare themselves and provide a voice and hope for their community.

We march with and for them. Together, we, all of us, will fight, resist and oppose every single action that threatens the lives and dignity of any and all of our communities. Make no mistake: We are, every single one of us, under attack. Our safety and freedoms are on the chopping block and we are the only ones who can protect each other. If we do not stand together, march together and fight together for the next four years, we will lose together.

Our opposition knows how to stick together. They are united in their agenda to hold this country back and to thwart progress. It is in their slogan. So, we, too, must stand united. If we, the millions of Americans who believe in common decency, in a greater good, in justice for all, if we fall into the trap of separating ourselves by our causes and our labels, then we will weaken our fight and we will lose. But, if we commit to what aligns us, if we stand together, steadfast and determined, then we stand a chance of saving the soul of our country.

So, let's march together. This is only Day One in our united movement. Let's march, united, together!

❧

AMERICA FERRERA is an award-winning actress and producer who is perhaps best known for her breakthrough role as Betty Suarez on ABC's hit comedy *Ugly Betty*, for which she won a Golden Globe®, Emmy® and Screen Actors Guild Award®, as well as ALMA and Imagen Awards. Ferrera currently produces and stars in the NBC workplace comedy *Superstore*, which was recently picked up for a third season. She recently executive produced Refinery29's *Behind the Headlines* and *Only Girl*. In July 2016, America spoke at the Democratic National Convention in Philadelphia on behalf of women's rights and immigration in support of Hillary Clinton.

Behind the scenes, America has started her own television and film production company, Take Fountain.

Hope, Justice, Feminism, and Faith

Dr. Musimbi Kanyoro

Everywhere, poverty wears the face of a woman.

Sixty million girls lack education and three-quarters of them belong to ethnic, religious, linguistic and racial minorities. These girls not only lack opportunities to realize their potential, they lack power, voice and influence; they are extremely vulnerable to sickness, violence and disasters, both natural and manmade.

Over my three decades working with women to alleviate poverty, I have learned that creating safe places for women can be difficult and frustrating, but this is the essence of social change: changing the lives of women, and thus children, and thus societies.

Women have been at the margins for so long that work to correct the imbalance is a full-time job for me and millions of others. There are enormous—and troubling—gender inequities in our families, institutions and society.

The Global Fund for Women began as an idea to correct these imbalances by doing things differently. Our idea was to shift the approach of international development by putting funds in the hands of women, as well as for initiatives that improve the lives of women and girls. We give over six hundred grants per year, worldwide, and we go to countries and communities that are usually not addressed by other donors or organizations.

We prioritize populations who usually can't get a meeting with donors, or populations who are shunned by the church and other religious institutions. These are populations who are constantly asking for justice for themselves and their communities; hard-to-reach women such as widows, rural women, single mothers, women's rights activists, peace activists, sexual rights activists, environmental activists, women in slums, women in conflict and post-conflict countries, women farmers and indigenous women.

Those of us who serve as leaders in traditional institutions such as our churches must be courageous enough to develop policies that eventually become our guiding principles. Such principles help us to implement justice and fairness and to be consistent so that we do not become ambiguous in the way that we act. In following the path of faith, we are reminded again and again that in our compassion for others, we must exercise the principle of "justice for all," not "just us."

To hope for justice and peace is to work for elimination of injustice and to become a peacemaker. Therefore, the way to correct injustice is to provide justice. My persistent search for justice is rooted in my belief that God is just and wants us to be equals, one with another.

As such, hope for justice is not merely an intellectual frame of mind, but something to be practiced in our daily lives. When we hope for democracy, this means we practice democracy in all of our relationships; this means we must be prepared to go through the pain of self-examination, which leads to change.

Time and time again, we learn from women living with AIDS and other life-threatening illnesses that hope does not always change one's condition, but it does change one's psyche. As a principle to live by, hope keeps us in motion. Principles are not substitutes for passion, nor do principles move us the way passion does, yet principles are able to guide our passions and groom them into compassions.

Since hope is the refusal to accept a single reading of reality, it incorporates the belief that reality can be changed for the better. Therefore, hope is a form of resistance: It actively resists the void of hopelessness by working for and toward alternatives.

We should not make the mistake of thinking that communicating hope alone brings about transformation—nor does it bring food to the table, nor does it remove despair from a patient dying of AIDS. It does, however, help those who are suffering manage their issues and learn how to persevere in conditions they cannot change.

Women have finally broken the silence on the oppression and violence toward them; they have finally accessed education and they continue to struggle to better access health care, economic stability, environmental security and human rights for themselves, their communities and their families. Women have done all of this with limited resources, all while continuing to work as career women, public servants and educators; all while continuing to nurture and grow as mothers, grandmothers, aunts, daughters and sisters to all the human beings in the world.

᷍

DR. MUSIMBI KANYORO is president and CEO of Global Fund for Women. Born in Kenya, she is an activist for women's and girls' health and human rights and promotes the use of philanthropy and technology to drive social change. She holds a Ph.D. in linguistics from the University of Texas, Austin, and a doctorate in feminist theology from San Francisco Theological Seminary. In 2014, she was named one of the twenty-one women leaders for the twenty-first century by Women's eNews. In 2015, *Forbes* magazine named her one of ten women "power brands" working for gender equality.

Outlaw

MATILDA SMITH

Every time we protested the laws of the country, we were breaking the law; thus every peaceful protest in South Africa was met with teargas and violent whipping with a quirt. Police action was not considered violence but, instead, "law and order." Law and order meant teargassing groups larger than three standing in silence with a placard. Law and order meant chasing and whipping children who said that they did not like the way they were being treated. Law and order meant shooting children with birdshot and rubber bullets and live ammunition. "Violence," however, came in the form of children who walked and sang "Senzenina." So, my first "violent crime" was perpetrated at the tender age of five. At least that is the first crime I can remember. My mother took me to the Dalebrook Tidal Pool in St. James. She had grown up in the area and wanted to share her favorite landmarks with me. We had just arrived and were looking for a nice place on the sand where there was not too much sun, as my fair skin burned easily. I was excited to see a number of children running and playing; I could see that they were having fun. The ocean waves pounded in the distance, and the salty air moistened my cheeks. A policeman approached us and said we would have to leave, as we were committing a crime by being there.

I could see tears escaping from the corners of my mother's eyes as she savagely grabbed my arm and dragged me after her.

I was confused and I didn't want to leave. This was a beautiful place and the first time I'd been to a beach. I wanted to stay. I asked why we couldn't as I flew like a kite behind her at the end of her hand. Because we are Black, she replied angrily.

This confused my five-year-old mind even more than other confusing situations, like the fact that my cousin Rhoda was able to ride in the comfortable white carriages of the train while we had to get in the crowded Colored carriages. Being in the same family but different was an easier challenge to accept than this new dilemma. You see, I had not been exposed to the sun yet that season, so my skin looked much lighter than those tanned children who were running around on the beach— although I did notice that their hair was straight while mine was curly. I didn't understand my mother's upset and why she was so angry.

I was twelve when I committed my next series of "crimes." Firstly, I felt implicated and complicit because my principal, an Irish Roman Catholic nun of the Dominican Order, was told by the apartheid state that she had to leave the country because her students were boycotting classes.

How did a Bride of Christ get to be a criminal and thus need to leave the country where the church had sent her to do missionary work? She who had drummed personal integrity into us because our school motto was "Veritas." She who ensured that we understood that we were not only to speak the truth but also to walk and live the way of the truth. She was being extradited because she explained "Veritas" to us by her own example of being true to her religious principles and values.

My brother, who was ten years older than I, was a major criminal: He read banned literature—magazines written by the Teachers' League with articles about what history children should be learning. I was scared because my older brother argued with my dad and said Dad was a coward because he did not want my brother to join in the student protests—this at a time when white men in white utility vehicles rode into the townships and brutally beat up Black children without cause. Of course, you could not report these actions, because everything the white man did was right and you were just a little terrorist trying to bring down the fatherland.

Yet the more I grew up amidst these conditions, the less it mattered that my whole community and I were criminals. In fact, it became obvious to me that the more "criminal" you were—defying an apartheid state—the more of a hero or heroine you became.

And that's how I became interested in this thing called "The Law."

The Law was all powerful: It determined what sea water you could swim in, which train carriage to get in, what bus you could take and whether you had to sit upstairs or downstairs—not a matter of age or pregnancy or infirmity, but a matter of your racial classification.

The Law regulated *all* things: from little things like which entrance to a government building you could use and where you were allowed to eat to bigger things like where you could live and study and whom you could marry. "What's love got to do with it?" Nothing. It only mattered what The Law said about it.

So I studied The Law, but the only places teaching The Law were the same places that had taught all those people who had made and implemented the apartheid laws. And so I, the child of a factory worker and a postman, learned The Law and the mechanisms of The Law and the philosophy of The Law of the Master from the teachers of the Master in the manner and the language of the Master.

∾

MATILDA SMITH has a bachelor's of social science and bachelor's of laws and is an admitted attorney of the High Court (CPD) who currently practices and teaches law in the Law Clinic of the University of Cape Town. She has worked with poor urban and rural communities in South Africa, taught and practiced *inter alia* human rights law, legal practice and poor law with barefoot lawyers (community based paralegals), law students, lawyers, court officials, oppressed and oppressors and anyone willing to teach and learn.

The Problem with Evolving

ETHEL MORGAN SMITH

After 9/11, Sarah and I agreed to not talk about politics. I found our new reality strange and difficult. My oldest friend was a new person; now we have rules about what we can and cannot speak of. I knew that her husband, Saul, was a German Jew and had escaped the Holocaust, yet I had never heard Sarah mention the Holocaust in the more than thirty-five years we'd been friends.

Then it happened; I was so excited that I slipped and forgot our agreement. We hadn't talked in a while when Sarah called me. I was always careful not to express my excitement about Obama being president, since she and Saul sounded like FOX News when they were talking about the president, and I wasn't willing to listen. I had other friends with political views similar to mine. After all, we can't get everything we need from one friend.

"What's going on?" Sarah asked.

"I am so excited. Angela Davis is coming to my university and she requested that I sit at the dinner table with her." Sarah was quiet, then she had to go. I thought nothing of it since we're all busy. When I didn't hear from her for a while, I replayed the telephone conversation in my head and kept reminding myself that I didn't think of Angela Davis as politics. By that time, Obama was in his second term as president.

About six weeks later, Sarah emailed me, saying that she

was sorry to just be getting back to me, but she had been so put off with my love of Angela Davis that she couldn't talk to me. Angela Davis had been negotiating for peace between the Israelis and Palestinians, and for that, Sarah hated her. This is what the woman does, travel around the world, including South Africa, trying to negotiate peace. I was shocked and angry.

I re-watched the documentary *Free Angela and All Political Prisoners* and felt even more proud of her. She was hunted down like a criminal, but she never broke. I wanted to be on her side of history.

Finally, I wrote Sarah back. The first thing I said was: In the words of Nelson Mandela, your enemies are not my enemies. Then I went on to ask her what she wanted from me. Was I supposed to contact her and ask for permission to admire and care about folks she hated? I was damn angry by then.

We wrote each other a few emails. I was puzzled and hurt and didn't know what to do with my emotions. Sarah told me that her mother had been a Holocaust survivor. I wrote her back and told her she didn't own all of the pain in history. My mother worked as a maid for fifty years earning $15 per week, and when our father was killed when the gas truck he drove exploded, we did not receive one dollar.

With the killing of Trayvon Martin, Michael Brown, Tamir Rice, Eric Garner and too many other Black bodies, along with the incarceration of Black bodies, my political radar was on high alert.

～

Months later, in mid-May, I finish grading finals for the semester. Around midnight, my telephone rings. Sarah cries into the telephone: She's afraid because Saul's health isn't good. And her kids are sick of her.

"Of course they're sick of you," I say. "We get sick of them, too." We both laugh.

Then I say, "Do you need me to come visit?"

"No, I just want to talk to you. Did I wake you?"

"No," I lie. "It doesn't matter; I'm done with classes for the semester."

"I'm sorry," she says.

"Don't be. I can pack up the dog and move in for a week or so. Just let me know."

And just like that, the sun is shining on our friendship again, as we navigate our way through our wounded pasts.

∾

ETHEL MORGAN SMITH is the author of two books: *From Whence Cometh My Help: The African American Community at Hollins College* and *Reflections of the Other: Being Black in Germany*. She has also published in the *New York Times*, *Callaloo*, *African American Review*, and other national and international outlets. Smith has received a Fulbright Scholar–Germany, Rockefeller Fellowship–Bellagio, Italy, Visiting Artist–The American Academy in Rome, DuPont Fellow–Randolph Macon Women's College, Visiting Scholar–Women's Studies Research Center at Brandeis University, The Virginia Center for the Creative Arts and Bread Loaf Fellowship. She is an associate professor of English at West Virginia University in Morgantown.

What Is Said

HOPE WABUKE

On June 16, 1944, George Stinney, a fourteen-year-old Black boy, was executed by the state of South Carolina for the murder of two white girls. George was so short that he carried a Bible to use as a booster seat for the electric chair. He was so young that the death mask would not fit his face. He took five full minutes to die, the mask slipping off to show his eyes melting and his body convulsing.

There was no evidence that George had committed the murders. There were no actual witnesses to the murders—in fact, George had an alibi for the whole day in question. The "confession," which George denied having made and which had not been recorded or written down, was the fabrication of three white police officers. But after a single-day trial, an all-white male jury returned a conviction and death sentence in less than twenty minutes for the fourteen-year-old boy.

George's family had been run out of town by its white citizens, so he did not even have the comfort of his mother's arms in the days he was imprisoned before his one-day trial and ensuing execution.

On December 17, 2014, the state of South Carolina overturned this conviction as wrongful and unjust.

On November 22, 2014, Tamir Rice, a twelve-year-old Black boy, was playing by himself with a pellet gun in a park in Cleveland, Ohio. Police arrived and immediately opened fire on Tamir. In the minutes that the twelve-year-old boy was bleeding out onto the pavement, the shooting officers did not deign to attempt CPR and save his life. Tamir Rice died at the hospital a few hours later.

One cannot avoid noticing the similarities in the cases of George and Tamir. Both Black boys, both executed by the state without cause. One was given the farce of a "trial," the other was not. We have regressed, it seems, from allowing even that when it comes to Black boys.

Tamir Rice's shooting happened two days before a grand jury decided not to indict another white police officer for shooting another unarmed Black boy named Mike Brown six times. I couldn't process it. I understand this is what is called shock. I was numb. The only conscious thought I had was to love my two-year-old baby boy, love every minute with him because I did not know how many days it would be until he, too, could be shot down to contain the "threat of his skin." Aiyana Jones, a Black girl, was seven and also unarmed when white police officers—again uncharged—shot and killed her.

That day of Tamir's death, I heard the echo of June Jordan in my head saying self-love is the most revolutionary act. My baby boy is the best part of myself. I committed to spend the day with him, loving him. I would take him to the park and his favorite places. That would be my protest.

We took baby boy's buckets and shovels with us, and like magnets, a small group of boys flocked to us in the sandbox. They looked so young, with their knocking knees and beautiful afros, I thought they were seven years old. "Are you in second grade?" I asked them. "No," they told me, "we are in seventh."

I did the math in my head and realized they were twelve. Twelve was the age Tamir Rice was when he was shot. "Twelve,"

I repeated. "Twelve." They did not know why I started to cry. But they looked so young. They looked like babies. I was seeing their bloodied brains and stomachs bleeding out onto the playground. Twelve, with a gun, shot down.

All that day I had moments of sudden tears; not crying, just water slipping out from my eyes.

In April 2014, Cliven Bundy and a group of armed militant white men drew guns and yelled threats at federal agents and police officers. "I've got a clear shot at four," one of Cliven Bundy's men is alleged to have threatened.

Assistant Sheriff Lombardo stated, "They pointed weapons," and "We were outgunned and outmanned." But Bundy and his men, unlike the unarmed Black children, were not shot dead, or arrested at that time.

It is, you see, about unequal application of force and justice depending upon race. It is about police brutality and racial profiling.

Darren Wilson, the white cop who killed Mike Brown, called him a "hulk," a "demon." A witness called him a "nigger." This is how they see us. Not as human. It has been documented by psychological studies that Black children are seen as criminal and not as young as white children are perceived, and the police act with increased violence accordingly when facing Black children.

∽

When I was a young girl of color growing up in Los Angeles, I wanted to become a writer to help end the virulent racism and sexism I had experienced, beginning when a white classmate called me "nigger" and pushed me off the swings in second grade. But now, as a Black mother of a Black boy, the systematic, often state-sanctioned acts of violence by white men upon Black bodies have become more real to me than they have ever been. Trayvon Martin, Aiyana Jones, Jordan Davis, Renisha McBride, John Crawford, Akai Gurley, Mike Brown, Eric Garner, Tamir Rice. The list is endless. I realized that the only way I would be able to keep my son safe would be to use my writing to help make the world a safer place for Black boys walking.

I would then be described as a "political" writer, as if that were bad. But everything is political. "Political" is only given a negative connotation when it is thrown at people of color for writing about our experience of living.

"How many of us have been told not to write about race? That, just by writing about your experience in the world as a Black person your book is 'too political' and will not sell?" I asked my peers at the Junot Díaz workshop at the Voices of Our Nations Arts Foundation. Nearly all of my brothers and sisters of color raised their hands.

I know I will be told this again and again—as will many writers of color. In workshop, "too political" is touted as critique. By those in the industry, it is dismissal of the content of your piece. But there are more important things. There are some things that need to be said. There are some moments in history when, if you are a writer and have been gifted with this uncanny ability to observe and make meaning in harmonious forms, you have a responsibility to look. To bear witness. As Junot Díaz says, "Those of us who have been systematically erased or marginalized throughout history have a right, a responsibility, to speak for those of us who now cannot."

~

HOPE WABUKE is a contributing editor at the *Root* and a contributing writer for Kirkus. Her work has also been featured in *Guernica, Ms.* magazine, *Salamander, Fjords Review, Ruminate, NonBinary Review,* and the *North American Review* and on The Daily Beast, Salon, Ozy, DAME, The Hairpin, Gawker, Literary Mama, and many more. Her work has also been featured in the anthology *All About Skin,* and her chapbook, *Movement No. 1: Trains,* was published in 2015. Wabuke was also a finalist for the 2015 Brunel International University African Poetry Prize.

Invisible Women

MENEN HAILU

Seventeen women living with HIV/AIDS in Ethiopia shared their stories with me by keeping their identities anonymous. Most women living with the virus keep their status a secret to be able to protect themselves from discrimination; few of them take the risk of becoming activists.

In Ethiopia, the rate of HIV/AIDS infection for women is twice as high as that for men. Inequalities characterizing the lives of women including poverty, violence and lack of protection make them more vulnerable to the disease. One of the main impacts of HIV/AIDS in Ethiopia is the growing number of children who have lost either one or both parents to the epidemic.

A girl named Yeshi, who lost her mother to HIV/AIDS two years ago, tells us that she has made a decision to go to Dubai for domestic work in order to later send money home with the help of her friend who is already there. We ask her, "Are you aware of what life would be like there?"

"I haven't found opportunities to be informed in detail about domestic work in the Middle East," she responds, "but I am determined and willing to work hard. It would have been ideal to only go to school. But that would have been possible if the basic needs were met at home. I must work, regardless."

Like Yeshi, young Ethiopian women are increasingly

migrating to the Middle East for domestic work, where several of their human rights are breached. The International Organization for Migration states: "the majority of workers leave through a diversity of illegal channels, facilitated by individual brokers and illegal employment channels. There are at present [only] 80 registered legal employment agencies in Addis Ababa, among a much larger set of illegal recruiters. At pre-departure, the women experience exploitation by traffickers and smugglers. At their destination, they experience labor exploitation, over-working, deprivation of food and sleep, withholding of salary, mistreatment and abuse: verbal, emotional and physical (beating, sexual exploitation, killing)."

According to UNAIDS, women living with HIV/AIDS are discriminated against because they tend to be blamed as vectors of the epidemic (to partners and children) and are labeled "promiscuous" and morally unworthy. Thus, they are rejected by their families, friends and the community. This results in being marginalized, abused and denied access to services such as employment, education, housing and other rights.

Suffering discrimination and the denial of human rights makes them less able to cope with the burdens of HIV/AIDS. Some living with the virus tend to alienate themselves (self-stigmatization) after facing discrimination or in fear of being discriminated against, with the thought: *What would people say about me?*

The following are some of the stories they have shared.

One says, "I keep my HIV status a secret. If I were open about it, my brother would not let me stay in the house."

"My family hid me for five months and four days in a room," says another.

"They did not want to live with me," says one woman, "they did not want to eat with me, they did not even sit on a chair on which I had previously sat."

"I used to be a cook," says yet another woman we interviewed. "Once I was aware of my HIV status, I wanted to be transferred to another type of work since my work was tiring. The employers were not willing to transfer me to another job, and so I had to quit."

"A woman living with the virus once fell from the stairs. The ones around her reacted by saying 'Do not touch her!'"

Many said, "They love me less."

"Because of discrimination, I had once almost reached the stage of committing suicide, but did not do so for the sake of my children. It is a fire that I have to carry every day."

"It brings psychological problems such as hating myself."

"My children are labeled 'AIDS children.'"

"My daughter is HIV positive. In the classroom, she is made to sit on a separate high table in the back of the room. Because of the discrimination she faces at school, I have kept her at home for a year. She now has mental problems."

"I go out and teach others about HIV/AIDS, but it has effects on how my daughter is perceived."

"The solution for me is to be open and to serve as an example to others."

"Love is what is most important. But people are governed by laws and not love, so it would be good if people were forced to follow anti-discriminatory laws on HIV/AIDS."

"Self-confidence enables me to live. Keeping one's HIV status a secret could result in mental instability. It is being untrue to oneself."

"Women have a lot of responsibilities within and outside the household. A woman needs to have her rights respected and to be at peace with herself."

❧

Yeshi and women living with HIV/AIDS may be made invisible in the society today, but they have spoken. A voice is invisible, yet audible. I hope that we have heard their voices, and respond.

❧

MENEN HAILU, originally from Ethiopia, is a graduate of Columbia University, with a master's in human rights studies, concentrating on women's rights and children's rights. She has researched women living with HIV/AIDS and street children from Addis Ababa, Ethiopia. Her documentary film, *Young Voices New Dreams*, stems from her thesis, "Human Rights of Street Children in Addis Ababa: A Gender Analysis and Perspectives of Street Children." Hailu has taught human rights in combination with the creative arts to youth at risk, ages twelve to nineteen, in New York City at IMPACT Repertory Theatre. She is also a photographer and poet. To see the film, visit www.youngvoicesnewdreams.com.

A Hairy Situation

WANDA M. HOLLAND GREENE

The telephone conversation began with a question laced with worry and a hint of vanity.

"Cheree, can you do me a large—I mean, very large—favor?"

My beloved hair stylist, Cheree, waited patiently for me to drop the proverbial other shoe. I paused, momentarily stunned by the audacity of the request emerging from my throat.

"Well, here's the story, Cheree. I am in San Diego right now with my family. We're enjoying spring vacation, and we won't be back in San Francisco until Sunday evening. I have to give an important speech at Fort Mason on Tuesday evening for my dear friend and mentor Jake, who is retiring as a head of school, and I have VACATION HAIR! Girl, I do NOT have head-of-school hair!" I shook my long and heavy dreadlocks and watched countless grains of sand from Imperial Beach fall to the floor. Something small with wings took flight from my scalp. This was not a cute picture.

"Cheree, I know the hair salon is closed Monday, but would you consider opening up for me? I would really like to feel more pulled together than this. I wouldn't ask if it weren't important."

"Of course," she replied instantly. "I'll call you back on Sunday and let you know what time to come in." Cheree couldn't see me dropping to the floor of my hotel room in blissful relief, quietly mouthing the words "Thank you, Jesus." I exhaled deeply and thanked her profusely.

Monday evening on my way to the salon for the 6:00 p.m. appointment she had given me, my cellphone rang. "Call me when you get to Sutter Street," Cheree said. "I'm sitting in my car because there is a homeless man who has set up his temporary dwelling in the doorway of the salon. We have to figure out what to do."

I paused for a moment to take in her words, tried not to panic about the possibility of a thwarted hair appointment, and then quickly agreed to call her when I arrived. As I continued to walk, I wondered what we should do about the homeless man. Should we ask him to move aside so that we could enter? Should we call a police officer to help us? How long would it take to manage this and get my hair done?

With each step toward Sutter, I could feel the more serious and less selfish questions poking their fingers into my flesh: Does this man live in the salon doorway on Sundays and Mondays when the shop is closed? Where does he live from Tuesday through Saturday when the shop is open? Why is he sleeping on the street? Is he mentally healthy? Is he hungry? What is his name? Where is his family? I became engrossed in my thinking and was suddenly at the salon door.

There in front of me was a man whose clothes were so filthy and tattered that it was difficult to make out the shape of his body. His face was hidden from me for the most part, but I could see that his eyes were closed. I didn't know if he was sleeping, thinking or praying for me to go away. The stained and damp flattened cardboard covered the sidewalk and part of the walls of the entryway, and there were bags and boxes containing the man's personal effects. In a strange way, this temporary dwelling looked quite permanent to me, and I had the overwhelming sense that asking him to dismantle his home and relocate would be incredibly disrespectful. I called Cheree.

"Wanda, we can't ask that man to move," Cheree sputtered before I could say a word.

"I had the same thought," I replied.

The next evening, I stood in my power at Fort Mason and delivered my speech with joyful flourish. Jake could feel my admiration and respect, and I was honored to be a part of his West Coast salute. My exquisitely styled hair glistened with its Aveda humectant pomade. As it had turned out, Cheree figured that we could get into the back door of the salon by walking to the next block and winding our way through a parking lot. We successfully reached the back door, went in and began the familiar two-and-a-half-hour ritual of washing, conditioning, palm rolling and styling my locks.

After the appointment, I had sashayed home on my urban runway of concrete slabs, feeling like a cross between Beverly Johnson and Nefertiti. As Tuesday came to an end, I carefully laid my freshly coiffed and tightly wrapped head on the pillow as my late father's words filled the chambers of my heart: "There but for the grace of God go I." I whispered a prayer of thanksgiving as I nestled in the comfort of my Pacific Heights home. How easy it had been for me to bend resources to my will and reclaim my beauty and professional dignity. With one telephone call, I could baptize my head in water, rise triumphantly and walk in the newness of life. Where would the homeless man go to feel whole again? Would his hair ever be clean? I fell asleep in a bed of questions, drifting off in the chasm between gratitude and shame.

∾

WANDA M. HOLLAND GREENE is native New Yorker who has been head of The Hamlin School in San Francisco since July 2008.

An experienced leader in education with a powerful voice and presence, Wanda has focused her attention on academic and ethical excellence, teacher evaluation, diversity and inclusion, adolescent health and global citizenship. The daughter of a Pentecostal preacher, she is well known for infusing her inspirational messages with poetry and song.

In 2014, she was named one of San Francisco's Most Influential Women in Bay Area Business, and in 2015 she received a Women Making History Award to honor her leadership in education.

What's in a Name

V.V. Ganeshananthan

It's all in the name.

Every day of the past nineteen years: ten syllables, twenty-four letters. My last name alone is five syllables and fourteen letters. It's a long time to live with anything, wouldn't you say?

G as in, "God-damn!" A as in, "Are you kidding?" N as in, "No way!" E as in, "Everyone must have a hard time remembering that." S as in, "Seriously?" H as in, "Hell no—I'm calling you by your first name." "Ganesh" is actually the short form of my last name. After the first grade, when I used the short version to make things easier for everyone else, I figured I could handle the whole thing just fine. I grew angry and thought, "Why should I make things easy for anyone? It's my name and if you can't handle it, that's your problem." I was going all out. As far as my last name was concerned, it was fourteen letters or bust.

Even my parents questioned the sudden choice. My brother went all the way through high school "making things easier," despite my arguments. My dad still goes by "Dr. Ganesh." People have suggested various alternatives to me. "Use the first name solo," like Cher, Roseanne or Jackée. I roll my eyes. I don't think I bear any great similarity to any of those people. No, I want to be just like everyone else. First name, last name, middle initial—thank you for coming, thank you for going.

It's been interesting over the years. First grade: People

attribute my success with the alphabet to "lots of practice." Second grade: My teacher expresses concern. People wonder if I get less time on tests because I spend so long writing my name. I assure them that my academics have not suffered as a result of my surname. I do, however, learn that if I want my name to fit in the upper-right-hand corner of a piece of notebook paper, I should start in the middle of the page, not four-fifths over to the right, where everyone else does. Fifth grade: In an unsuccessful bid for school president, I realize that "Vote for Ganeshananthan" isn't exactly, well, pithy. And absolutely nothing rhymes with it. It also makes posters and stickers expensive. I lose. I also begin to realize that when I leave phone messages with people who don't know me, I get the comment "wow" a lot. My mother and I get a similar reaction at the grocery store when she hands over her credit card to pay.

"How do you say that?" the cashier asks politely, eyebrows shooting up.

"Gun-ay-SHAN-an-than."

"Oh." Silence. "I get it. That's long."

Thank you.

Middle school: A bunch of teachers mispronounce my name when I first arrive. They are still mispronouncing it when I leave. "You're missing the second-to-last N," I try to explain to them.

"Are you sure it's phonetic?" they ask.

Yes, I'm sure.

High school: I take the SATs and the APs and similar standardized tests for people with short names. They turn me into "Ganeshananth, Vasug" or variations thereof. Rumor has it that each test-taker gets 200 points for writing their name. Someone asks if I get extra. When I am a sophomore, one of my friends is the editor of the school paper. When stories are a few lines short, she gets her reporters to call me for a quote so they can use my name to take up space. Before graduation, I have to spend extra time with the student announcing my name so she can get it right. I catch her in the bathroom before the ceremony, practicing the fourth and fifth syllables furiously.

College: One of my stories runs in Harvard's *Crimson* magazine. The column isn't wide enough for my name to fit on one line, so I become what is believed to be the first person in history to have a hyphenated byline without a hyphenated name. When I look to purchase a Crimson softball jersey, Crimson President Joshua H. Simon '00 tells me he's pretty sure my last name won't fit above my number. No, not even if they make the letters smaller and stretch them across the sleeves.

Ganeshananthan. Ganeshananthan-andonandonandon andonandon, as someone once said. But you know what? It's my name and I like it. I even like that some people think it's a pain and that I'm a pain for making them use it.

And we're not even on the topic of my first name yet. Relentlessly misspelled, mispronounced and misgendered, my first name has been an experience. Example 1: a recent job rejection letter addressed to Mr. Sugi Ganeshananthan. (It's hanging over my bed, the "Mr." circled in red.) Example 2: This past pre-frosh weekend, I went to dinner with three friends from high school. We were at Uno's, and the hostess had an abnormal amount of energy. The restaurant was crowded with a mixture of what looked like pre-frosh and frosh. It had been a long day and we were hungry. "Four, please," I said.

"Name?" the hostess asked, looking up expectantly. I hesitated for a moment, turning back to my friends, tired and not in the mood to be called "Susie." The male among us just laughed, but one of the two women came to my rescue. "Emily," she said, stepping up.

The hostess handed her a timer with a name on it, telling us it would be about fifteen minutes. We sat down and Emily shook the timer. Then she laughed. It said, "Elimy." You see my point.

But strangely, my name crops up where you would never expect to find it. Granted, I never find a Sugi mug or keychain or, for that matter, a Sugi anything in the card store aisle with all the name merchandise. (There are about a zillion varia tions of the name Alissa, though. Alisa, Alysa, Alyssa, etc.) But there's a restaurant near Fort Lee, New Jersey, with my name. I've never actually been there myself, but a friend handed me an advertising card. "Fine Japanese Cuisine...Sugi features Six Tatami Rooms accommodating up to 20 people." What? There are at least a hundred Sugis on America Online. Sugi.net is a website. I hope to buy sugi.org upon graduation. Or maybe ganeshananthan.com. I'm torn. I'm pretty sure no one would ever make it to ganeshananthan.com because they'd forget that pesky second-to-last "n."

So what, in the end, do I think of my name? What should I do when I get married, for example? Keep Ganeshananthan? Change? What if I marry someone with a really long last name? Oooh, I could hyphenate. The excitement!

No, I don't think so. I like my name the way it is.

This essay was originally published in the *Harvard Crimson* on April 22, 1999.

❦

V.V. GANESHANANTHAN'S debut novel, *Love Marriage*, was long-listed for the Orange Prize and chosen as one of Washington Post Book World's Best of 2008, as well as a Barnes & Noble Discover Great New Writers Pick. A recipient of fellowships from the NEA, the Radcliffe Institute and the American Academy in Berlin, she has been visiting faculty at the University of Michigan and the Iowa Writers' Workshop and presently teaches in the MFA program at the University of Minnesota. Her work has appeared in the *Washington Post* and the *New York Times,* among others. She is at work on a second novel, excerpts of which have appeared in *Granta, Ploughshares* and *Best American Nonrequired Reading.*

The Girl from the Ghetto

Deborah L. Plummer

I first met Beany Malone the summer following sixth grade on the day we called "library day." Library days alternated with museum days, replacing our schedule at St. Thomas Aquinas. Absent the nuns' regimen and lacking financial resources for day camps, Mom decided our summer educational experiences would consist of either visiting the county library located at the end of the street or visiting the city's art museum, a ten-minute walk if we cut through the playground of Doan Elementary School. Both public places had free admissions with librarians and museum guards serving as the best kind of adult supervision. With the exception of one sister, who had to be repeatedly reprimanded for sliding around the museum floors in her socks or flipping through the library's *Seventeen* magazines and tearing out pages of outfits she liked, my five sisters and I were all well-behaved kids.

At eleven years old, I had read the majority of the books in the children's section of the library and had no appetite for the childish rhymes in the books that I hadn't read. My favorite librarian, with the kind of enthusiasm white adults have for helping Black kids, decided that I was ready for the young adult section. There, she introduced me to her favorite books: a series about an Irish American family from Denver, Colorado, featuring one daughter, Beany Malone. The Malone family had no more in common with my family of Jamaican-Panamanian immigrant parents living in Cleveland, Ohio, than a family of ninja turtles from Mars. Yet after reading the first book of the series, I became enraptured by the pristine life of this white family and especially liked Beany, who had nothing else to do but cook, clean, decorate her room and dream about getting married.

Reading the series introduced me to a world very different from my beloved inner-city neighborhood. Spending evenings turning ice cream freezers making peppermint-stick ice cream was nowhere near as exciting as the street parties in my neighborhood with everyone line dancing to the latest Motown hit. The happy hullabaloo of teenagers running through the Malone household wasn't as interesting as the visits to our house from fast-talking men who sold jewelry, clothing and even groceries door-to-door—goods that my sister secretly told me were acquired through "a five-finger discount." Yet, I found a comforting stability in the world of the Malones.

On Saturdays, I was active in our neighborhood Girl Scout troop, a predominantly Black troop with Mrs. Hazel Ford as our leader, a voluptuous woman who taught us Negro spirituals along with the traditional Girl Scouts songs. At an all-city Girl Scout meeting, I overheard two white Girl Scouts from a troop across town whisper that we were Black girls from "the ghetto." I didn't have to look up the word to know that ghetto was not a good place. Their persnickety tone and superior glares defined it for me. I had experienced my first sting of racism without any warning from Beany that this was how white people actually thought.

I completed reading *Something Borrowed, Something Blue,* one of the final books of the series, in which Beany gets married, the summer our family moved to a predominantly white rural area. Their intense desire for us to "get a good education" in a "good neighborhood" meant a move was in order. I would be educated and socialized with the Beanies of the world. At thirteen, I found myself a ninth-grader in an all-white, all-girls Catholic high school where my struggle with racial identity intensified. Thirty miles from my Black girl friends, my new friends were all white girls who lived like the Malones. Their families owned stunning homes, and, compared with my paycheck-to-paycheck family, were multimillionaires. Like Beany, my new white friends asserted their wants and opinions aggressively to their parents; some even had freckles across their noses and harbored Irish tempers. Straight out of the pages of the series, many owned and rode horses.

My parents had purchased a home under construction with plans to complete it as finances dictated. Like the physical space in which I lived, my racial identity needed resolution. I wasn't Beany and I was no longer the girl in the ghetto. I was the "only one" in my class. I resolved it by being the "race mascot." I made jokes about race. I laughed at their jokes about race. I never confronted. I blended into a comfortable existence of becoming more and more like Beany despite the fact that I didn't have freckles.

Then the summer of 1966 came and race was no longer a funny topic. My internalized white identity, honed over the years from lessons from Beany, completely dissolved. While my classmates took summer trips to visit relatives in Europe, I went back to the inner city to babysit for family friends. Spending my summer in an apartment without air conditioning with three kids under the age of ten gave me the opportunity to connect with my Black friends, whom I desperately missed. It also placed me in the middle of Cleveland's race riots, a week of civil unrest during which four people were killed, many more were critically injured and the Hough community destroyed.

When the riots began, I watched with detached interest from the apartment window. As people I recognized spilled onto the streets, I described the chaos like a newscaster to the kids who were lying flat on the floor by my feet. Smoke churned through the air and a sharp blast compelled us to quickly move to a huddle in the bathroom where we stayed until the uproar tapered off.

I wasn't scared. In fact, I approached the riots with curiosity and an uncanny understanding of the root causes. These were people who were tired of their identity being defined by social problems that they had no control over and that had created their neighborhood conditions. I suddenly felt the weight of having to live in close proximity to white privilege without ever being able to experience its benefits. It was an idyllic experience to read about the Malones and now a distressing experience to exist in a community like theirs.

The next day, I defied my parents' order not to go anywhere near the streets where the riots were still active, and joined my friends for what we knew would be a real-time history lesson. Our goals were to actually see national guardsmen and to witness the looters. We were confident that we could avoid the rocks being thrown and were simply naive about gun fatality. It would be a show to surpass any movie we had seen. Except it didn't have that impact.

The anger was explosive, the violence physically and emotionally jarring, the tension between the police and the community members frightening. My neighborhood, the ghetto.

After several days, the riots dissipated. My parents took me back to the land of Beany Malone and its own culturally encapsulated ghetto. The roar of the fires and the ripples of gunshots would forever be etched in my racial identity. My white friends, unaware of race riots and absent any personal racial identity struggle, would now become acquainted with the girl from the ghetto.

༄

Deborah L. Plummer, Ph.D., is the editor of the *Handbook of Diversity Management* (Rowman & Littlefield) and author of *Racing Across the Lines. Changing Race Relations through Friendship* (Pilgrim Press), which received the publisher's Mayflower Award for best publication in the category of church and society. As a psychologist, university professor and chief diversity officer, she has also authored several book chapters and published numerous journal articles for the academic community. She has written for *Diversity Executive* and *Globe Magazine* and is a proud board member of GrubStreet, one of the nation's leading creative writing centers, located in Boston. You can find more information at www.dlplummer.com.

In a Family Way

Family and Friendship

A Pink Dress

Jennifer De Leon

Spring of my senior year in college I needed to buy a dress for graduation. *Not just any dress, of course,* Vaya, my mother, had said. So we drove to the mall, our special mother-daughter terrain. We were experts at tracking discounts. Tuesdays were retail markdown days. The salespeople at Macy's gave out coupons, and twice a year, if you purchased full-price bras at Victoria's Secret, you got a free lip gloss. That day, weeks before I would be the second in my entire extended family (next to my older sister) to graduate from college, my mother and I had a clear goal: find the dress.

Then, suddenly, there it was underneath the glow of soft lighting inside Ann Taylor. Magenta, magical.

My mother and I gazed at the silk fabric through the storefront window. A headless mannequin showed off the exquisite A-line cut. Sleeveless, sophisticated. Nothing but a pane of fingerprint-proof glass between us. We stepped inside the store and were greeted by the sweet smell of leather and cashmere-blend tops as the aura of credit card transactions hovered around us like a mist.

"How much?" my mother asked.

I massaged the crisp white price tag between my thumb and forefinger.

"How much do you think?"

We left the mall that day, defeated. The dress cost one

hundred dollars, well over what we could afford. I was a scholarship student at Connecticut College, a private liberal arts
school that resembled a country club. My mother worked as
a housekeeper. I made six dollars an hour babysitting for families near campus. I would need to buy a suit for upcoming
job interviews, not to mention outfit an apartment in Boston
where I planned to live with two friends from college come
September. My mother and I, expert shoppers, knew storefront
items wouldn't be marked down for weeks, maybe months.
Graduation was in seventeen days.

"I'll find a dress at the mall near school," I assured her, my
voice rinsed of confidence as I pictured the crowded racks
inside the mall in New London. She pursed her lips, lowered
her lashes.

My college graduation dress was as important to her as
a wedding gown. Ever since my mother was a schoolgirl in
Guatemala, where she had often carried the flag in the annual
school parade (an honor for the students with the highest
marks in each grade), she had dreamed of going to college.
Education was like a religion in our household. She preached
the importance of straight As. She snuck in *consejos* like
mashed-up vitamins in our morning mosh. "If you study hard
you can get a good job and then you can do whatever you want,"
she'd say. Or, "Books are your friends." When she was driving
my sisters and me to gymnastics or Girl Scouts or church, and
we couldn't escape, she'd tell us about a family whose house she
cleaned, how the son went to Duke (the name made me think
of a prison) and how he got a scholarship (the word sounded
like a disease).

Thanks to my mother's persistence, I eventually learned the
true meaning of a scholarship when I earned one to attend

Connecticut College. One semester she spoke to my Women & World Studies class. Seated at the far end of a rectangular wooden table in the snug classroom of an ivy-covered campus building, my mother crossed her arms and described her experience moving from Guatemala to the United States at the age of eighteen, and we discussed the ways in which globalization played a role in our family's economic, political and cultural trials. I got an A.

Then she visited me at the offices of *Ms.* magazine in New York City where I interned one summer. I'll never forget the moment that Gloria Steinem's long-fingered, delicate hand knotted with my mother's coarse hand with chipped nail polish—just for an instant. "How lovely to meet you," Ms. Steinem said. "You, too," my mother replied.

The next fall, when I studied abroad in Paris, my mother came to visit. She insisted on taking pictures of the small cars she said looked like sneakers and then asked me to take photos of her posed in front of them. In between visits to the Louvre and the Sorbonne, where I was taking a feminist philosophy class and attending lectures by Hélène Cixous, my mother bought miniature replicas of the Eiffel Tower for relatives in Boston. Throughout the years, she held tight the picture in her mind of each of her daughters on that all-important day: graduation.

∽

The final weekend before college graduation, my mother came to visit me on campus. She had packed a weekend bag and driven the two hours to campus. By now she knew where to park and how to type in the seven-digit code required for entering the dorm. There, inside my room, she relaxed on the purple comforter (the one that she had sewn herself) and talked to my grandmother on the phone while I wore headphones and worked on a final paper. That night we ate dinner in Mystic, a quaint seaport town fifteen minutes away.

We sat upstairs in a restaurant overlooking the bridge, where we ordered piña coladas and split an entrée of stuffed scallops. Afterward, back on campus, we drank frothy beers from plastic red cups and met up with my friends. By then they knew and loved her. The following morning, my mother and I ate brunch in the dining hall and then took a long walk in the school arboretum. Before she returned home, she handed me a department store bag with hair gel, toothpaste, shampoo and raspberry-flavored Fig Newtons. I stood on the dorm entrance steps and watched her drive away, the car a little lighter, both of our hearts a bit heavier. I could tell she was already mourning her visits to Connecticut College. Monday passed. Tuesday.

Finally, on Wednesday morning of my last week of classes, I dug in my closet for a shirt to wear to my final presentation in women's studies. There, tucked between a sparkly tank top and a white button-down, I felt the crinkle of a cream-colored plastic garment bag. I pulled it out gently and immediately recognized the magenta fabric peeking out the bottom. I didn't have to look because I already knew what was inside.

∽

JENNIFER DE LEON is the editor of *Wise Latinas: Writers on Higher Education* (University of Nebraska Press, 2014). Selected as a tuition scholar in fiction at the Bread Loaf Writers' Conference in 2015, De Leon was also named the 2015–2016 writer-in-residence by the Associates of the Boston Public

Library. She is using her office space in the Boston Public Library and stipend to work on her young adult novel, *Don't Ask Me Where I'm From.* Jennifer's short story "Home Movie," originally published in the *Briar Cliff Review,* was also chosen as the 2015 One City One Story pick as part of the Boston Book Festival. De Leon is now a freelance writer, editor and consultant, as well as a creative writing instructor at Emerson College, GrubStreet creative writing center and elsewhere. She also has an active career as a public speaker on issues of diversity, college access and the power of story.

Offerings

JAIME LEON LIN-YU

What do you call forty-plus relatives who span three generations? A gaggle? A clan? A tribe? A tribe is a community whose members interact with and support each other. When tragedy strikes (death, illness), they rally, but call them on a Saturday to chitchat? No thanks.

When my husband and I started dating, I knew I had a lot to overcome, but I did not realize just how much. His father had died when he was seventeen; his sister was eight. As the oldest, my husband took on a father-like role and assumed the mantle of crown prince among the family. (It is not uncommon for relatives to tell me how lucky I am to have married such a perfect man.)

Meanwhile, their mother was forced to speak the English she abhorred and take control of the family, both financially and emotionally. She did it like a boss, using the life insurance money to buy a new home and renting out the old one for additional income. She was a vibrant butterfly: trips to Australia, dance lessons, shopping...always on the phone with friends. When you look at her now—post-stroke—she is frail, a halo of frizzy gray hair framing her face. Her mind is still sharp, her emotions closer to surface. Tears hover perpetually at the edges of her eyes.

We had moved away from Seattle in the mid-aughts, me relieved and almost giddy to leave the city notorious for its

Freeze (which refers to its citizens more than its climate), and my husband slightly intimidated, perhaps a tad resentful of having left a place where he had lived almost his entire life. We relocated to New York City, which—in my mind—was home. Unlike in Seattle, here I was loved, cherished even, by old and new friends. Moving saved our marriage and revitalized our careers.

Multiple jobs and two children later, we found ourselves back in Seattle, after more than a decade away, called "home" by my ailing mother-in-law.

❧

I had sworn I would never return to Seattle. When I had first moved there, I realized quickly that the city and I would never fall in love. It's a maze of twice named streets and lawns mushy with the drizzle that arrives in October and stays well into the summer. Despite its purported laid-back nature, Seattle can be cold, unyielding. I was desperate for warmth, which I did not find in the weather—or in my in-laws. What I failed to understand was that the cultural code is passive aggressive; my direct ways and honest nature were seen as hostile.

It is not an understatement to say I was not what my mother-in-law had envisioned when she and her daughter met me. I understand now that I was the enemy, a threat to take their beloved son and brother away. They could barely meet my gaze, preferring to look at my husband when I asked a question or at a spot somewhere over my head. At our first luncheon, my husband's sister sat across the table, hunched over, eyes only for her heroic brother. Later, when asked what she thought of me, she replied, "At least she's prettier than your last girlfriend." At our wedding, she would cry ugly, brokenhearted tears and hug her brother, desperate to lay claim to him.

My mother-in-law had said my right eye was smaller than my left. Baffled, she would repeatedly ask my husband (sometimes in front of me in Chinese), "Why is it like that? Is it because she is not full Chinese?" My husband shrugged. His mother continued, "Must be her Filipino side."

I did not speak Chinese, but I did honor the traditions, except mine were not "right." My mother is half-Filipina; both my parents grew up in the Philippines. My husband's family is from mainland China and they sought refuge in Taiwan with Chiang Kai-Shek. To put it bluntly, I was not the same kind of Chinese. But I could not explain the Chinese diaspora to my in-laws. They relied on their own singular experience to guide them; they had never taken an ethnic studies class.

When my mother-in-law announced her plans to host a red egg party for my niece when she reached one hundred days, I reminded her that the red egg ceremony is performed one month after birth, not almost three months later.

"We did this for my kids, remember? You came to visit when they were four weeks old."

My mother-in-law shook her head. "You're confused. Red egg is done one hundred days later. That is Chinese. You did it the Filipino way. Or maybe the Korean way."

But I knew—indignantly, furiously—I had not. She was the confused one. Later I learned she had tweaked the rules because she had wanted to give her premature granddaughter time to grow stronger before her big debut. Rather than admit that, my mother-in-law accused me of not being Chinese enough.

❧

What could I do? What could anyone have done? When all one sees is disappointment and resentment in the faces of those meant to be family, what can one do? You seek counsel with your dead father-in-law, of course. Because you figure his absence set off the chain of events that led you here.

$\backsim$

I often think about my father-in-law and what life would have been like had he lived. He is in a handful of photos, serene with a *cha-siu-bao* face. I had fantasized what I would ask, what I would say. I had it all planned out: drive to the cemetery, the sun shining its blessings. I would bring ritual offerings that my mother and aunts had done. I would bring Coca-Cola—the drink of American prosperity—oranges for luck and sticks of incense. I would bow three times and feel...something.

I never got around to driving out there. Maybe it was laziness or embarrassment or inertia. I told myself the sticks of incense would not light due to the damp air. I imagined other mourners staring at me, distracted from their grief by the imposter posing as the dutiful daughter-in-law. I wanted to feel mystical, empowered...and accepted.

Instead, I felt stupid.

Mythicizing my father-in-law wasn't the answer. Thinking like this was another form of whining—to a dead person. My problem was with the living, not the dead. I did wonder if he would've liked me, but I never asked, partly because my husband would have been a very different person had his father survived. He might have been so different that he may not have loved me at all—or I him.

And in the end, I am reminded it's about love, which is a very Western notion. It's also about duty, which is a very Eastern belief. I love my husband enough to bring him back to his mother and sister. Love brought me to Seattle the first time and love made us leave. Hopefully love will help us to stay.

$\backsim$

JAIME LEON LIN-YU earned her MFA at Mills College, where she received the Marion Hood Boess Haworth Prize for YA fiction. She was twice a resident fellow at Hedgebrook, accepted as a fiction candidate at Voices of Our Nations Arts Foundation (VONA) and attended Bread Loaf Writers' Conference on the prestigious work-study-waiter scholarship. She was also a part of the Emmy-winning writers' team at *One Life to Live.* Her work has appeared in the anthology *Philly Fiction, Seattle Weekly* and *MetroKids* magazine, and on SoapNet.com, ABC.com, York Daily Dispatch, AsianAve.com and haveuheard.com. She lives in Seattle with her husband and two sons.

A Note to the Boy
Who Was My Son

TARA DORABJI

When you were in fifth grade, you put your hand on the square of my back, so you could feel my heart beat right into it. You knew that I came back for you. To take care of you. Because you asked me to. The plan was that I would leave before your dad came home. But he left work early.

"Stop, Dad," you said. And you put your small, thin frame between us. Your father stepped back and released his hold on me. That is when you put your hand on my back. I was sitting on the stairs. "It's okay. You can go. Go." You gave me permission. Somehow, I needed it.

Days before, I'd left you sobbing on your bed when I said that I was leaving your dad. Lanky in form, arms lean, muscles reaching to cover bone. Even though I was raising you, I had no legal or biological claim to you. Leaving your dad was leaving you.

I came back a few days later to take care of you. Your moon face beamed at me, and we pretended like nothing had changed, your hand warm in mine as we walked home from school. Your shoelaces dragged, untied, through the gutter as we crossed the street. Without being asked, you did your homework. If you were good enough, sweet enough, maybe I would stay.

When your dad and I finally split up for good, you were

sixteen and no longer good or sweet. Your voice dropped and hung flat. *I don't give a shit,* you said. *It doesn't matter to me.* The gaping holes in your teeth had been replaced by braces. The rounds of your eyes were bloodshot red and lidded with weed.

You moved out a few months later, taking the posters from your wall. You couldn't stop shaking your foot. Even your voice trembled. I could not see the scabs under your shirt, but I knew they were there, trying to stake a claim to the pain you tried to cut away.

Years later, when I took you to MOMA, you told me you saw the Columbia poster I'd given you on a TV show. You still have it hanging on your wall. A piece of revolutionary street art passed from me to you.

I recycled the empty bottles of tequila in your room. Convinced that you would come back, I waited nearly a year before clearing out your room. But even the calls had stopped—the substance abuse program, your CPS worker, the counselor from the county shelter. The worst was when the calls stopped from you on birthdays, on Mother's Day.

But then, they started again.

Calls from you wanting something. A place to stay. A tent. Money.

My stomach tightened and heat rushed to my cheeks when you told me what you wanted. Joy, longing and anger collided. I told myself that I didn't hunger for you. We, for a moment, pretend not to be strangers. Mother and son. And that still exists even if not bound by blood or law. On your eighteenth birthday, you called me back to ask me to sign over your college account to you. You're not in college, I said.

I wanted to be angry because it gave me something to feel that took the pain away.

When you were twenty-one, I called you and asked you to be a pallbearer for my grandmother. You took the day off work. I pulled your suit out of the closet that I'd emptied out all those years ago. It still fit. You cut your hair and shaved. Dark suit. A young man. Three days later, you called again and asked me to pick you up at the Caltrans station. You came home for Thanksgiving.

On your twenty-second birthday, you texted me and asked if I'd buy you a passport. Yes, I said. We are both waiting for you to save enough money to buy the ticket.

I remember how we were. And we start becoming something new.

Still, I realize that after all these years, I never said thank you for that time you put your hand on my back and told me it was okay to leave.

Before I walked out that door, I held you. All 46 pounds of you, balled up as if you could become a fetus that would fit inside of me and go into my womb and be born again as my child.

❧

Tara Dorabji is a writer, strategist at Youth Speaks, mother and radio journalist at KPFA. Her work is published or forthcoming in *TAYO Literary Magazine, Huizache, Good Girls Marry Doctors: South Asian American Daughters on Obedience and Rebellion, Center for Asian American Media, Mutha Magazine* and *Midwifery Today*. Tara is working on novels set in Kashmir and Livermore. Her projects can be viewed at dorabji.com.

Beloved Halmoni*

MIRIAM CHING YOON LOUIE

You press your blade into the bellies of cucumbers sweating with salt. Slice them long ways. Stuff the slits to bursting with slivered carrots and an eye-watering, nose-burning, hair-curling red mash of pepper, garlic, ginger, chives, onions and salted shrimp.

We're in Auntie Esther's backyard in Pico Rivera in southeast Los Angeles where you and your earthenware crocks of fermented Korean sauces and pickles reign supreme.

Your white hair is parted in the middle and secured at your nape and your floral apron is tied around your thick waist. You are the oldest surviving member of the Yoon tribe and you allow Mom and her big sis Esther to tell each other their news in the kitchen as my one-year-old brother Kenny keeps us company outside.

My rice-bowl haircut swishes sharp. You let me help you stuff the cukes, and I am thrilled to be trusted with such a big-girl job, until I accidently rub hellish pepper in my eyes, forcing you to perform an emergency "eye wash" with the garden hose. You scold me in Korean, which I don't understand since we live up north near Dad's family in San Francisco Chinatown. But your deep growl is a ringer for Mom's. Scary. Foreshadowing a switch. A belt. The closest torture instrument.

Thankfully, you guide me back to your sweating cukes. You

carefully tie a chive around the waist of each one to contain its swelling tummy come bubble time. You teach me that a grass blade can be a belt if its wearer is small enough.

My brother Kenny falls hard and cries out in pain. His undershirt and diapers are blotchy with dirt and snot. That's when you scoop him up and park him astride your hip in one smooth motion like a galloping horsewoman stooping low to rescue a lost child. At that moment, I realize that you must have made this movement a zillion times.

Let's hop, skip and jump to years later when Mom—the youngest of your eleven-child brood—makes the same swooping motion to save Kenny's life as he is going down for the third time. One minute he is chasing a lizard up a tree that overlooks an angry river. Then he is a splash, scream and bubbles. Then he is choking up water in Mom's arms. Dad's, my and li'l bros Matt's and Ernie's mouths round in soundless fish o's. Miracle Mom gifts Kenny with another two decades. Before Alcohol King spirits him off to the grave at age twenty-nine.

But now, on this L.A. morning, Kenny the explorer grins from the safe perch of your hip, able to survey the yard's four corners from a greater height. He points and rides your hip to a crock, where, still holding him, you stack the stuffed cucumbers with your free hand. You show me how to tend babies and keep on working.

The heat readies the kimchee for rice in no time. You slice and serve the cucumbers with fragrant sides you've made from wild weeds like dandelion, mustard greens and bracken fern. I have never tasted cucumber kimchee as good as the batch you made that day.

Beloved Halmoni*, your kids know it is you, the unnamed
patriot and woman warrior, who keeps your family and nation
alive through radical acts of daily devotion. Your plantation
hands crack, furrow and thicken with the seasons. Jesus feeds
the hungry multitudes with fish and loaf miracles; you, with
pickles and rice magic.

You toil as laundress, migrant farmer and domestic worker
while Grandpa, your Methodist Minister husband, fights for
liberation and shepherds flocks of Korean migrants working
Hawaii's plantations and West Coast farms. Historians familiar with Grandpa's leadership and sacrifice to the Korean
independence movement against Japanese colonialism tell
me, "Your grandmother was a baby-making machine!" I know
these men mean this as a compliment. But you lose six children along the way to poverty and overwork and Aunt Sarah to
suicide because of her cheating husband. Heavy is your sorrow,
Halmoni. Grief-strewn your path.

You teach your chicks how to squawk and fight back.
Five-foot-tall ball of energy, you are the original party animal,
singing and dancing with co-workers and fellow survivors
late into the night, then stumbling back out into the fields the
next morning. When you fight, woe be unto thine opponent.
Including Grandpa, who must flee through a window to escape
you and your trusty knife. His sin? Talking too long with a
white woman. Tip: Do not mess with a woman of color! Lest
she grab the closest instrument of torture. I saw you slice those
cucumbers head to toe. I know the power of your blade.

I get to see you only a few times before you ascend to
that great church picnic in the sky. I have clay crocks full of
questions about whether Mom's madness and my sadness
visited you, too. I journey to your home province, walking

where the grass grows back thick, green and crunchy after U.S. carpet-bombing and napalm. I play the *janggu* hourglass drum so your spirit can party upstairs while we dandelion drummers—and your great-great-grands—rock the beat downstairs sending you armfuls of love.

---

*   Halmoni—Grandma, Grandmother

∽

MIRIAM CHING YOON LOUIE is a Korean Chinese American writer whose works feature kick-butt heroines and their movements. A former member of the Third World Women's Alliance, Louie was co-founder of the Women of Color Resource Center, Oakland, and served as media coordinator for Asian Immigrant Women Advocates and Fuerza Unida. Voices of Our Nations Arts schooled her in fiction and poetry; and Jamaesori, SisterSound and the Korean Youth Cultural Center taught her farmers'-style drumming. Check out her books, including *Not Contagious—Only Cancer* and *Sweatshop Warriors: Immigrant Women Workers Take On the Global Factory*, at www.rabbitroar.com. Louie is working on a tale of men of color who build a road through Burmese jungles as they fight enemies, both foreign and homegrown.

An Exceptional Father

Vicki L. Ward

My parents and their friends took turns hosting bid whist card parties. My brother Preston and I loved when it was our turn, because the house was filled with the music of Little Richard, Jackie Wilson, B. B. King and others. The adults sang and danced and we did the same in our room. There was lots of laughter, cards slapping on the table, and someone would shout "Boston," taking all the points and winning the game to the howls of all.

My older brother and I had our own party where we were shuttered in our bedroom. We would open the door a few inches to spy on the party and then close it, doing our silly imitations of the adults, falling on the bed in laughter. My dad instructed us not to come out unless we had to go to the bathroom, which gave us our only glance into the living room as we were ushered down the hall. Our limit was two trips, and we learned not to push that.

Those were the good times. Apart from the bid whist game nights, my father sometimes came home drunk. Maybe he'd gotten into an argument with his boss. He was a cook on the ship and worked long hours, so maybe something went wrong and he'd been reprimanded. Or maybe he lost some money gambling. These were reasons I used to believe were responsible for his drinking. Often, hearing his heavy stomps up the stairs signaled what kind of night it would be.

My dad was a career Navy man and received transfer orders to relocate every three years. Each time, my parents packed up their growing family, moving up and down the West Coast— Washington, Oregon and a third and final move to California. I was eight when we lived in San Diego and can distinctly remember how calm the house was when my father was on a ship out to sea. Upon his return, there were calm nights, and then there were two very different houses: the party house and the alcoholic house.

Those dark memories of cowering beneath the covers in fear were a marked contrast to those lively, colorful nights of parties filled with laughter and music. If my dad arrived home after drinking, we heard volatile arguments and bumps against the thin walls from their bedroom. Mother's voice got louder and firmer. She had given my brother and me firm instructions to comfort our two year old sister, Denise, when these arguments began.

"No, I'm not gonna do this tonight. Quiet down before you wake the kids! Stop it! You are not coming in here with that BS tonight," Mother shouted angrily.

Ashamed, I never breathed a word of these events to anyone. I was too embarrassed. I swore no husband of mine could ever touch alcohol. As a teen, spending time in the homes of friends, I learned alcohol-fueled arguments and warring parents were often the norm.

My father retired from the Navy, yet the alcohol-fueled scenarios continued. I was fifteen and knew alcohol was the scourge and our family was its prey. We lived in apartment buildings near the Navy base—buildings so old that the city had scheduled them for demolition. This was the catalyst my mother needed. After seventeen years of marriage, she summoned the courage to break the cycle of a wife battered by an alcoholic husband.

She silently crafted a change for her family and never revealed her plan. She found a small house, secured additional work and relocated all of us within two months. When the timing was right, she dealt the final blow: She changed the locks to the house. That night, my father retuned home late and he fumbled, attempting to unlock the door, yet his key didn't work. We were all awakened by his slurred cursing, his banging on the door. "Let me in the damn house!" My mother stood tall and comforted us, but she refused to open the door.

"You can't stay here anymore!" She said it sternly and loudly through the closed door. He knocked and continued to twist the knob. He kept at it for a long while. But he finally left, cursing his way down the street. She'd never stood up to him so defiantly, and he must have sensed the change in her. With little drama, they later divorced.

∽

We're all products of the environment in which we've been raised. I spent a lot of time trying to make sense of alcoholism, domestic violence and parenting, and was left confused. I carried with me insecurities from not having a loving, nurturing father raise me to adulthood and beyond, and knowing what a broken family was.

Years later, I married, gave birth to a son and later divorced my son's father. My ex rarely came to school plays or soccer games, and probably because of that, I became like a mother bear, so much like my own mother: I was on a mission. I would make sure my son didn't grow up the way I did. I didn't want him to feel the loss I felt, so I watched his development carefully, paying particular attention to the kind of environment I was providing for him.

I surrounded him with positive, strong Black males like his Uncle Prentice, who took him to the barbershop and fishing whenever he went, and Uncle Preston, who always talked to him about moral values. There were also great male friends of mine like Daniel, who took my son to T-ball games, basketball games and soccer games.

In our conversations, I stressed to my son that his father loved him but just didn't know how to be a father. I didn't want to poison him by putting his dad down, and eventually God led his father to contact me, telling me that he wanted to reestablish a permanent place in his son's life.

Much of what I taught my son and what he picked up was by instinct. Yes, I had my mother's blueprint for raising four children ages seven to sixteen alone. She fled from an abusive father into the arms of a troubled young man who became an alcoholic husband. She was just months shy of earning her high school diploma. As a single mother armed with new determination, she obtained her GED and a job to support her brood.

Watching her taught me about strength and resilience. I became that strong and empowered woman charged with the physical, emotional and mental development of a young Black male. Through my developing faith, inner strength and perseverance, I raised a strong young man. His training came from his surrogate fathers and me. Today, at forty-one, he is the married father of five boys.

He easily assumed the roles of father, husband and head of household for the two boys his wife brought to the marriage at ages eight and twelve, as well as the three boys they later had together—bringing their brood to five boys. He became a caretaker for his mother-in-law, a wheelchair-bound stroke victim. He is a professional child development specialist working with youth in the county juvenile detention facility.

He stands big—over six feet tall—and is incredibly patient, forgiving and understanding. He approaches decisions rationally and logically. He has three boys under fourteen years old at home. He models positive behavior for them, demonstrating character, teaching life skills, imprinting moral values and cultivating responsibility. He takes his family on annual winter vacations—providing snowboarding lessons—and on trips to water parks, to picnics, professional baseball games, new car shows and monster truck rallies.

His drives them to school each morning and attends school events and parent–teacher conferences. He and his wife own a family catering business through which they teach their boys life skills. I asked him whether he gets tired juggling his work time and family time. He answered, "Yes, but it all dissolves once I see the smiles on their faces." At home the boys love to snuggle under each of his arms, napping with their hero. He would never be a father in name only; he would live with, love, nurture and raise his children.

I wanted to know how he'd done it. "How did you learn to be such a giving and nurturing father without your own father in your life when you were young?" I asked.

He thought before he answered. "I watched my uncles, and the men in your life. I also watched my friends who were fathers, and above all, knew in my heart what I wanted for mine."

He said he was watching the hurdles I jumped over, saw how I juggled so much as a single parent and how determined I was to return to college to get my B.A. degree. He witnessed me purchase our first home and develop my professional career. Our bond was strong, communication open and honest as we shared love, values, goals and faith—all of which he incorporated into being a father.

I am blessed to have had a strong mother who provided a road map to follow when I faced raising a child into a man alone. I understand that God places many opportunities and people in your life. I know He placed this young man in my life and gave me the humility, wisdom and compassion to teach him and show him the way, even when I didn't know he was watching.

❧

VICKI L. WARD is an author and publisher of several award-winning books, including *Life's Spices from Seasoned Sistahs: A Collection of Life Stories from Mature Women of Color; Savvy, Sassy and Bold after 50! A Midlife Rebirth* and *More of Life's Spices, Seasoned Sistahs Keepin' It Real.* Her latest book, *Supercharge Your Life after 60: 10 Tips to Navigate a Dynamic Decade,* was released in 2016. She publishes books that help educate, inspire and illuminate women's lives and that highlight and enrich their journey. She believes in empowering women to become motivated self-advocates, both to seek and exceed their needs—to dream bigger dreams and learn how to achieve them.

Rewriting the Story

MEILAN CARTER-GILKEY

Driving my younger son, Mateo, to his private co-op school in our two-year-old SUV, dressed in yoga pants accessorized with a cliché coffee cup, I am a stranger. I don't recognize this woman. She looks like a typical suburban mother and housewife who shuffles her seven-year-old to extracurricular activities after school, but she is not.

She *is* a wife and a mother, but she is also a writer, a renter with too much student loan debt and a professional caregiver of her mother. Mateo's mother is also Kamau's mother, and sixteen years ago she drove Kamau to public school in her "previously owned" Toyota Corolla (an upgrade from the salvaged Volkswagen Rabbit), before attending classes at San Francisco State University and then going to work. Her mother, Mateo and Kamau's grandmother, was like her wife: helping with pickups, meals and homework. There was no husband.

⟳

My mother cried when I told her I was pregnant. Not just because I was nineteen and a sophomore in college, but because I was alone and she knew what it was like to be a single mother without a degree. She had worked hard to return to school as a wife and a mother and eventually as a grandmother. My mother was a free spirit who talked honestly about sex and introduced me to Planned Parenthood at a party when I was twelve (much to my horror). Despite her efforts, I was a stereotype and I hated it. Black, young, single and pregnant with a son destined to have no relationship with his father. However, up until that time I felt anything but stereotypical. Born to an immigrant Jamaican mother and a Black American father who was once a monk and made his living as an artist, I grew up with white stepparents, stepsiblings and siblings who did not have the same father as I—some Black, some white and some of mixed race.

My parents and stepparents were all friends who also shared gurus. I attended a Quaker school and my father lived in a teepee for years. As a child, I wanted to be inconspicuous and more conforming, but my family and I were always a curiosity and that defined who I was. We were not anything the mainstream would associate with conformity or with Blackness, but my identity soon changed.

Getting pregnant at nineteen by a member of a famous rapper's entourage made me classically hoodwinked and naively optimistic. Despite declarations of love, Kamau's father's long-distance calls whittled into silence and I joined a population people shook their heads about. Suddenly my choices were textbook mistakes that even strangers felt qualified to speak on. *How could you bring another fatherless child into the world?* My colorful family and unique experience were replaced with a stereotype, and it was infuriating. These attitudes strengthened my commitment to my son and pitted me against the world and his father. In his absence, my anger and pride as an underdog grew. I perfected my answers to all invasive questions and taught Kamau his own: *My dad wasn't ready to be a dad.*

My husband, David, and I met when I was in graduate school and working, both full time. Kamau was in middle school and had reunited with his father only to be quickly abandoned again. I had just lost my father and ended a hopeless long-term relationship. Those losses made me want more for our lives.

Getting involved with David, especially when our relationship became more serious, made me reflect on what a family could be, what a husband/father could bring to our lives, and it reminded me of the beautiful, sometimes embarrassing, blended family that I had grown up with. For fourteen years, I had celebrated my small family of two, fighting to make Kamau feel loved and complete without a father. It was crucial to teach him to define himself and to never succumb to stereotypes about himself or anyone else, but sometimes it was difficult. I had tried to help him navigate an experience unfamiliar to my own. My father and stepfather brought me so much love and I wanted that for my son.

My stepparents came into my life at five, so I easily accepted them, but David and I worried about Kamau accepting him as a father as a teenager; Kamau wasn't resistant, but it was foreign. They liked and respected each other, but it took adjusting for everyone. David had to become a husband and a father; I had to let go of my single-mother persona and learn to partner with someone besides my son. It took time. Kamau and I had grown up together; we had struggled and we had fun. Sometimes we reminisce about the funny stories, the heartbreaks and the places we lived; his fake New York accent—*sausage, chocolate*—it was another lifetime, a happy lifetime with a plot twist.

Soon after we became a family of three, we discovered the family was growing. We assured Kamau that having another child did not mean he was not enough for us. Pregnant and mother to a teenager, I was a nontraditional bride, but getting married pushed me closer to conformity. I adopted "husband" and "children" into my lexicon and used them frequently. During my second pregnancy, I looked at single mothers with empathy and I felt oddly excluded and sometimes guilty for being married. It was a dynamic I couldn't have imagined at nineteen.

Not only were my experience and perspective different, so was the way I was perceived. At nineteen, shopping for baby clothes and going to the doctor alone defined me; I was stained by strangers' stares and their spoken and unspoken words. My second pregnancy evoked smiles and pleasant conversation. "Is this your first baby?" was a common question and I shocked everyone when I mentioned Kamau. I wouldn't forget my sixteen-year-old or let go of my past; it made me strong, it made me proud.

Now I am mother to a seven-year-old, a twenty-four-year-old and my seventy-eight-year-old mother, who is a stroke survivor (that's another story). Our lives are filled with love, but it's not easy. I cherish my journey and who we are as a family. I may have upgraded my car and my house and gotten married, but I am the same woman who rushed home after work with dinner cooked by *her* mother to help Kamau with homework and then started her own at 10 p.m. Now I watch the boy who left unanswered heart-wrenching messages for his biological father call David "Dad." I watch Mateo adore his father (and brother), oblivious to what that means, and I have watched my husband discover the joys of parenting and his identity as a father. I see this new woman unfold. The daughter of hippies, a former single mother and gypsy, master's degree holder, wife, caregiver, child chauffeur, old-school dancer, published writer and suburban mom lookalike.

I learned in childhood to stop deferring to other people's stories and to claim my own, and I have. It's a love story.

MEILAN CARTER-GILKEY holds a B.A. and an MFA in creative writing and English from Mills College. Her essays have been published in the anthology *Who's Your Mama?: The Unsung Voices of Women and Mothers, Mutha Magazine* and the *Huffington Post*. She is a contributing writer for *mater mea* and *Heart & Soul* magazines. Recently, she won a James D. Phelan Literary Award for her family memoir in progress. Meilan lives in the Bay Area.

A Letter to My Son

Nuris Terrero

Dear Jayden,

There is so much that happens in my life that I believe that writing it is the only way that you can know your history. So I write in an effort to give you insight into my story, my life. Me, who I am, your mother, an extension of you. I am thirty-three years of age, and as I grow into my thirties, I've learned how to honor my testimony instead of being ashamed for some of the choices I've made, such as the choices I've made in relationships. I stopped trying to erase my past instead of facing it and accepting it as part of my process and, most importantly, using my voice in a culture where women aren't expected to be vocal.

Jayden, you truly changed me. You push me to change. I want to break some unhealthy generational cycles—especially family violence. Don't get me wrong, there are many traditions that I want to continue but also many that I will fight to change. I know you are too young to understand the dynamics that have led to some of the violence in our family, but I have hope that one day my writings will give you further clarity.

My childhood wasn't as bad as some stories I've heard, but its impact on me, emotionally, has caused severe emotional scars. Papi wanted to protect us from the world, yet he caused much harm. Our home should have been a safe haven, but it wasn't. For years, he struggled with alcoholism, and when he drank, he was volatile, breaking things in the home and making threats. He wasn't the best stepfather to my older siblings (their father had passed away back in the Dominican Republic). He was very cold toward them, barely spoke to them and told my mom they couldn't be enrolled in high school. I feared him. Yes, my own father. Some days, even as an adult, I still do. Just because I have witnessed what he is capable of. I remember that I always got in trouble in school for talking, yet at home I was a selective mute. To imagine that fear had that much power, to even take my voice! Well, after twenty years of his abuse, Mami found her courage and left him. Mami, I love her, but she's always been very critical and emotionally cold, detached in some sense, even to her own kids. Name-calling and cursing rants are what she is known for. I never understood as a child why she didn't leave earlier, but then I later understood her fear.

It wasn't until 2013 that I realized how our family's chaotic, unstable behaviors played a role in your development as a young person. You showed signs of behavioral problems at age four, but then it continued to worsen and got extreme, to the point where you had to be hospitalized and I had to leave my career to care for you and your emotional well-being full time. I knew it was deeper than what the natural eye could see. I had to detach from the family for some time, especially for your sanity. I had to take control. I had to break this unhealthy cycle of violence your young eyes had been exposed to. I couldn't live like this anymore. Of course, they didn't take it well. They attacked me verbally and your grandfather even threatened to hurt me physically. I later realized I was being attacked because they couldn't make sense of me. They told me I was being disrespectful when I would not do what they (my elders) wanted of me. They did not like it that I—a female—spoke my mind on things I was opposed to. My way of living and seeing life was greatly different from what not only my family but the culture expected of me. How can I, a single mother, be so headstrong? So instead of trying to understand me, and actually support my decisions that were meant to contribute to your well-being, they judged me and verbally attacked me with insults, saying I was making you "crazy" and trying to "get a check" for you!

So, for the following year, I ended contact with most of the family. I lived off my savings and when that depleted, I sought out government assistance. Here I was, a young woman who fought to defeat all the odds society placed on me because I was a teen mom and a woman of color. All my education didn't mean a thing when I was in those government offices. I was just another black face who didn't know her child's father's whereabouts. I was humiliated and made to feel ashamed. Workers would roll their eyes and look at me with judgment, and some even commented on my age. And so, slowly, I became depressed. Then eventually I became so physically ill and I was diagnosed with lupus, was hospitalized four times in one year, and began chemotherapy. Our family eventually came around. We never spoke honestly about what transpired in 2013. I suppose near-death situations just seem to take precedence in life. I still felt alone in the midst of my pain. It was all too overwhelming, especially emotionally. I felt vulnerable. I felt unaccomplished and worthless.

At the end of it all, even with all that has transpired, you keep me going. On those days, when I lay on the hospital bed, fighting for my life, my mind was always on you. I prayed and pleaded with God to restore me. The thought of being taken from your side was painful and so I fought. I know you needed me but I needed you just as much, even more. When God gifted you to be, He promised me a friend for life. I share all this in hopes that you can continue the work, internally, that is, as you walk into your seasons. I will guide you along the way, through the good and the bad. If at any time I fail you as a parent, I apologize in advance. Just know that I will fight for you until the end. You have captured my heart in ways unimaginable. Thank you for being my son.

∽

NURIS TERRERO is a Black Latina of Dominican descent who grew up in the Bronx. She obtained her B.A. in sociology and political science in 2007 and earned her master's in social work in 2009 at Lehman College. Nuris has worked with young people in foster care, with pregnant teens and teen-aged parents, with victims of violence and with children in the child welfare system. She has great passion for social justice issues, reading and children. Nuris resides in East Harlem with her thirteen-year-old son, Jayden.

Prison Parenting

Rhonda Turpin

I am currently incarcerated at Danbury Federal Prison Camp. I have been in prison more than eleven years in the process of serving a fifteen-year sentence for a white-collar, nonviolent offense. It is almost over for me. It did not take almost twelve years for me to be punished for my crime. Many murderers have served fewer years in their sentences, but I will not complain, because this is not the time for that.

When a woman is sentenced, her children and grandchildren automatically become victims of the criminal justice system also. The moment Mom is snatched up, if they are lucky, the children are placed with relatives who try their best to maintain normalcy in the children's lives. If children are not so lucky, they suffer all kinds of abuse that is not limited to physical and verbal abuse, but is sometimes at the worse end of the spectrum. Children's Services steps in and takes control of their lives if they don't have the proper family support. There are not many things that bring tears to my eyes, but the suffering and mistreatment of mothers and children do. I serve my time in a positive manner and look at my blessings daily. God has kept me, and because He does not make mistakes, whether I like it or not, this is part of my destiny in life. I don't complain. I make the best of every day.

When a woman comes to me crying about her children, it throws my entire day or week off. Even something as simple as overhearing them in their pain causes me dysfunction. When I was on the phone a few days ago, I could not help but hear one of the women talking to her young son. She was prompting him to answer her questions, and he seemed to be doing a good job for a small period of time.

"Why are you crying?" she asked the child suddenly, then told him, "Don't cry. Mommy will be home very soon."

She did a lot better than I ever could have. She was able to talk her child out of his tears and to a better place. I, on the other hand, on the phone next to her, had to hang up because her conversation was tearing me apart.

Last month, Dr. Belica from the Education Department put together a family event where mothers and grandmothers could spend the day outside with their children and grand-children in a playground setting. My grandchildren said that the entire time was like a giant playdate. It was the first ever at Danbury Camp. At count time, there were close to one hundred mothers and grandmothers. Four hundred partici-pants total, counting the inmates.

Paradoxically, seniors are the majority at the camp. When the federal law was expanded, it became a federal crime for a wife to cash her husband's Social Security check after his death. I talked to several women from sixty-eight years old to seventy-six years old. They stated that they had cashed the check of their deceased spouse because they needed the money to maintain their quality of living and not give up their homes. They were treated like any other inmate. They had to get jobs in prison, although they were already retired at home and had worked all their lives. They also have to share rooms with younger women. This is often a disaster because some of the younger women are disrespectful.

We have experienced a large wave of Russian women who were sentenced because they were not able to prove that they were survivors of families who lived during the Holocaust. Every last one of these women was well over sixty-five years of age. They stated that the government asked for hereditary survivors, and began to pay them $1,700 a month. When the government decided to conduct an investigation, if the family link could not be verified, these women were sent to federal prison. The federal indictments have hundreds of women on the same indictment. We do not have enough lower bunks to accommodate them at Danbury Camp; therefore, they are on a waiting list and are at home waiting to come to prison.

Many in the older population enter prison with extensive health problems. I don't understand why they cannot be allowed to remain on home confinement or house arrest in lieu of coming to prison. They are not a threat to society in any way. It is mind-boggling to their loved ones and very hard on the families who visit and support them. After release, most return to live with their adult children because the federal government automatically confiscates all their assets to pay back the monthly allotment they received.

The tide is changing somewhat, but real reform is a long way off. Politicians are realizing that a lot of prison sentences for nonviolent offenders are not only unjustified, but also an unwanted burden on America's taxpayers, who include the same family members who ultimately have to foot the bill to care for loved ones. For them, it is always a double-edged sword.

∽

RHONDA TURPIN calls Cleveland, Ohio, home. She is a grant writer by trade, with more than thirty years of experience. She started her own publishing company, World Books Etc. She is currently in prison at FMC—Satellite Camp and has been incarcerated since October 18, 2004. She was once housed with Martha Stewart, who mentored her in writing her first book. Turpin's background is in assisting women and men with barriers to success. Her blog depicts the facts of daily prison life. She lives by the quote, "You are only as imprisoned as your thoughts and dreams."

Scolding Other People's Kids

Soniah Kamal

"I hate you. You're the worst mother in the world. You're dumb. You're stupid! You will buy me that toy!"

My steps slowed as I approached the coffee shop on a sunny Atlanta afternoon. An adolescent son and his mother stood in the patio. The mother's back was turned toward me, and I could only guess at her expression as her child publicly bullied her, his tone both disparaging and menacing. A young couple, hand in hand, came out of the coffee shop. They glanced at the situation, the grip of their hands tightening, and hurried on. Surely this was not right. Surely if this were the other way around, if it were the mother screaming abuse at her son, someone would have done something. The fact is that American society—and all societies that value privacy—puts such a premium on each of us minding our own business that we think once, twice, thrice and more about intervening, no matter what's going on before us. Of course, the flip side of intervention is interference, and the two straddle a fine line.

I'm originally from Pakistan, where your business is everyone's business and so parenting remains a village activity. No matter how big the city you live in, it is quite common for one parent to reprimand another's parenting or scold someone else's child for misbehavior. Growing up, I had my share of public parenting, and though as a teenager I was irritated by it, as I grew older, I realized that, when done with good intentions, this is part of the caring and sharing that builds a society. Still, there must be a balance. There are pitfalls to moral policing— it can morph into citizen watchdogs with too much power. America is not a country where citizens traditionally keep each other in check, and I appreciate this freedom in certain ways, as well as the ethos of individuality it can birth. It's one of the reasons I moved to this country, chose to have my children here and have lived here more than twenty years.

And so, I began to walk past the situation outside the coffee shop, even as the boy continued yelling at his mother on this sunny afternoon. But with each step, I wondered: *Don't I have a civic responsibility if I see a parent berating a child or a child abusing his parent?* These are not the same things, some people might claim. A parent is in a position of power, while a child, no matter how offensive his behavior, is defenseless—hence, I should leave parenting to the parent. But...should I? Could I?

"I hate you and if you don't get me that toy, then I'm going to call the cops." I stopped in my tracks. Pretending to fiddle with something in my bag, I caught a look at the woman's face: distress. I could hear her clearly, despite her voice low, begging her son to please, please behave. I assumed she didn't dare raise her voice for fear that she might come across as the aggressor. Here was a white mother being yelled at by her child. Here I was, a brown mother, obsessing over whether I should intervene because, truth was, I was terrified of being told some variation of "Get out of America." I had been told that before, in Georgia, in a lovely public library not far from this very spot. I was told that by a white woman in a smart outfit holding an expensive handbag. I was told that the likes of me and my kids—brown and Muslim—are not welcome here, that we need to get the hell out of this country and go back to where we came from. (For my two elder children, that would mean Denver.)

Outside the coffee shop, I knew the wise thing to do was to move along even as I hated measuring the cost of intercession in terms of race instead of simply one human to another. I tried the easy way out. I told myself it wasn't my problem. I told myself the woman's parental skills were at fault for allowing her child to speak to her with such insolence in the first place. But it was my problem because, being a mother myself, I know how difficult it is to bring up respectful children in a culture where parental respect and values seem to clash with the concept of being "cool." As I stood there, I knew that if I didn't intervene, didn't say something, I would never forgive myself. That would outweigh my regret in the event that the woman was rude to me.

So, I approached the boy. "Do you think you should be talking to your mother like that?"

The boy seemed stunned.

"Apologize to your mother and, next time you disagree with her, do it without yelling, threatening, cursing or name-calling."

The mother was staring at me and, as I backed away, I mouthed, "I hope that was okay?" She mouthed back, "Thank you."

Entering the coffee shop, I went straight to the single restroom, where I locked the door behind me and sank into the chair in the corner. The mother and son were stunned, one with shock and the other with gratitude, but I, too, was stunned at having gathered the courage to intervene, at my terror for the consequences that may have resulted for myself, at how tired I was of having to think—once, twice, thrice and more—before doing the right thing.

∿

Soniah Kamal is a Pushcart Prize-nominated essayist and fiction writer. Her novel *UnMarriageable: Pride & Prejudice in Pakistan* is forthcoming from Penguin Random House. Her debut novel, *An Isolated Incident,* was a finalist for the Townsend Prize for Fiction and the KLF French Fiction Prize and is an Amazon Rising Star pick. Her short story "Fossils," judged by Claudia Rankine, won the 2017 Agnes Scott Festival Fiction Award, and her short story "Jelly Beans" was selected for the 2017 *The Best Asian Short Stories Anthology.* Soniah's TEDx talk, *Redreaming Your Dream,* is about regrets, second chances and reinventions. Her work has appeared in the *New York Times,* the *Guardian, Catapult, Chicago Quarterly Review,* the *Missing Slate, Literary Hub,* the *Normal School, BuzzFeed,* the *Atlanta Journal Constitution, Huffington Post* and more. Soniah's website is www.soniahkamal.com.

Thoughts on Mother's Day

Nayomi Munaweera

At ten years old, I had two rules about life: I would never get married; I would never have babies. I have broken my first rule twice. I have never wavered about the second.

I came close to becoming a mother once. Not by choice, but in an entirely brutalized way. I was twenty-four and breaking up with a man I had been with for eight years. We had met when I was sixteen and he was twenty. He had been a tremendous part of my formative experience, romantic and otherwise. At twenty-four, engaged and planning our wedding, I realized through a series of events that I did not love this man and did not want to marry him. I realized that the life I would create without him would be so much fuller, wilder, freer than the life I would have with him.

My fiancé did not want to break up. He cried, he threatened suicide. He called my parents and my friends at all hours of the night weeping and asking them to convince me to return to him. He told my parents he had lost his job over pining for me. It was a lie, one of many that kept me trapped in a crucible of guilt and shame. Who was I to hurt someone so deeply? Who was I to destroy his life, as he said I was doing? As a South Asian woman, I was not expected to choose a man so easily and then so carelessly give him up. I knew that breaking up with him would ruin my reputation in my communities both in

L.A. and back home in Sri Lanka. He, too, was Sri Lankan. But because I was a woman, the breakup would cast a certain taint on my character, not his. I didn't care. I had tasted freedom, and I wanted it more than anything else. It was a desire so sharp and clean I could feel it in my body like an ache.

In that final chaotic month, my fiancé begged me to go on one last trip with him and stupidly I gave in. In the neon wastelands of Las Vegas, he begged me to have sex with him one more time. That crucible I mentioned before had become a vice. There was an added ingredient: pity. I slept with him one final time. I had stopped using birth control. He promised he would not come in me and then immediately he did—I knew with a gutting fear that he had impregnated me. I rolled over and wept while he showered. It was 1997 and I had never heard of the morning-after pill, even though it existed then. I took a pregnancy test two weeks later and it was positive.

When I told him, there was a spark of glee in his eyes. I realized that he believed this meant I would stay with him, that I would bear his children and live in his house for the rest of my life. I felt the bars of a prison closing around me. South Asian women are not supposed to sleep with men. We are not supposed to get pregnant outside of marriage. We are not supposed to get abortions. I "failed" on all counts.

Getting an abortion was the hardest thing I've ever had to do in my life. There was a girl volunteering on that day. I held her hand so hard I think I could have broken it. I stared into her green eyes and I think she saved me. I wish I knew her name so that I could thank her. A few weeks after my abortion, my fiancé revealed to a mutual friend that he had planned to get me pregnant. He had thought this was the way to get me to stay. If I had the baby, we would be a happy family. If I decided to get an abortion, he would stand by me and prove how support-ive he was and win me back that way. I broke up with him and I've never seen him again. This feels like a blessing.

I deeply regret the circumstances that led me to get preg-nant and have an abortion. I wish I could have talked to that younger version of myself and told her that her body belonged only to herself, that she did not have to please the man or the community. I wish I'd had the inner resources to walk away at the first sign of danger, but that only came with time and experience.

I do not, however, regret the abortion. I am deeply grateful that I had the privilege of choice. I am grateful that my younger self had the intuition to follow her own path, to remain child-less and claim the life that she had only glimpsed then.

In the almost two decades since, I've never felt those deep maternal urges other women talk about. I've never felt that painful desire for my very own baby. Still, I think about her every now and then. The daughter I might have borne. She's always a girl. Of this much I am convinced. I calculate how old she would be now. It astounds me that in a parallel life I could have been a mother to an eighteen-year-old. I am thankful that I was not forced to be her mother. These days, I am learning compassion, for the naive young girl I was, for the baby girl who was never born and perhaps even for that other, the tor-tured man who committed this sin.

On Mother's Day, we are always reminded of our own mothers and extolled to call them, to appreciate them. But I am also always reminded of the mother I never was and never will be.

∽

NAYOMI MUNAWEERA is an award-winning author. Her debut novel, *Island of a Thousand Mirrors*, was short-listed for the Northern California Book Prize and the DSC Prize for South Asian Literature. It won the Commonwealth Book Prize for Asia. Her second novel, *What Lies Between Us*, was considered one of the most exciting releases of 2016 in publications from *Elle* magazine to Buzzfeed and won the Sri Lanka State Literary Prize. The *New York Times* has called Nayomi's writing "luminous," and her voice has been compared with that of Jhumpha Lahiri, Michael Ondaatje and Louise Erdrich. Her work has been widely anthologized in both fiction and non-fiction collections. Nayomi lives in Oakland, California, and is at work on her third novel. Find her on Facebook and Instagram.

But Beautiful...

The Beauty Myth

Doppelganger Dreams

NARI KIRK

When I peered into mirrors, I'd startle at the Korean girl gazing back at me. Bulky hair, beige skin, those tiny eyes—*almond*, people called them, as if they were a viable source of protein. That girl was not whom I was used to seeing. And while she didn't repulse, she seemed like an alternate reality, the kind experienced only when I encountered my reflection.

For years I considered myself white. Adopted as a baby from Seoul, I'd grown up in middle-class white America. Brown-haired, blue-eyed relatives and friends surrounded me, and our shared world was simple and light. There were a few suggestions of a larger universe—the servers at El Ranchito Mexican Restaurant on Burnside, the Tongan family who sang at church concerts, Vusi from South Africa, whom my parents helped through college. But these dark people seemed to flit in and out of my life like exotic visitors. Later I would understand that my family and I flitted into their lives and retreated. Back then, however, as my adopted mother and grandmother home-schooled me through elementary, as I went off to a small private high school, everyone familiar and ordinary was white.

❦

In my college cafeteria, the pale blond server scooping rice onto my plate announced, "You look like Sandra Oh."

I'd never been told I looked like a celebrity. Except for

serious K-culture fans, most Americans don't know Korean celebrities. Sandra Oh from *Grey's Anatomy* happened to be the only one I knew of, and immersed in whiteness as I was, I hadn't thought we might be alike.

While the blond server's words could have meant any number of things, her smile suggested she meant them as a compliment. She handed my plate back to me. I reached for it and mumbled, "Thank you."

Back in my dorm room I Googled photos of Sandra. I scrolled through shot after shot, some from *Grey's,* others from *Sideways* or the red carpet. I held up my hand mirror and studied myself, pondering what the server had noted that I did not. Sandra was taller, sparer, her face longer, her lips wider. The outer corners of her eyes tilted upward, the ends of her brows swooped down. We did not resemble each other and would not, ever.

A hazy feeling puddled within me, unsettling me. I couldn't name it then, but I can now: It was disappointment. I'd hoped to recognize myself in Sandra, to detect some echo in each of us of the other, to be able to believe it if anyone else said I reminded them of her.

Two years later, I borrowed a friend's blue scrubs to wear to a Halloween party. The costume was unimaginative, and I wondered if people would figure it out right away. How many famous Korean doctors—real or fictional—were there?

"Who are you?" people asked again and again.

Instead of answering "Dr. Cristina Yang," I barreled through the fourth wall: "Sandra Oh."

"Oh," they said. One remarked, "You're prettier."

A friend arrived late, her accessories a cigarette holder, long gloves and pearls, her hair in an updo, her dress sleeveless and black. Even though she was Latina, everyone knew who she was.

Soon after I Googled Sandra, many of my Facebook friends changed their profile pictures to photos of white celebrities they resembled. A sense of delight underscored this brief trend; having a famous double like Christina Hendricks or Reese Witherspoon carried with it a shift in status, a glimmer of glamour. I wanted to join the fun but couldn't think of anyone who could be my celebrity lookalike—the options were too limited. I left my profile pic as it was.

The disappointment was identifiable this time. I felt the loneliness of color, the non-ness of non-whiteness. The self-perception that had flickered couldn't now be ignored: While I might imagine myself white, no one else would. The strangeness of the El Ranchito waiters, the Tongan family at church and Vusi from South Africa was a strangeness I shared, a strangeness I was a part of.

I hunted with growing hunger for a Korean American celebrity doppelganger of my own. I was surprised to discover that Grace Park, known as Officer Kalakaua on the *Hawaii Five-o* reboot, was Korean. She was lanky and square-shouldered, her wide eyes popping against her dark skin, laugh dimpled. My reason for not guessing her Korean was a poor one—she didn't look like me. Nor did Jamie Chung or Nicole Bilderback or Margaret Cho.

Jenna Ushkowitz was my closest match. When watching her as Tina on *Glee,* I saw myself in her broad face and stocky frame. Reading about her, I saw myself in her story; she'd been adopted as a baby from Seoul by American parents and had cofounded Kindred, an adoption advocacy organization. But as I greedily sifted through photos of her beaming at parties and awards shows, I started to realize that wishful thinking had muddled my vision—her eyes angled far more steeply than mine, her jaw was more heart-shaped, her body daintier.

In other words, she was not "The One."

Nobody has "The One"—a friend observed recently as I vented about the scant numbers of Korean American actors. The entertainment industry's array of bodies, faces and skin tones is far too homogeneous for any of us to find anything but vague approximations of ourselves there. And why does superficial similitude matter at all?

To me, it matters because mirrors do not show me who I am—people show me who I am (or am not), whether they're in real life or pop culture. My self-sight is referential, like a light bouncing from surface to surface, a complex zigzagging between data points. Gazing in the mirror when I was younger did not tell me that I was Korean; I had to be told that I looked like a particular Korean—a Korean I didn't actually resemble— for me to start connecting my reflection to myself.

I struggled to apprehend this self in part because of pop culture's limitations. Though Hollywood does not depict reality, it is a formidable component of reality. Its narrow storytelling diminishes people of color—via monochromatic scripts, whitewashing and racial stereotypes—so they all but disappear, so that they become anomalies rather than the beautiful norm. More accurate representation would not only have helped me recognize myself, it would also have helped humanize the Latina and Black individuals I considered strange as a girl. And it would have humanized me when I registered what others already knew: that I wasn't white.

My search for a famous doppelganger was in vain, but at least mirrors no longer surprise me. My image and I are merging. The world that I once considered white now appears bigger and better. I do worry especially for young people of color, whose points of reference are inaccurate and few, who don't yet know that they are looking for something and it will be hard to find.

An American family, good friends of mine, adopted a little Chinese girl. Her new parents, brother and sister, all tall and white, keep her happy. She has a horse and a room with a window seat. One afternoon, I'm told, she noticed a framed photo on a table in their big Victorian house—it was an old graduation portrait of me. She stilled, focused. Then she pointed to my face and said her name.

⌒⌒

NARI KIRK earned an MFA in creative nonfiction from the University of New Mexico. She has work published or forthcoming in *Blue Mesa Review*, *Hobart* and *Poetry Northwest*. Her writing ponders race, faith, family and gender. During 2015, she read books exclusively by women and plans to devote future years to reading works by other marginalized writers. She lives in the greater Seattle area, close to the mountains and the sea.

Black Dolls for Everyone

MERCY L. TULLIS-BUKHARI

"She has a Black Barbie?" asked our concierge, as we walked out of the building.

The concierge was a woman of color, whose skin was the same hue as mine. She and I were different ethnicities—she of West Indian descent and I of Honduran descent. If I can assume anything about her life, because she and I were of the same color, she experienced discrimination not only from white people but also from other people of color. She may have been told her hair was not good enough, that her nose was too big, that her skin was too dark.

My daughter, whose father is South Asian, is of lighter complexion than the concierge and I. The texture of her hair is loosely curled, which is a combination of her father's and my hair. Many times, because of the stark difference in our complexions, people have either told me that my child looked nothing like me, or assumed that I was her nanny.

Although my daughter's Barbie collection can easily represent a United Nations conference, a darker brown Barbie with tightly curled hair happens to be my daughter's favorite. This particular Barbie has become a staple of our daily outings.

Our concierge saw my light-complexioned daughter with her favorite Barbie, and, without hesitation, inquired. (Her question, actually, felt more like surprise than actual inquisition.)

When I looked at the concierge with my right eyebrow

lifted, since she had infiltrated my child's personal space, she caught the inappropriateness of the "question" and asked, as an attempt to sweep her impropriety under a rug, "She has a Barbie?"

"Why wouldn't she have a Black Barbie?" I responded. "Her mother is Black, she is Black, so why wouldn't she have a Black Barbie?"

She could not respond. Instead, she changed the subject by offering to hold packages for me until we returned from our outing.

I was initially upset, because I thought about the audaciousness of the question, and even considered complaining to building management. However, I eased my anger because the interaction reminded me of a past situation where the tables had been turned.

Two years ago, with my daughter in a Colorado mall, I saw a white woman handing her white daughter a dark-complexioned American Girl doll. The mother and her daughter looked like Malibu Barbie dolls themselves.

The girl, with excitement and joy, immediately tore open the box that contained the Addy Walker Civil War American Girl doll. The girl attempted to remove the attachments on her own; when she could not, she passed the packaging to her mother. Her mother, with a careful firmness, tore off the attachments. The last piece was much stronger than the others, and the mother used her teeth to break it. Addy Walker was freed from the box and the attachments. The mother handed the freed doll to her daughter. The girl put her arms around this doll as if it were an actual person, as if she had finally met the long-lost friend who was not in her collection of dolls. I stared with wonderment. In the name of dolls of color everywhere, what business did this white woman have buying her child a Black doll?

My daughter was in her stroller then, and when I looked at their process of opening the Addy Walker box, I slowed down the stroller. I stared at the Malibu Barbie prototypes with the Addy Walker. I questioned what seemed unreal yet what I saw in front of me. But was I really questioning what I saw, or questioning my own beauty as a Black woman? As a Black child in a Honduran household, I had learned that I had *pelo malo* and that lighter skin was always better skin. As mother to a biracial child, I had already been told many times that my daughter was beautiful because she was a child of mixed race. With my own preconceived notions, I did not understand why the blond woman with her blue eyes, along with her blond daughter also with blue eyes, would find joy in a doll that looked more like me than them. The well-known Kenneth and Mamie Clark doll experiment had become such a reality in my subconscious that I could not conceive how they would wholeheartedly accept a doll that looked like me. Instead of a celebratory look of approval, my eyebrows crinkled in an evident stare of confusion.

When the white mother noticed my stare, she gave me the what-the-fu#$-are-you-looking-at look: one eyebrow raised, head slanted.

I looked away quickly. With shame, I pushed the stroller at a fast pace, and turned the corner toward the exit of the mall.

Now my assumption about the concierge who had my same skin color made me think she experienced discrimination not only from white people but from other Black people. I assumed she thought that people who looked like my daughter did not "suffer" the way people who looked like her did. She had seen people who look like my daughter getting passes in instances that she did not, simply because of appearance. She was inundated with unrelatable images of beauty and, at some points in her life, questioned her own existence and beauty because she realized she did not measure up to what she had been taught was beautiful.

I got it. I knew what "She has a Black Barbie?" was about.

My annoyance turned to sadness after I thought about why she had asked about the Barbie doll. The concierge had a limited view of beauty. Her limited view was sourced by her images that did not include women who looked like her.

Among Latinos, we are haunted by the racial classification of *las castas,* where a person's value is based on how light or dark their skin is. The closer a person is to Eurocentric features, the more value that person has in society. The West Indian concierge, also a product of the transatlantic slave trade, experienced *las castas* from her angle of Blackness. *Las castas* has led to self-hatred for people of color, because a standard of white perfection and beauty has been set for how we should value ourselves and others. The mother and daughter in the Colorado mall would be at the top of this racial classification. In other words, they would represent perfection, beauty and acceptance. My daughter would be midway toward this high bar of beauty in this racial classification system. Women like the concierge and myself would be at the bottom.

Proven by the Clark doll experiment, and continuing to be proven in many current YouTube videos, dolls have historically been created to represent this racial classification that influences our standards of beauty. The created standard of beauty and perfection fosters a strong lack of self-love and self-acceptance among girls of color. *Las castas* created the historical basis for the confusion the concierge and I felt when we saw the two little girls with their dolls.

We, as women of color, need to fight against everything we were taught about ourselves in order to see our unique cultural exquisiteness. To "go natural"—in other words, to stop chemically straightening our hair—becomes a true fight against our parental restrictions and societal expectations. To talk Black pride and accept our African heritage have been deemed as attacks against the white norm when, really they are acceptances of the Black ideal. To accept our Blackness—regardless of how others may want to categorize us because of how we look—is to wholeheartedly accept our African heritage.

My daughter and I are Black. The doll my daughter most closely identifies with illustrates the importance of us, as a race, accepting that we are each uniquely beautiful.

To own a doll that represents Africanness is a subtle yet poignant protest against the formula that we have all been brainwashed to see as beautiful and acceptable in our society of whiteness. My daughter did not celebrate whiteness with her Black doll (to the surprise of the concierge) as the blond girl in Colorado did not celebrate whiteness, either, to my own surprise. Both girls celebrated universal beauty, and to celebrate universal beauty—an idea where beauty is not defined by race, culture and ethnicity—becomes an acceptance of oneself and a genuine acceptance of others.

As my daughter and the girl in the Colorado mall get older, they will confront situations in which race will be a dominant factor in their decisions and in their discussions. They will encounter the concierges and the women rudely staring at them in the mall. Their views of themselves and others will drastically change because of how our society treats the groups they represent. Our duty as parents is to maintain and foster what our children naturally see as beautiful, so that when they are in positions of power as adults, they can annihilate the social construct of race. The social construct divides us, and ultimately victimizes many groups of us.

As mothers, as long as we encourage the pure and the right, our daughters will crumble the current racially driven, media-supported status quo of what is considered beautiful and aesthetically acceptable. My daughter and the girl in Colorado are trailblazers; they will create a new world of feminine beauty, woman power, self-love and self-acceptance.

My daughter gets stares all the time when she is with her favorite Barbie doll. As many people assume that I am her nanny, I am sure people stare wondering why she has a Black Barbie. I take my cue from that mother in the Colorado mall whenever a distasteful stare encroaches on my daughter's innonence and happiness. That what-the-f$#%-are-you-looking-at look always works.

◦↝

MERCY L. TULLIS-BUKHARI is a poet, essayist and fiction writer who finds inspiration from being a Bronx-bred Afro-Latina, Honduran and Garifuna, of Jamaican descent. She is a Callaloo Fellow, and has performed at the Bronx Library Center, the Bowery Poetry Club, the Nuyorican Poets Café and for the Caribbean Cultural Theatre. She is currently writing her first novel through the MFA creative writing program at the College of New Rochelle. An excerpt of her novel can be found in Issue 33, the Winter/Spring 2017 issue of *African Voices*. Mercy can be found at mercytullisbukhari.com.

The Gift of Hair, the Gift of Joy

Emma McElvaney Talbott

Hair was never more important to little Black girls than on Easter Sunday. I remember how the Saturday evenings before the day were spent prepping; we endured stiff necks and the wince-worthy heat of curling irons. Our hairlines had to be "in order," meaning we might get "surprised" by a few unfortunate encounters with the hot comb around the edges—all to be appropriately coiffed as we sashayed down the street to Sunday school. After church, we'd stand around in our new dresses, black patent leather shoes and Easter bonnets, mutually admiring each other's Shirley Temple curls.

On those Easter Sundays, no one's curls were any more admired than mine—thick, long and completely glossy from Royal Crown pomade. Fast-forward decades later to find me mortified to discover a clump of hair the size of a golf ball clogging the shower drain. Did all of that come from my head? Surely not. But the evidence was staring back at me. I'd been told that anesthesia from surgery and several weeks of prescription drugs might cause hair loss, but it was something else entirely to witness tufts of hair defecting from my head like lemmings plunging over a cliff.

My hair continued to fall out at a rapid rate. The following days and weeks, it was almost unbearable to witness a brush or comb full of hair that a single pass would bring. I began saving the fallout in a brown lunch-size bag—but instead of lunch, mine was stuffed full of hair.

One day, I rushed to my husband's home office carrying my lunch bag full of hair and lamented, "Look at all this hair. What if I have to wear a wig?" I dreaded the thought of wearing a wig—I'm the kind of person who can barely keep a hat on my head. My husband, Cecil, an electrical engineer and analytical to a fault, shrugged, half-listening as he searched through his electrical code books.

Eventually, the gravity of what I had just said weighed in on him and he looked up and asked, "What did you just say, Emma?" Reading the panic in my face, he got up from his desk and gave me a reassuring hug and said matter-of-factly that it was probably temporary. "You still have a lot of hair, so stop worrying—because that'll only make it worse. Why don't you make an appointment with a dermatologist?"

He was right. I would call a dermatologist in the morning, but in the interim, I needed a shoulder to cry on. So I called my friend Margie.

"Girl, I'm so sorry," Margie said. "What are you going to do?"

After an hour of commiserating with me, she finally hit upon the idea that I visit her hairstylist, Joy. A few days later, I walked into Joy's Hair Salon with my bag stuffed full of hair, wanting to cry. Joy sat me down—she exuded professionalism and matter-of-fact confidence as she analyzed my hair, reassuring me that the little white tips of my hair strands meant that the hair had been falling out for quite a while but would eventually grow back. Instantly relieved, my eyes welled up with tears. I could see she didn't want to raise my hopes too much, as she meted out her warning: "It'll come back. But it might take a long, long time."

She gave me special homemade concoctions she'd made up herself, like something from an alchemist's book of potions, and I slathered them on my scalp every other day. Within two short weeks, my hair had stopped falling out. Over several months, my hair was gently nurtured back to health. Needless to say, Joy was a lifesaver.

Prior to my hair loss, I had always gotten haircuts on impulse. Not anymore. Losing so much hair so quickly had shaken me.

I thought of cancer patients, whose chemotherapy brings about complete and utter hair loss within a month with possibly no chance of restoration. I also thought of women who suffer from alopecia, wherein the hair loss is permanent. My plight over losing some hair that would eventually grow back was trivial compared with theirs. In addition to battling and surviving cancer, they suffered permanent or semipermanent hair loss at the very moment they sought to believe in their own vibrant survivor status.

Whereas even the thought of wearing a wig gave me hives, I knew that for many cancer patients or those with alopecia, wigs were a necessity. I also knew that wigs made from hair with varied textures and color must be rare, and so an absolute gift to those patients who needed them.

I thought back to Easter Sundays, and how important it was for us girls to be primped and styled. I thought about the anguish many young girls who have lost their hair must feel. As my hair continued to grow, the idea took root: I would donate my growing hair to Locks of Love.

Locks of Love is one of several organizations that make and distribute wigs to girls and women who need them following hair loss due to illness, scalp injury or alopecia—but the great majority of these wigs are for cancer survivors.

I thought about all the stories I had read about hair donation and realized I'd only seen images of Caucasian women donating to cancer survivors with hair colors and textures similar to theirs. Surely African American women had donated their hair to African American cancer survivors? After all, hair grows back. Why cut it, sweep it up off the floor and trash it when it can be made into a lovely wig for a young girl on the road to recovery?

I kept quiet about my plans to grow my hair to donate to Locks of Love. I'd grown up in the South hearing about "the power of hair." We were cautioned to guard our hair and not let a strand of it get into the wrong hands lest they use it to cast spells.

I'd already entertained questions and comments about growing my hair out long. "Is that yours or a weave?" someone once asked. Another acquaintance said, "I don't remember your hair ever being that long."

I tried to be patient and kept my plans a secret to everyone except Joy and Cecil, who always loved my hair long, though he grudgingly accepted that I mostly wore it short.

The day that Joy finally cut my hair—twenty-two months later—there was an air of excitement in the shop. Other clients seemed to get a vicarious rush as they watched Joy deftly section off the hair for cutting. She cut four thick 11-inch-long braids and prepared them for mailing.

There were lots of smiles, *ooohs* and *aahs* over the cut braids and questions about how I felt. One customer commented that if it were her hair, she wouldn't even be *thinking about* giving it away. Another customer seconded that emotion. I laughed along with them, but told them that I felt good about my haircut. I was happy that the hair was going on a worthwhile journey, and would find a new home.

"And I know there's a sweet little girl just waiting for her new wig."

Joy smiled and said, "If this makes you happy, Em, then I am happy to be a part of this process."

"Of course you were part of the process!"

Indeed she was: Without her expertise and nursing my hair back to health, I would never have had the courage to pursue hair donation. My experience taught me not to take my locks for granted: Hair itself may not have "power," yet what you choose to do with it—and why you've chosen to do it—can be empowering.

I realized that many African American women might consider donating if they only knew how to go about it, so I made a vow to spread the word about Locks of Love in whatever way I could.

Within another three years, I had yet another full head of hair, and I donated once again. Now for the third time, my hair has grown back and I am considering a third gift of hair. I have never known who received my hair, nor can the patient know me, since Locks of Love protects the identities of the recipients and donors. That's all well and good.

I must admit, though, that when I see children with cancer, I sometimes wonder how the girls who received my hair are faring. I try to imagine their faces the day they got their wigs—ones made specifically for them. Wigs that suit their faces and features, and remind them of the days of health ahead, rather than the days of illness behind. Though I will never meet these girls, my hope is that my simple gift brings each of them some small amount of Joy.

∾

EMMA MCELVANEY TALBOTT is a Louisville, Kentucky, native. She is an educator, author, freelance writer and genealogist. She participated in civil rights demonstrations, including the 1963 March on Washington, and is driven by a desire to write and speak truth to power and fulfill the dreams of her ancestors. Talbott holds state certifications in administration, supervision and reading. A former adjunct professor at the University of Louisville, Clark Atlanta University and Spalding University, she founded the David C. & Emma W. Miles McElvaney Memorial Scholarship for African American students.

A graduate of Central High School, Kentucky State University and Indiana University, she has extensive postgraduate studies at three additional universities. Her first book was *The Joy and Challenge of Raising African American Children,* and for seven years she served as parenting editor for *Family Digest* magazine and *Family Digest Baby* magazine and wrote two columns, "Ask Emma" and "Child Builders."

Touch and Go

MAROULA BLADES

So here I was finally, waddling like an overstuffed Christmas turkey, a flat-footed grizzly wearing a summer floral tent, hugging the white teddy bear that my friends Rainer and Daniela had just brought me. They came unannounced to the antenatal room where swollen profanities leaped into a gulch of pain, as the contraction monitor climbed Mount Everest one hundred times over. Initially I refused to see them, but they barged in, curious about the delayed birth. I thanked them for the gift, which I squashed immediately under my bulges as my husband ushered them out of the room.

Earlier in the morning, the nurse had given me a batch of tiny eggs that prickled the tip of my tongue. They were supposed to induce birth. It was the second day in succession that I was given them because "Little Wonder" didn't want to touch down on earth. He was fifteen days late. I was cursed with a spanking headache and still there was no sign of him, but his presence certainly could be felt, kicking like Maradona* and directing the passes, one to the right under a lung, one to my bladder and a direct hit on the solar plexus, scoring a breathless fifty points. It was pure torture for eighteen hours. During that time, I had a so-called calming bath in the industrial bathroom en suite as big as a factory packing room without

---

* A famous soccer player from Buenos Aires

so much as a terry towel to dry my body. I was subjected to a series of rigorous and humiliating medical examinations and suffered the loss of hair from my pride and joy, which I found rather irritating.

At eleven o'clock in the evening, one could find me straddled on a huge, red gymnastics ball, rolling to and fro like a monolithic squawking hen under a weak-dripping shower. I'd had enough of perpetual vomiting, screaming and hunger pangs to last me a lifetime. After all the preparations and suffering, "Little Wonder" still didn't want to say hello to the outside world. It must have been marvelous in his miniature water world where he had jet skied, scuba dived and surfed during the past months, but now there was not enough space to wiggle his Lilliputian toes.

I was happy to hear music, the same two tapes regurgitating pure artistry from a wacky parrot duo whilst I lay frothing in the labour room with my husband washing my brow and handing me delicious ice cubes to quench my ever-growing thirst. Time was running a four-by-four relay, pulling me like that scraggy, crazy rabbit you see in greyhound races, the one with bedraggled whiskers and clumps of fur missing that by the last round is totally bald.

A female doctor arrived, I was relieved, for I felt she could feel my anxiety, the tiredness, the hunger and above all the love I had saved for the past nine and a half months. She disinfected my skin with an acidic spirit and unleashed a hefty needle.

All I could say was, "Please, please, please do it right."

My husband held my arms as the spirit evaporated into the air, causing him to retch. "I've got to go, I feel really queasy," and with this he made a mad dash for the swinging white doors.

"Stay completely still; everything's going to be all right," the doctor said in a reassuring voice.

I was exhaustedly rigid, like a kyphotic badger with rigor mortis setting in. The pain of Hades vanished and I began to lift towards cloud nine, which was floating just above my bed. It felt good to be held within the bales of heaven for more than an hour until the red emergency light blinked on the monitor and panic ensued.

"He's in stress. Quick, call the doctor," the nurse said in a concerned voice.

The doctor explained the situation: "Your cervix has not dilated and the baby is not in the right alignment. His heartbeat has increased and he is experiencing fetal distress. I think it is best to operate. It could take a further eight hours for him to be born naturally, and you haven't got enough strength to continue. Due to the circumstances, it would be better to take the baby now."

Her sensitive voice seemed to cartwheel around the room as giddiness filled my orb. Feeling I could trust her with "Little Wonder's" care and my own well-being, I signed the mottled consent document. My heart plunged into a dark, formidable chasm and a thousand and one thoughts clambered the walls. I was in no mood to prolong the birth, but I desperately wanted to experience natural childbirth, for it was an important part of the bonding process. I had heard that caesarean mothers encountered difficulties with nursing and holding their children after the operation.

I started to cry with all the pain, the fear, the hunger and the love collapsing inside me. The green-coated strangers hovered around me as another injection was administered and a painful cry lit from the base of my throat for my husband. "Where is he? Where is he?"

There he was, standing in the second row, clad in a green Martian costume. "I'm here," he said as a voice counted down the seconds to oblivion.

Double vision tended me as I woke to see my husband holding a beautiful little bundle that had the fragrance of a Hawaiian orchid.

"Is he okay?" I asked hoarsely.

"He's just perfect. Hold him," my husband said with overwhelming pride, tears running down his cheeks. "Little Wonder" had finally arrived with footballer's calves. He was wrapped and protected in a fluffy white blanket, so very quiet in an angel's sleep.

I have never, ever seen a child with such beautiful black locks and a cherub face full of curiosity. God has blessed me with a seraph who looks at me with eyes as big as the illuminating moon, a moonchild who would live out the wonders on Earth. For a moment I entertained the thought, *I hope he likes me*, as I lifted him to feed on Mother Nature's milk. He held my finger with the same volume of love and warmth that I had in my heart, and the silly thought disintegrated.

Of course he loved me, right from the fountainhead; he knew the voice that had spoken and sung to him during the past months. It wasn't the easiest pregnancy with all the highs and lows, but from the beginning there was a sense of awe. It didn't matter what negative thoughts I had about myself; I was able to bring forth perfection with the aid of the Most High. The Lord had given me another chance to understand the meaning of life, love, responsibility, giving and sharing. But now, after such excruciating agony, it was time for a holiday.

Three years later, "Little Wonder" turned with a seraph's smile and said, "Mummy, you look like the moon and the stars."

That was the best compliment I've ever received. My "Little Wonder" is growing; he is the sunshine and the moonshine of every passing wonderful day. He is the morning spirit that capers in the light of the world.

∾

MAROULA BLADES is an Afro-British poet/writer living in Berlin. The winner of The Caribbean Writer 2014 Flash Fiction competition and Erbacce Prize 2012, her first poetry collection, *Blood Orange,* is published by Erbacce-press. Her works have been published in *Thrice Fiction* magazine, *Kalyani Magazine, Volume, Abridged 0-40* magazine, *Words with JAM* and *Blackberry* and by The Latin Heritage Foundation, Peepal Tree and other anthologies and magazines. Her poetry/music program has been presented on several stages in Germany. Her debut EP album, *Word Pulse* (Havavision Records, UK), can be found on iTunes and Amazon.

Invisibility

NIKKI ABRAMSON

Yes, I do have U.S. citizenship. No, I am not a foreign exchange student. No, I don't speak either Korean or any other Asian language. No, I don't like Asian food. Actually, I speak Spanish and love Tex-Mex food. This is conversation that I experience countless times.

Where am I from? I tell people I am from Minneapolis, Minnesota. Most of the time I get blank stares, as though people think I am lying. *No, really, where are you from?* I reply again, "Minneapolis, Minnesota." My heart sinks every time I answer the question, because I know what they are really asking, they just don't know how to say it. I guess you can say I am "really from" Seoul, South Korea. I was six months old when I was adopted and came to Minneapolis, Minnesota.

I have always wanted to fit in and not look different. I can't take off the Asian in me. I look Asian. I have to learn to embrace these features of mine. Every day I wake up and look in the mirror and here I am, Asian. There are things I can hide, such as having a disability. Being Asian is something I can't hide. There are times I wish I could blend in with the sea of people.

I was born with a condition called mitochondrial myopathy, a condition that falls under the umbrella of muscular dystrophy. This condition tires my muscles easily and lactic acid builds up, making my body weak. The condition has impacted me in many ways; however, at times I can hide the fact I have this disability. Many people often don't know until they really get to know me because it is somewhat an invisible disability of the genes, metabolic system and muscles. Being a woman of color, though, is not something I can disguise; it follows me wherever I go.

There are sometimes perks to this idea of being a woman of color. When I set up coffee networking meetings with people I don't know, I tell them I am Asian and it's easy for them to find me. It can be hard to find someone else when everyone looks like each other, but I am usually the only person of color in the room.

Wherever I go, I have a tendency to notice if anyone around me is a person of color. It is an instinctive thing. It is one of the first things I notice when I'm in a group of people. If I am sitting in a big group of people, I count the number of people of color in the room, and realize that usually I can count that number on one hand. While I feel "white" on the outside, it is easy for me to see others who look like me.

People don't understand: I look Korean, but I don't speak the language. They assume that because I look one way, I will be able to speak in some sort of Asian language—though speaking Korean has never held any interest for me. My parents are both Caucasian. They have tried to teach me about my Korean culture, but two white people teaching you about Korea is just odd.

My brother—also adopted—is originally from Paraguay. We flew to Paraguay to pick him up. I was only seven, and I clearly remember the piercing stares of the Paraguayans who watched my Swedish/Finnish parents holding the hand of their Korean daughter, meeting her new brother for the first time. Now, as adults, when we go out to eat as a family, it's clear to me that we're a family. Nevertheless, the waiter asks if we want separate

checks. No, we want one check, please. Giving us a confused
look, he moves on as though we don't belong with our parents.

Yes, these are my parents. What am I? I am Korean
American. No, I don't eat Korean food. No, I haven't been to
Korea. This is my reality as a woman of color. These are battles
I fight every day because I can't remove the fact that my skin
and facial features are Korean and I don't resemble the major-
ity of people living where we live.

As a child, I went to many Korean adoptee events. My
parents told me that going to these events would help me to
understand the Korean culture. I went to a Korean culture
camp along with other Korean adoptees so I could learn about
the Korean culture, language and activities. Some of the events
were ones in which Korean Americans show off their talents
such as Korean drumming and cooking, and still others were
language classes. My parents took me to these events and we'd
stroll along, gaping at the huge display tables. Vendors sold
everything you could possibly imagine: Korean kids' books,
Korean novels, K-pop music, Korean CDs, the latest Korean
magazines. Toys, candy, artwork—all handmade from Korea.

Most of the celebrations happened during Children's Day—
which, in Korea, is celebrated as a national holiday, and is even
bigger than Mother's Day or Father's Day. I soon realized that
these people were either from Korea, or went to Korea and
bought these items specifically to sell to Korean adoptees and
their families.

We listened to the music, watched dancers and ate the
Korean food my parents encouraged me to try. I remember eating the food and not liking it. There were a few things
I liked, but I mostly stuck with the rice. A typical American
food. Right?

At the end of the event, my mom said to me, "We want you to have something. Look around and see what you like. I will buy it for you." I looked around the tables that wound around almost two rooms full of items, yet nothing caught my eye.

I knew that my mom wanted me to have something that represented my Korean culture. I told her, "I'm good." She said, "No, let me get you something. What is it you want?" Finally, I picked out a Korean doll. Each year I found something: a Korean magazine, a book, a CD. Soon, I had a dresser drawer full of Korean items. As a child, I couldn't understand the significance, yet my adult mind realizes the impact this had on me. Now, thirty years old, even though I still can't read or understand these items, I cherish them. They are a part of me.

ᢙ

When there are women of color around, I feel secure, safe and free. I feel as though I belong and I don't have to pretend to be something or someone I am not. Sometimes, I feel as though people don't see me for me. People see Asian and they think, *She is different.* They think, *She has a different upbringing than we do,* when in reality, I have an upbringing similar to many people's. This is often frustrating. I may look one way, but don't judge me for that.

In high school, I looked at colleges all over the Twin Cities and the Chicago area. In the numerous college visits, I was asked what my ethnicity was. They told me that if I checked a box there would be many more opportunities to be involved in on campus as well as scholarships and grants. Why check a box? I didn't want to be labeled as something. At one point when I was applying for colleges, I was working with one admissions counselor, and as soon as I checked the box saying I was a student of color, I was moved to another counselor who worked exclusively with students of color. This frustrated me that I was boxed in for my race.

I decided to attend Bethel University, a small Christian liberal arts university in St. Paul, Minnesota. I loved the school and it gave me a great education. I was asked to be in an admissions video to represent the college. Little did I realize that not only was I representing the college, but I was also representing being a student of color for the campus. They wanted to have more people of color in this video. At the time, the school only had about seven percent students of color.

Six years ago, I graduated. I was interviewing for a teaching job with a school district representative. After asking the standard interview questions, he leaned over to me and said, "You know, Ms. Abramson, we would be honored to have you here. We are looking for teachers of color. We have many students of color here and it would really help them to have a face that is similar to theirs." I leaned back in my seat and thought, *Wait— you're hiring me because I am a teacher of color?*

I got the job. I was elated. However, did I get the job because I am a person of color or did I get the job because I deserved it? Which one was it? I don't know. They want me and that is what counts. I have a job.

There are countless times when people judge me for what I look like. It is a constant battle I am willing to fight. I am willing to explain who I am to people. I embrace the Korean American-ness in me. It makes me—me.

∽

NIKKI ABRAMSON is the author of *I Choose Hope—Overcoming Challenges with Faith and Positivity* and *Hope for Today*. Her first book is an inspirational memoir about the challenges she has had and how she is overcoming them as a Korean adoptee and someone living with rare medical challenges and disabilities. Her second book, *Hope for Today*, is an inspirational coffee-table book that is half inspirational quotes that will inspire someone in times of need and half journal reflections. Abramson is also a contributor to several anthologies, including *Women of a Certain Age Answer Seven Questions About Life, Love, and Loss; Surviving Brain Injury: Stories of Strength and Inspiration;* and *Stories from the Social Side: Advice from Marketing Professionals to Marketing Professionals.* She is also an actor, educator and speaker. She holds an M.A. and a B.A. in elementary and K-12 education. Her mission is to inspire others by sharing her story. Abramson also co-authored the one-woman play *No Limits* and the six-woman play *Beyond Limits,* about her life journey and how she is overcoming the challenges of being a person of color and having several disabilities.

Stumbling into Beauty

CHARMAINE MARIE BRANCH

My freshman dorm room, part of the original 1861 servants' quarters of Vassar College, was extremely narrow with
a window at one end and an oversized armoire at the other.
After a few months of practice, my roommate and I settled into
a dance of maneuvering the space without elbowing each other
in the face. I would stand in front of my dresser, a mess with art
history books and hairpins, fixing my curls in the mirror while
she leaned over my bed to scooch past me.

Vassar College was, in many ways, the island of misfits I had
hoped it would be. "Difference" was embraced in the circles I
treaded, but our community remained susceptible to the hege-
monic hierarchies I had grown up with in Madison, Wisconsin.

One evening in my first months of college, I stood in front
of my dresser getting ready for a party our dance company
was hosting. I didn't have any "going out" clothes from my
high school days, so I texted my childhood friend Nakatte for
advice:

"Should I wear my multicolored skirt with the belt?" I typed
into my flip phone.

"I don't remember that one," she wrote back. "Maybe the red
shirt you like?"

As I dug through drawers of clothes, I peeked up at myself in
the mirror to check the lip gloss I had just applied. I saw curls
swept up in a fountain-esque ponytail. I saw thick eyebrows

above almond-shaped eyes and a freckled nose. Then suddenly I saw something new that gave me pause: a beautiful brown woman.

And that beautiful brown woman, to my surprise, was me.

◦∾

Nakatte and I became friends in preschool and remain friends in part because we understand how difficult it is to make sense of our identities in a society that tells us we cannot be multiple things at once. We had both felt an underlying displacement throughout our childhood, but it wasn't until college that we were able to articulate it to each other. For Nakatte—whose American name is Margaret—that meant working to define her bicultural identity as both a Ugandan and American woman. For me, it meant many years of searching for the vocabulary to express myself as a biracial woman of color. Although my parents created a loving home where Blackness was celebrated, it was also a home where racism was rarely discussed. Even to this day, my sister Sarah and I attempt to make sense of situations we couldn't put into words at eight, twelve and seventeen by discussing them with each other.

That year I flew into Madison's small airport for winter break. I was greeted with a tornado of snow and the familiar gridded farmland that slowly morphed into a cityscape. Not long after arriving home, I borrowed my dad's car to drive to Nakatte's freshman dorm on the University of Wisconsin–Madison campus. Nakatte would eventually join the School of International Business, but freshman year she was busy acclimating to college life at the same level of exhaustion and awe that I was. She met me at the door with a giddy hug and we climbed the steps to her room equipped with Christmas lights and a futon couch.

The roads outside were icy, so we stayed in, exchanging stories of our very different college experiences. We began with the everyday of being eighteen and in college: daunting course loads, potential new friends and reflections on how it all compared with the not-so-distant high school of our past.

Then, without quite knowing how to articulate it, I began to tell Nakatte about the small event that nevertheless substantially shifted the way I thought about myself. I explained how sudden it had been, seeing something so different in the mirror than I had moments before. For many years I hadn't realized I had subconsciously compared my appearance with that of my white peers and the idealized "girl next door" image our high school coveted. I had wanted naturally straight hair and skin that didn't scar in dark melanin marks. It took a chance encounter with a mirror on the way to a party for me to realize the necessity of redefining my previous understanding of the word "beauty." I had to wipe away its many societal connotations in order to fully recognize it within myself.

Nakatte nodded in understanding and leaned in to tell me that she, too, had recently stopped comparing herself with a singular image of white beauty. Through her own journey, Nakatte had come to the same realization about herself and we had both found an openness of thought unknown to us before.

Nowadays I don't see Nakatte as often as I would like—one of the many plagues of adulthood—but we still text and call each other about new adventures including parties, job interviews, finding love, fellowships to Argentina, business trips to India and more.

My phone calls are full of the ramblings of a twenty-something who isn't sure she turned the kettle off before getting in the shower but was somehow accepted into an

M.A. program in art history. Perhaps this mindset is a reflection of the transient space I find myself in today. I'm moving to New York City, taking out student loans for graduate school and coming to terms with the fact that adulthood does not bring the answers to many of my questions. Instead, adulthood will probably surprise me with answers to questions I didn't know I had.

༄

CHARMAINE MARIE BRANCH is an incoming M.A. student in modern art: critical and curatorial studies at Columbia University in New York with a B.A. in art history from Vassar College. She plans to specialize in art of the African Diaspora in the Americas. Charmaine is a recipient of a Fulbright scholarship to Argentina and the Weitzel-Barber Art Travel Prize. In pursuit of becoming a curator, Charmaine has interned at institutions including the Metropolitan Museum of Art, the National Museum of African American History and Culture, the National Museum of the American Indian and the Smithsonian Center for Folklife and Cultural Heritage.

Not Shirley Temple Curls

Dera R. Williams

I remembered giving my mother the blues the night before
Easter Sunday; it had to be either 1959 or 1960. I loved to
watch Shirley Temple movies over and over, enchanted by
her dimples and bouncy curls, singing and dancing on The
Good Ship Lollipop and tap-dancing with Bill "Mr. Bojangles"
Robinson. I also remember those curls and how much I wanted
some "Shirlies," as we called them, for Easter. I was eight or
nine years old and I had it all pictured in my head just how I
would look. I was going to wear my new pink frilly dress and
white patent leather shoes, and I was going to be a brown
Shirley Temple. Just like Amos' daughter, Arbadella, the little
Negro girl on the Amos 'n' Andy Show. She had the Shirley
Temple look. That was the look I wanted and expected to have.

Saturday night before Easter, I sat down in the kitchen chair
ready to be made over after going through the ritual of washing
and the horror of detangling my knots and naps and "kitchens"
but enduring the torture because I could picture the result: a
mass of bouncy curls that would rival my childhood idol's. I
sat still in one spot, not fidgeting as I usually did. My hair was
going to be magically transformed.

Mama took the curling iron out of the drawer and put it
on the stove. She worked nonstop, curling my hair and then
carefully pulling and twisting each curl. When she finished,
she took a deep breath, frowned and told me to go look in

the mirror in the bathroom. I ran fast, expecting to look like Shirley Temple, or rather Arbadella. But the image staring back at me was neither of them. I had thin, limp curls, not full and fluffy. I was not happy. I ran back into the kitchen whining. "No, no, like Shirley Temple, Mama, I want my hair like hers." I cried.

So how does a mother who always had a head full of lustrous hair handle the care and styling of her daughter's hair, which was thinner and not able to adhere to the popular styles that the world deems as beautiful? I recall the words Mama said when I asked her what having "good hair" meant. She said, "God made your hair the way He wanted it to be. There is no such thing as good hair; if you have any, it's good."

But I didn't want to hear or think about that. I wanted what I wanted. I knew not all hair was created equal. Not only was Negro hair different from Caucasian hair, but within our own race there are different textures and lengths. Pictures of my mother as a girl show her with a head full of thick waves. I had always had pigtails that reached my shoulders, but they were soft, and thin. That had been fine with me for the most part. When I desired more hair, I did the Whoopi Goldberg thing by putting a sweater on my head and twirling around the room, the sweater arms blowing like white girls' hair.

My sister and I had Black baby dolls in the '50s and '60s. We would heat up the hot comb and press their hair. Seeing the dolls' burned-out white scalps, Mama told us we sure treated our children badly.

I cannot remember a time we did not have *Ebony, Sepia* and *Jet* magazines in our home, the latest issues proudly displayed on the coffee table in the living room. In those pages we saw famous celebrities and everyday people whose skin ranged from the lightest tones, like my mother's, to the darkest brown, almost black, like my father's. The hair textures ranged from Kunta Kinte-tightly curled to wavy to straight and long. That is the beauty that makes up our race, the Black race.

Mama stood there a minute with a dismayed look. "Well, I thought I did what you asked. Sit down and let me see what else I can do." I sat down and she brushed out the curls and started curling again. I went back to the mirror again and burst into tears. I ran to my room, "These aren't Shirley Temple curls, this isn't it!" Mama just stood there, a look of helplessness on her face. I had to have known I was being a big brat. My mother had always been supportive of her three children, even indulgent. I could see how hurt she was that she could not give me what I wanted. My beautiful, smart mother, a teacher who taught me to read in kindergarten, who worked hard to make sure I had a pretty dress and accessories for Easter.

Weary and drained from the entire ordeal, I finally fell asleep, but she later woke me up and tied my hair up with a scarf. I got up the next day resigned to my fate of having curls but not Shirley Temple curls. I had to accept the reason I could not get the hairstyle I desired was a combination of my fine, thin hair and my mother's lack of expertise in hairstyling. She was pretty basic: Braiding cornrow plaits and curling bangs was the extent of her repertoire. She could do a mean press but she was no stylist. My aunt and sister laughed about this at a family reunion when we were looking at some of our childhood school pictures. Had my mother been a little better stylist, I might have had better formed Shirlies, but they would never be full and thick; my hair was just not that kind. So, that morning I went to Easter Sunday service in my new pink dress, shoes and purse and with a curly 'do and was told by several people how pretty I looked and how nice my hair was. It was the Dera Jones curls, not Shirley Temple curls.

As the late 1960s dawned, there came an awareness of Black pride. That included embracing and loving one's self—kinky hair, curly hair, semi-curly hair and straight hair that was the full range among people of African descent. My sister and I wore our afros proudly. They weren't big and thick like Angela Davis'; as I said, we did not have that kind of hair. Our 'fros were beautifully shaped, smaller and becoming to our faces. The new awareness of embracing our individual images and feeling pride in who we were was further instilled by our parents. They had been doing it all along.

∽

DERA R. WILLIAMS lives, works and plays in the San Francisco Bay Area. A retiree of a local community college, she now mentors students in family history research. This Cali girl with Southern roots is a freelance writer and contributor to anthologies, journals and academic encyclopedias and is her family historian. Dera is co-author of the fiction book *Mother Wit: Stories of Mothers and Daughters*. She is completing a story collection about growing up in Oakland and a children's book about Alzheimer's disease. Her most recent publication can be found in the anthology *Our Black Mothers, Brave, Bold and Beautiful*.

New Year's Day

NIRA A. HYMAN

My grandmother, a Southern woman from Virginia, always made New Year's dinner, including collard greens for money/ prosperity, and black-eyed peas and pork for good luck and health. Unfortunately, my family enjoyed every part of pork I hated: pigs' feet, pigtails, hog maws, fatback, chitterlings/ "chitlins" (the smell of which still makes me dry heave) et al. To make fun of me—the only child and the youngest in a small family—my aunts, cousin and uncle all exaggerated eating their meals, dramatically gnawing on gristle and fat, shoving a pungently vinegared pig's foot under my nose for my horrified Pavlovian response, and generally making me nauseated.

Grandma, however, always had my back. She went out of her way to fry one lone pork chop just for me. "No one eats Nira's chop!" she'd yell, wrapping it in foil and setting it on the pilot light to stay warm while she finished making cornbread and other sides. While everyone mixed their food together, I had my sides on a dinner plate and my chop on a separate little saucer. Nobody was feeling my pathetic little piece of meat— which never looked like the picture on WordPress—unless I couldn't finish it. Then, everyone was putting dibs on the bone. But the inclusion always made me quietly pleased.

My aunt grumbled when she later took over the cooking: "She needs to try these pigtails. Does she know I can't buy just *one* of these things?" I was around twenty when I gave this any real thought; I never remember Grandma buying a pack of pork chops. There were still butcher shops in the area, though, and I'm guessing she was able to politely request one chop, every year, for her granddaughter, who was a picky eater but needed to be a part of this annual family tradition. Because of her I always think of New Year's meals with fond, giggly memories. I was the one-chop girl, and she helped me be proud of this.

∽

Nira A. Hyman has been copyediting and proofreading for more than fifteen years with publishing companies such as Scholastic, Bloomsbury and Wiley. Well versed in the *Chicago Manual of Style, The Gregg Reference Manual* and *Words into Type* and familiar with the *AMA Manual of Style,* Nira is experienced with rewriting and editing copy; fact-checking; and developing and executing story ideas in magazines and manuscripts and on websites. A novelist in her own right, she currently edits for Bloomsbury Books and individual clients, covering a broad range of fiction and nonfiction.

Re-Searching for a Truly American Art

TEREZITA ROMO

As an art historian in the era of the Obama "post-racial" discourse, I am asked to accept that we have moved beyond identity politics and its art, which was characterized as sacrificing aesthetics and quality for the sake of political statements. Yet as a Chicana art historian, I have come to believe that art has *always* been—and still is—about identity politics. But that has been hidden behind "art for art's sake" notions of aesthetic universality and artistic purity. Within art history, Western European art has been created, patronized and later canonized in exhibitions, scholarly catalogs and artist monographs as an artistic expression stripped of ethnicity and thus rendered "universal." In fact, I was taught that the clean lines and symmetrical form of an African mask rendered it "ethnic" and "primitive." It was only when Picasso transformed this mask into recognizable Western European art that it became "universal." I was told that the art created by artists of color constituted "hybridity," whereas a Western European artist's appropriation of other cultural/traditional art forms transformed it into "art." And one only needs to look at the art and artists included in mainstream institutions to see that identity politics have everything to do with who is included and who is excluded. Thus, considerations of ethnicity, race

271

and gender are not just fundamental to the non-white artistic world, but continue to uphold a mainstream institutional practice of exclusion.

For me as a Chicana art historian, the challenge has been to move the discussion beyond advocating for a "revisionist art history," which only serves to create a wider schism between white, mostly male artists who transcend "history" and the rest of the world relegated to creating an art that can only be explained as historical and/or cultural markers. In reality, artists do *not* exist outside of history and their cultural heritage. Thus, even though all art created by artists represents an "ethnic art," we have come to accept that Western European-derived aesthetics are universal. I saw this schism most clearly in two paintings that, though created almost fifty years apart, illustrate how little has changed within American art history.

Norman Rockwell's painting titled *Freedom from Want* (also known as "The Thanksgiving Picture") was created in 1943 and used to promote the purchase of war bonds by American citizens during World War II. As such, I can deduce that Rockwell was re-creating an overall image that would appeal to the Americans he was trying to reach. It is a sentimental version of a family celebrating an American holiday with its origins in the 1600s and commemorating the idealized reunion of the Native Americans and Jamestown settlers. In Rockwell's painting, the focus is on the grandparents lowering the turkey onto the food-laden table. Along the sides, one can see three generations of family members leaning in as if making sure they are in the picture frame. All but a young man in the lower right corner stare back at us with a contented gaze.

In 1988, Chicana artist Carmen Lomas Garza painted *Tamalada*. It, too, shows an American family, but this one is making *tamales*, the signature food for another holiday celebrated in the United States, Christmas. The three generations in this painting depict the different aspects of the assembly line needed to produce the labor-intensive main dish. The painting's composition is very open with a perspective from above, allowing us to view all the various activities. There is also an attention to the realistic details of the all-day endeavor, such as Lomas Garza's placement of toys to keep the children busy on the floor and various pots and pans on the stove.

Lomas Garza's painting is based on her memories of growing up in south Texas where blatant racism was the norm. It is telling to note that as Rockwell was calling on Americans to buy war bonds, African Americans, Asian Americans and Mexican Americans were dying in disproportionate numbers on the battlefield. In fact, Lomas Garza's father joined the GI Forum, a WWII Mexican American veterans' organization established to obtain the basic civil rights they had fought for. Thus, Lomas Garza's family is as American as Rockwell's and *Tamalada* is no more ethnic than *Thanksgiving*.

Yet this fallacy continues. The *Washington Post* art critic Paul Richard had this to say of Lomas Garza's 1995 solo exhibition at the Hirshhorn Museum, "They pound you with their niceness... these images of barrio life are never quite believable. Poverty? Forget it. Bitterness? No way. There are no roaches in these kitchens. No drunken macho meanness disturbs the perfect kindness of this little Texas town. Not even Mr. Rogers has a neighborhood as benign as this."*

---

* Richard, Paul. "Tejana Nostalgia." *The Washington Post* (December 3, 1995): G5.

Thus Richard, an art critic for a prestigious national newspaper, would have us believe that Lomas Garza's artistic portrayal of her home is not correct (i.e., not stereotypical). Yet, one wonders if he would have given her a good review even if she had portrayed his stereotypes. It may be true that art critics have toned down their overtly racist remarks over the past decade, but they, along with museum directors and art academia, continue to use Western European ethnic criteria to evaluate all artwork and act as de facto aesthetic gatekeepers.

For many years, Rockwell's art was dismissed and often shunned by art critics and art historians as illustration and devoid of artistic merit. But even his work has been reevaluated recently. In 1999, *The New Yorker* art critic Peter Schjeldahl said of Rockwell in *ARTnews*: "Rockwell is terrific. It's become too tedious to pretend he isn't."* Two years later, the Guggenheim Museum exhibited his work, and in 2006 his painting *Breaking Home Ties* was auctioned for $15.4 million. As a result, more museums have exhibited and collected his work. Yet, artists such as Lomas Garza continue to be limited to battling stereotypes.

I believe we need a paradigm shift that disrupts museums and art academia across the country. However, this paradigm shift necessitates a major transformation on the part of all artistic institutions, one that reflects diversity at *all* levels, from directors to curators to docents. It requires an acknowledgment there is nothing "new" or "emerging" about the artists from the excluded public we represent increasingly in the United States. I, for one, believe that there is enough room

---

* Jim Windolf. "Keys to the Kingdom." *Vanity Fair*, 2008. http://www.vanityfair.com/news/2008/02/indianajones200802. Retrieved April 28, 2012.

to reflect a more accurate, inclusive American art. It would not only change the power relations inherent in the art world that exist now, but also do away with the need for perpetuating a false argument around defining diversity and quantifying inclusion. We may even be able to finally have an informed debate regarding what constitutes art from a truly universal perspective.

∽

TEREZITA ROMO is a lecturer and affiliate faculty in the Chicana/o Studies Department at the University of California, Davis. An art historian, she has published extensively on Chicana/o art and is the author of the artist monograph *Malaquias Montoya*. An independent curator, she also served as the arts project coordinator at the UCLA Chicano Studies Research Center (CSRC). Romo was the curator of *Art Along the Hyphen: The Mexican American Generation,* one of four exhibitions in the CSRC's "LA Xicano" collaborative project within the Getty Foundation's regional initiative, Pacific Standard Time: Art in LA 1945–1980.

The Cure for What Ails You

Transcending Illness and Trauma

Labor of Love

SAMINA ALI

When my son was three years old, he announced that he was the Buddha. We were standing together in the bathroom, he on top of a three-step stool next to me, facing the mirror, as I pushed toothpaste onto his Elmo brush. "Mama," he said, staring at himself in the mirror, "I'm the one and only Buddha."

How could he even know who the Buddha is?, I wondered. Finally, I managed to say, "Thank you for telling me."

For what else are you to say to the Buddha when he announces his presence?

My son, he was like the breath within the breath, the life within the life, his great and ancient soul filling my small one with a fullness of happiness I had never experienced before.

On his birth certificate, my son's official name is Ishmael. Ishmael was one of the few names that incorporated his Indian-Muslim heritage from my side and his Anglo-Irish-Scottish-Welsh-German and Native American heritage from his dad's side. The Qur'an, the Bible and the Torah all historicize Ishmael as the firstborn son of Abraham and Sarah's Egyptian slave, Hajar. Then of course there's the literary Ishmael: *Moby-Dick* begins with the invitation, "Call me Ishmael..." There's one more literary reference to Ishmael that many may not be aware of, in a book titled *What NEVER to Name Your Child!*

My husband and I knew of no other name with such a beautiful blend:

A desert Ishmael and the Ishmael of the sea.

I experienced some of the happiest months of my life while pregnant with Ishmael, a calmness I'd never known before. I felt his energy emitting from the center of my belly, radiating through me so that I was at complete peace with my surroundings.

It wasn't anything like what I'd ever experienced before. I'm the kind of person who rushes through meditation and wears yoga pants as a fashion statement. When I first learned I was pregnant, for instance, I didn't call my parents with the announcement, as Ishmael's father did. I instead called the 800 number on the EPT test and argued with the customer service representative, telling her that the test was defective and I couldn't possibly be pregnant! Even though my husband and I had planned to have Ishmael, I went into a panic. I was twenty-nine years old. I was in the midst of writing my first novel. My husband, whom I'd met in our graduate writing program, had given up writing poetry in order to teach full time to support us, support me, while I finished writing that first novel. It just wasn't convenient to be pregnant with a baby when I was already in the process of birthing a story. How would I ever complete the book?

The customer service representative at EPT listened patiently to my rant and then calmly said, "Ma'am, it's not hard to pee on a stick. Congratulations on your pregnancy."

My pregnancy started off appearing to be a textbook example of a healthy, normal pregnancy, the baby's development progressing through the months just as expected—which of course filled my husband and me with pride, as though the fetus was already a model of a well-behaved child.

"We wouldn't expect anything less from our baby," we often joked to friends when reporting on how the pregnancy was going.

But then, in early August, when I was seventh months along, I began to notice strange symptoms. It began one afternoon when I was sitting at my desk, my arms uncomfortably extended past my belly to reach the keyboard as I furiously wrote my novel, trying to get as much done as I could before the baby arrived. While I was typing, the flesh of my fingers kept grazing against flesh. It was so uncomfortable that I stopped typing and stared down at my hands. Just that very morning, I had slid on my wedding ring with ease, yet now, within hours, the band was so tight it wouldn't even turn. Over the next few days, my body continued to swell like a puffer fish under attack until I became self-conscious about my appearance. I would stand in front of a mirror and push a finger into my fleshy cheek, horrified by how much I'd swollen up. But I didn't bring it up with the doctor. Aware of my neurotic tendencies, I told myself I was just retaining water, that it was entirely normal.

What I did complain to my obstetrician about later that month was the constant, jabbing pain in my abdomen, right beneath my ribs on the right side. My obstetrician suspected my muscles had grown tender from being stretched by the expanding uterus and prescribed Tylenol. When I found that it didn't help relieve the pain, I began to eat less, believing that less food would place less strain on the muscles. I also upped my water intake because I'd read that water helped flush out fluids, reducing bloating. In late August, at my baby shower, a friend remarked with some astonishment that, despite how much water I was guzzling, she hadn't once seen me go to the toilet. Instead of wondering if low urine output might be a sign of kidney trouble, I considered myself lucky. At least I wasn't one of those expectant moms always rushing to the bathroom!

What finally caught my attention, forcing me to accept that something might be wrong, was when I began to itch so severely that I dug my fingernails into my flesh, leaving long scars like claw marks across my enormous belly. At the same time, I began to be assaulted by headaches and noticed floating specks in my vision.

"Migraines," my doctor assured me. "It's a normal pregnancy complaint."

"And the itching?" I asked, doing my best to hold back that familiar rise of panic.

"Your skin is being stretched beyond limits, that's all."

"Even my palms? The soles of my feet?"

"I can prescribe a lotion if you want."

When I began to throw up after my meals, as I did in the first trimester when I had morning sickness, I finally broke down.

"Something's wrong!" I cried to my husband, listing the strange symptoms I'd been having.

"Why didn't you tell me earlier?" he asked, as alarmed as I was.

I didn't know what to say. The symptoms were so vague, so dangerously innocuous, that it was hard for me to know, as a first-time mother-to-be, what was normal and what wasn't. So each time my doctor, who does have the training to know, dismissed the red flags, I left the appointment doubting myself, feeling increasingly crazy.

Together, my husband and I began to plot. He would join me at my next doctor visit. He would be the one to talk to my doctor. Maybe the doctor hadn't been taking me seriously because I'm a woman of color? Or maybe simply because I was a woman? As a man—a white man at that—my husband wouldn't be ignored.

At what turned out to be my last prenatal visit, my husband said exactly what we'd prepped: "She's itching all over, she's vomiting, she's not peeing at all, she's so bloated she's unrecognizable, and now headaches and floating specks. We would like you to perform some tests. We're not asking you if something is wrong. We know something is wrong. We want you to find out exactly what that might be."

"Tests?" The doctor sounded incredulous. He had an indulgent smile on his face as he said, "By next week this time, you'll be home from the hospital with your baby, both of you healthy and happy."

That very night, I went into early labor. Within twenty-four hours, I was in the Neuro ICU, the intensive care unit for patients with brain trauma, fighting for my life.

During the course of labor, my symptoms worsened. My headache felt like someone had squeezed a hard ball at the very center of my head, so intense that it blocked out the agony of labor.

"Shouldn't I be having more pain down there than up here?" I kept asking the obstetrician.

In the final two hours, when I was pushing my son out, my heart felt so strained I thought it would pop out of my rib cage. I begged the nurse for pain medications. I was given Alka-Seltzer.

"I'm seeing double," I cried. "Triple!" Eventually it got to the point where I couldn't count anymore. I went in and out of consciousness.

"Maternal exhaustion," I vaguely overheard the doctor assuring my husband.

Twenty minutes after delivery, while my son was being weighed and bathed, I was struck down by a grand mal seizure. My husband later told me it was the most frightening scene he'd ever witnessed, my body wracking and rattling the bed, my arms and my legs thrown up in the air, violently shaking. I have no memory of it, nor of the following days. What follows is what I was told by others.

Eight hours after my seizure, I was finally wheeled down for a CT scan of the brain. It showed what the doctors weren't expecting: two hemorrhages, one in front, one in back. One was a subarachnoid hemorrhage, which, my younger brother, who was a resident in neurosurgery at the time, told me kills 60 percent of patients. Kills, that is, patients who have no other medical condition but the subarachnoid hemorrhage to deal with.

I had other things going on.

Liver failure. Kidney failure. Pulmonary edema. Single-digit blood platelet count. Blood that had stopped clotting. And the chest pain I'd been given Alka-Seltzer for? Turned out to be a heart attack. I also had brain swelling so severe that it refused to respond to medication and the doctors were planning to drill a hole in my head to relieve it of the excess water.

"She won't need anesthesia, of course," one of the doctors offhandedly mentioned to my husband.

I am told I went into a coma. I am told the doctors were frequently awakening me to prevent me from moving even deeper into a coma. When awake, I am told, I did not recognize anyone, not my brothers or parents, not my husband.

Hundreds of strokes, the doctors said—that was what they believed was happening in my swollen brain: It had become a galaxy of popping and shooting blood vessels.

The neurologist told my family that if I was lucky, I would die. If not, my husband would be my legal guardian. The hospital asked my husband if I'd thought to make a living will. My husband fell into a state of shock. Several times a day, he took the elevator up to the fifteenth and top floor of the hospital to visit our newborn in the nursery, then took it back down to the eighth floor, where the Neuro ICU was situated behind locked doors, entrance denied to anyone but immediate family. My mother told my doctor she refused to prepare for the worst, for my becoming a vegetable or for my death.

"A mother's heart knows better than any doctor if she's going to lose her child," she reprimanded the neurologist. All day, she sat by my side in the curtained space in the Neuro ICU ward. At night, when she got home, she spread open her prayer rug and touched her forehead to the ground, not rising again till morning.

So, what is it that I remember?

I remember my son, shoving and winding his way out of me and thinking he had a long body. I remember the shock when I finally saw him, his face so different from what I'd imagined. For nine months, I had been preparing my white husband for a brown baby. Yet, here he was, born with skin fairer than even my husband's ruddy complexion, and gray-blue eyes. I remember wanting to hold him, but the doctors had whisked him to a table far from me to be wiped and cleaned, his lungs sucked of impurities.

Then there is darkness. And two people inhabiting this darkness.

The best way to describe it is by the epidural I'd been given during delivery. I hadn't wanted it, enjoying each spike of pain that brought me closer to my son, but the nurses had insisted. Then the doctor injected it incorrectly so it numbed only half of me. I was thrilled and, during delivery, reveled in the left side of my body, the side alive to the pain of emerging life.

Like that, there were two selves in the darkness where I was and only one was "waking up" at the doctor's insistence. This self, whenever she was awake, thought of Ishmael and screamed that he was still inside her, wanting to come out. It seems the internal clock had stopped during delivery. So the one who had her eyes open, shouting for her son, was the one who was asleep. And the one awake was the one inside the darkness.

Darkness. That is what I remember. An enveloping darkness where there are no relationships, no ties, no love, no fear, no creation, no connections. And, in this way, there is peace.

It is said that at the end of Buddha's life, when he was asked what there was to know about death, he turned over his bowl. Meaning, an emptiness within an emptiness.

I was living inside that turned-over bowl.

A week following my delivery, while the doctors were preparing my family for my inevitable death, my organs unexpectedly started to rev back up, one after another—my kidneys, my liver, my lungs, like lights in a house switching on. My blood started clotting. My platelets got a modest boost. Even my brain stopped swelling. My neurologist later told me that in his twenty-five years of experience, he'd never seen anything like it. I'd had a leg through death's door, he said. Nobody comes back from that.

Fifteen days after I'd gone to the hospital to deliver my son, I was released with a brown paper bag full of medications, sent home to recover as best I could. On the day of my discharge, the director of obstetrics came to see me to explain that the condition that had left me so debilitated was called preeclampsia. In the brown paper bag full of medications was also a printout describing the disease. When I looked it over, I saw every one of my symptoms. Even though I was a patient at one of the best hospitals in the world, I'd fallen through the cracks. There was no other way to explain what had happened: These esteemed doctors at this esteemed institution had missed my telltale signs. Undiagnosed, my preeclampsia had morphed into eclampsia and then into its most lethal form, HELLP syndrome.

The brain damage was so severe that when I was discharged the neurologist warned my husband that the woman he was now taking home wasn't the same woman he'd brought to the hospital. He was right. Although my brain had stopped swelling, it had ballooned out until the outer edges were pushed up against my skull. For weeks, I suffered from debilitating headaches that kept me balled up in bed in a fetal position. Even if I wanted to, there was no way I could stand by myself, or walk from my bed to the bathroom—let alone take a shower, brush my teeth or sit on the toilet in privacy. Because the wires in my brain were faulty, my right eye would go intermittently blind. I had no short-term memory or depth perception. My speech was broken by severe aphasia, so that what I wanted to say wasn't what I ended up saying. I was a writer whose words had left me. Almost immediately, I sank into depression. Although I was now a mother, I was as helpless as my newborn. My mother had been forced to move in to help care for us both.

A month after my release, when I saw a neurologist for a

follow-up appointment, I asked him when I would be able write again. My husband was at the appointment and I could tell he was taken aback by the question. On his face, I could see what he was thinking: *There is so much else to worry about!* To him, to my mother, to the doctors, there was a distinct before and after. Pre-delivery. Post-delivery. Pre-Samina. Post-Samina. There was no way to reverse course, go back to the time before the big disruption. We had to move forward, picking through the debris, recovering what little we could.

But in my mind, I was the same person. I just couldn't do as much as I'd been able to before. As I saw it, the best way to become my old self was to pick up and continue doing what I'd been doing before the catastrophic delivery. And what I'd been doing then was writing my book.

"To write," the neurologist told me after a moment's consideration, "you need this part of your brain and this part and this part and this part." He pointed to various parts of his head. "And I'm afraid there's no part of your brain that hasn't been damaged. Your brain is currently so swollen it will take an entire year just to reduce back down to normal size. At that point, we'll know better what functions you've permanently lost. For now, I would be leading you astray if I didn't tell you that you've lost the higher mental processes to imagine, to plan, to create, those functions that are intrinsically human, those very things that make us human...and which also allow a person to write."

"So I can't write again?" I asked, speaking slowly to get the right words out. I hoped he didn't see that I didn't understand anything of what he'd just said, didn't have the capacity to. I just needed a short, simple answer. I peered into his face, concentrating.

"No," he said.

I stared down at my hands for a long while, thinking of the last time I'd sat in an exam room like this one. It was the day before my delivery, when my husband and I had gone in together to get the obstetrician to see that something was wrong. The doctor had brushed off the warning signs and, afterward, had kept dismissing the red flags all the way through my labor and right up until I had my seizure and it was too late to do anything.

If these esteemed doctors at the hospital had missed my disease, telling me I was fine when I repeatedly pointed out my telltale symptoms, desperately seeking their help, how could any of them be right about my recovery? The neurologist was wrong, I decided right then in the exam room, and I'd prove it by finishing my novel.

I asked my husband to move my desk to our bedroom, place it in the corner near the bed. Days later, when I'd recovered from the exertion of visiting the neurologist, I asked my mom to help me to the desk. I pulled up the file for my manuscript, stared at the last scene I'd been working on. I had no memory of what I'd written. I went through other pages, then more, right back to the first chapter. Nothing, no recognition that this was my work. It was as though I'd taken a book off my bookshelf and begun reading. That the novel was based on my own life experience made no difference. It was entirely foreign to me. Feeling myself beginning to panic, I quickly shut down my computer and went back to bed.

The following day, I sat at the computer and opened up a blank file. I decided to start a new novel. It did not occur to me that I did not have a story in mind to write nor even that I needed an idea for a story in order to write. I simply put down words, then did so again the following day and the day after for weeks. Almost immediately I realized that writing wasn't as easy as I'd allowed myself to believe. With my aphasia, I couldn't type the words I was thinking. Other words would emerge that weren't even on my mind. Worse, there were days when my brain was too impaired to grasp that the words I was stringing together were random at best, pure nonsense. The gibberish actually made sense to me! My debilitated brain was seeing something that wasn't in fact in front of me. The very act of forcing my brain to put words together at my command, to create the very beginnings of a scene (if it can even be called that), instantly brought on a headache. But I continued to write even as I felt my head growing hazy from exhaustion, heavy from pain. Finally, when I could no longer keep my eyes open from the agony, I would swivel my chair around, away from the desk, and simply let my body fall to the ground. There I would lie, curled up, my arms wrapped around my head, my eyes squeezed shut. From some other part of the house, I would hear my mother cooing to my son. A half an hour later, twice the time I'd been able to sit at the desk and write, I would lift myself off the ground and slowly crawl back to the bed. To get myself up, I'd grab hold of the sheets and pull with all my might.

On bad days, I hit my limit in under five minutes and would again let myself fall to the ground. Good days, I had ten minutes before I was assaulted by the headache. I told myself it didn't matter, none of it, not the reality that the sentences weren't making sense, and not that, even on my best days, I wasn't able to function for more than fifteen minutes. I didn't let anything stop me. I struggled forward, too scared to acknowledge that the doctor was right, that at twenty-nine years old, as a result of having a baby, I was disabled.

I set other goals. From the bed, I'd walk the six paces to the desk by myself. From my bed, I'd walk the twenty paces to the bathroom. I would sit on the toilet in private, even if I had to keep the door open, my mom or my husband standing just outside in case I called for help. I accepted that I wasn't able to shower without assistance. There was something about the pressure of the water spraying down on my head that aggravated my already aggravated brain. More than once, I had to shut the water off mid-shower and lie down on the tile floor, naked, wet, feeling dizzy and weak. It was after I showered that functions I thought I'd recovered—my right eye could see, I was walking farther and farther—would disappear again. For several hours or several days—it was entirely unpredictable—I would be right back to square one, as broken as the day I'd been released from the hospital.

Like this, the healing process was tedious, marked with uplifting breakthroughs and then heartbreaking regression. There were countless times during that period when I wanted to give up. But I happened to be raising a newborn while I was recovering and I actively made the decision (then remade it over and again during my all-too-frequent dark moments) to use my son as my inspiration.

In all, it took me approximately three years to recover. In that time, I learned to walk again alongside my son's first steps. Together, Ishmael and I each met our milestones: learning to speak, to write, to shower, to brush our teeth. There isn't anything special in my story of recovery, no secret I can impart. Life has a way of backing us each into a corner and we do what we can to survive; the roulette wheel of fate doesn't spare anyone. For that reason, I'm not even sure I'd say it was courage and tenacity that saved me. It might have instead been stubbornness and denial. And of course, a great deal of luck. Even though I didn't know it going in, the repetitive process of working on a story based on my personal experience forced my brain to excavate my past, to imagine a trajectory for a future through planning and plotting, to correctly match the words I was typing/speaking with those I was thinking, to create a story populated by multiple characters, each with a different mind of his or her own. In this way, for months and then for years, each day I sat down at the computer, I forced my brain to create new connections between brain cells, called neural pathways. These pathways branched out to connect cells that weren't connected before and this new wiring in my brain means I overcame my deficits *not* by regaining what I'd lost but by relearning those tasks and functions.

By creating new neural pathways, my brain didn't do anything special. Our brains are flexible enough to work continuously to build new circuits. It's exactly what a newborn's brain does as it develops, exactly what my son's newborn brain began doing from the moment he was born. He and I just happened to develop neural pathways at around the same time.

The same day of my last neurological exam, the one where the doctor pronounced me fully recovered, my husband and I decided it was time to part ways. My son was three years old, right about the age he announced he was the Buddha. The doctor ended up being right. The woman I became after the delivery was not the same woman who had gone into the hospital, nor the same one who'd gleefully gotten married right after graduating from the writing program. The new neural pathways had created a new person. By forcing myself to recover, I had reinvented myself. Our struggles to survive—mine as I recovered, my husband's as he helped me recover—depleted us. We felt bound by a wound, by trauma, and couldn't ignore the overpowering urge to leave it behind and start fresh.

Even as we divorced, I finished up my novel and sold it. Long ago, when I'd called the customer service number for EPT, I'd been deeply worried I wouldn't be able to birth my son and a book at the same time. The task seemed insurmountable. I had no idea then that I would also be called upon to rebirth myself.

There is a saying in Islam that encapsulates how I feel as a mother—a mother to my son and a mother to myself: I am God, and God is me. Yet, God is God, and I am me.

In Sufi Islam, we say a small fire burns in each of our bellies, the fire of life that only Allah has the power to extinguish. When I think of Buddha turning over that bowl, I see an image of a full belly, of pregnancy, of creation.

Life: It is not simply to be alive; it is to be awake.

This is what I've learned from this labor of love.

෴

SAMINA ALI is an award-winning author, activist and cultural commentator. Her debut novel, *Madras on Rainy Days,* won France's prestigious Prix Premier Roman Etranger Award and was a finalist for the PEN/Hemingway Award for Fiction. Ali's work is driven by her belief in personal narrative as a force for achieving women's individual and political freedom. She is the curator of the groundbreaking, critically acclaimed virtual exhibition *Muslima: Muslim Women's Art & Voices*. A former cultural ambassador for the U.S. State Department and a regular contributor to the *Huffington Post* and *Daily Beast,* Ali has spoken extensively at universities and other institutions worldwide. Her work has been featured in the *New York Times,* the *Economist,* the *Guardian* and *Vogue* as well as on National Public Radio (NPR) and elsewhere. She is currently working on a memoir about her near-death experience delivering her firstborn.

A Photograph of Martin

Marti Paschal

Remembering the last photograph I took of my brother, Martin, is how I sit in the charnel fields. In every photo I have of him, he is smiling—even the last one, as if he had to smile for me, knowing it would be the last picture I would take of him, knowing our days together were dwindling. I don't like thinking about that photo. His smile is stretched from his teeth as if he were grimacing. His once handsome face ghoulish, his skin darkened and hair straightened and thinned by the toxic drugs he took daily. His left leg was amputated below the knee, his skeletal body propped in a wheelchair.

He was so close to death, I see now. He was heading to the charnel fields.

I would never show anyone that photograph. In my favorite photo of Martin, he is on a train to Zell am See, Austria, a white Panama hat framing his thick, dark eyebrows, his navy polo shirt contrasting with his golden skin. His lips are full and he smiles with ease; his skin is glowing in the bright afternoon sun; his muscular and tanned arms are akimbo. He is looking into the distance toward the left, as if he is looking into the past.

I would read Zen parables to Martin while we waited for his medical appointments, whispering as we sat in the waiting rooms. Our favorite story was of a monk who found a lost boy, took him in and loved him as if he were his son. Years later when the mother found her son, the monk easily gave him up. The lesson was: "Hang on tightly, let go lightly."

Martin believed that one never died without first accepting death. Even in murders and accidents, there would be a moment when the spirit said, "Yes," and let go. As we watched the ward fill up with AIDS patients in different stages of the illness, as he cycled in and out of the hospital with kidney damage and Kaposi Sarcoma and seizures, I wondered when he would say, "Yes."

During my last visit home before he died, he scheduled surgery to replace the shunt in his chest, a device to receive the caustic drugs he took. The morning of the surgery, my mother and I woke up early to take him to his appointment. When she went into his room to wake him, he was already up and determined. He said no to the surgery. My mother was overcome with fear, fear cloaked as fury and irritation. His appointment was in less than an hour. He needed the shunt for his medication. Why was he giving up? As she called the hospital to cancel the surgery, I went into his room and said, "Let go lightly." He smiled. I went back to sleep and dreamt that I was screaming at my mother, my face scornful, telling her that she had to accept his decision. I woke up, wondering if I had said something to her before I fell asleep, painfully aware that I could not tell a mother what to accept.

One evening I fell asleep in the living room and woke up after everyone else had gone to bed. I had slept through dinner, and went into the kitchen to get something to eat. As I ate, Death walked through the rear hallway to join me. Death was a tall man with wide shoulders and burnished, leathery skin the color of sunbathed mahogany, his body nude but as asexual as a wooden sculpture. His face was broad, rectangular and handsome. He sat at the head of the table and ignored me. I was not afraid because I was not the one he wanted. I finished my meal and went to bed. I do not remember seeing him leave. Yes, I must have been dreaming.

A hospital bed was in Martin's bedroom. I would stand at the doorway and watch him, barely able to lift himself out of his wheelchair as he climbed into bed. I never offered to help him. I watched as he pulled the four cotton blankets and the blue comforter over himself, then smiled at me, his smile a fading grin, his eyes weary. I would sit on the bed next to him and read passages from Buddhist texts, flipping through books, wondering what lesson might be appropriate at the moment. Appropriate for both of us.

I realize now that he was probably humoring me.

As he slept, I would stand again in the doorway and gaze at the dark blue walls he painted before losing his leg, the photographs from his not-too-distant trip to Europe, the Brooks Brothers pullovers in pastel colors stacked on an armchair, the bookcase filled with books from his contemporary civilization and African American literature classes at Columbia, and the books on nutritional healing, drugs, and AIDS care and research. I would watch him as he slept, his breathing noisy and labored, each breath a raspy struggle.

I was not home when he died. I was in San Francisco on the phone with our mother, who called to ask if he should be hospitalized yet again. I told her no, let him remain at home; there was nothing more they could do for him. While we were on the phone, the noise, the rasping, the struggle stopped.

Let go lightly.

Spiders began to symbolize death and reincarnation. I imagined my brother returning as a spider, over and over again, spinning beautiful webs high above me. Every spider I saw in my apartment was Martin, there to comfort me, to reassure me that all was okay.

I didn't realize that grief is a hallucinogen.

"She took it hard," my relatives said. I was always the laughing, dancing one in the family, but now there was a pool of darkness behind my eyes and underneath my skin. But I accepted his desire to let go, for that was not a life I wanted for him: his body failing him, the drugs and opportunistic diseases battling each other, thwarting any chance of true recovery.

It is not my death that I fear. I fear the deaths of others. Imagining the charnel fields containing my mother, my sisters and remaining brother, and my dearest friends. Imagining my life without them. According to Buddhism, it is the nature of everyone to change; there is no way to escape being separated from the people I love. I understand this but it is hard to accept.

I return to the photograph of Martin heading to the charnel fields.

But my brother is not a photograph. No matter how technically exquisite, photographs would not capture the laughs, the conversations, the joy we shared after the photos were taken. My brother was not his body, not when it was strong nor when it was ravaged by AIDS. Because the charnel fields contain more than the bones of our loved ones, they capture our relationships, our identities as sister, brother, mother. The charnel fields reveal our attachments to our hopes and plans, shackling them to the bloody ground, still visible but illusory and beyond our reach.

I still reach for Martin occasionally, twenty-three years later, wishing he were here to share in this life. Wondering, wondering, I reach, I wonder, then I let go.

∽

MARTI PASCHAL is a longtime member of Temescal Writers, a Voices of Our Nations alumna and a recipient of residencies at Hedgebrook and Blue Mountain Center. Her writing reflects her Southern upbringing and fascination with conflicts in urban settings and between cultures. A graduate of Stanford Law School, she works in local government and is currently writing her first novel.

Pressing Pause

MEERA BOWMAN-JOHNSON

"Stop and smell your flowers!" my childhood friend whispered, holding my wrist and bending into my lilies and roses. "This is your wedding day. You should take in every moment! Smell them," she urged. The last time I had seen her had been at her own wedding, six months prior. It was a lovely Hudson Valley event, straight out of *Martha Stewart Weddings*. But I wondered if she wished she'd taken in more of the details. Because even though I'd only been a bride for two hours, I was quickly learning how easy it is to miss the idiosyncrasies of one's own wedding day. How ironic that the little things people spend many months fixating on disappear into the ether on the Big Day. I was grateful that she was forcing me to stand there and inhale my flowers, even though it wasn't easy for me to do.

I always found it hard to slow down because I was too busy trying to move ahead. I guess that's to be expected of the goal-oriented product of two African American public school teachers. I maintained a vision board in my head before vision boards were a "thing." I carried a bullet list (on a clipboard, no less) in college before people were pinning them to boards on Pinterest. By the time graduation came, I'd carefully planned my career in magazine publishing. When I met Susan Taylor at my commencement, I thanked her for *Essence*. Five years later, I was an art director at the iconic magazine. I married a like-minded man who wrote me a letter in college saying he planned to become an author. I believed him, and then he did it. That's part of why we made a good team: We always had a plan and supported each other's dreams. We may not have had a GPS helping us get there, but we always knew where we wanted to go.

It was like that for years as we established our careers, and then a family. There was a frenzied, sometimes chaotic pace to our days and nights as we forged ahead, but there was a rhythm to it. Suddenly we had a mortgage and three young children. When I started experiencing headaches and fatigue, I didn't give it too much thought because there was too much to do. When I mentioned it to the doctor, she explained that it was probably due to dehydration and stress. I left her office promising myself I'd cut back on caffeine and go to bed earlier. Most days, I felt fine. I went to Zumba, yoga and belly dancing classes. I even began running, something I never thought I could enjoy. That fall, my husband and I ran a four-mile Turkey Trot on Thanksgiving Day in Memphis. I was running in real life, too, hustling the kids to school and to various lessons and starting a new career in higher education.

So, when I collapsed in our hallway one Saturday morning, I wasn't afraid because I thought I was still in control. Even when I came to, staring up at the angelic faces of my three children asking if they should call 911, I took a moment to think about it before giving them the go-ahead. I didn't even think I'd lost control as they were helping me up off of the floor. Or while my younger daughter was helping me change out of my pajamas and into street clothes before the paramedics came. I was still in control as they put me onto the stretcher and wheeled me down our driveway to the ambulance; I was taking a head count of the children. Someone was missing. I insisted that someone go back for my son and they allow all three to ride with me to the emergency room. And although I had no idea what was happening, I told them, "Mommy's okay," like it was my new mantra. My oldest called my husband on her iPhone.

The CT scan revealed one walnut-sized tumor in the third and fourth ventricles of my brain. There was also intracranial swelling that explained the headaches and, more recently, memory loss and moodiness. My husband and I stared at the screen in shock, as the attending physician gently told us that I would need emergency surgery. If there was any upside at that moment, it was that we lived twenty-five minutes from the world-famous Texas Medical Center. The local ER put me under sedation and transferred me there for the surgery. My husband called my aunt, a Philadelphia-based physician, and she flew in to emotionally support my family.

To this day, I don't know what we would have done without her support and that of my parents and my college roommates.

The surgery was six hours and we were relieved to learn that the tumor was benign. But my right side, while not paralyzed, was severely weak, so that I couldn't even wave "hello" or wiggle my toes. When my family asked the doctors how long it would take for me to recover, they said they weren't sure. My husband started pricing elevators for the house. My deepest gut feeling was that I may not ever run a Turkey Trot again, but I would be able to walk, eventually. I had to. There was still so much to do.

I began visualizing standing upright and walking by myself, before I was able to do either. Each morning, I slowly walked the floor in my hospital gown with the help of a physical therapist and a walker. But every afternoon when my husband came to visit me after teaching his classes, he massaged my right foot and asked, "Any movement today, baby?"

"No," I sighed. But that was only because my short-term memory had yet to catch up with my body. When the nurse casually mentioned to my husband that I'd actually been walking for several days, that I just didn't remember, you'd think she'd said he'd won the Powerball.

But even better than winning the lottery, I was soon told I was ready to continue my recovery at the number-two rehabilitation hospital in the nation. It was the same facility where United States Congresswoman Gabby Giffords recovered from her severe brain injury as the result of an assassination attempt in Arizona in 2011. I wondered if she, too, was rushing through life before that unfortunate, life-changing event. I arrived the night before my birthday, and woke up to light streaming through the flowers from friends and family wishing me good health and acknowledging another year. I was forty-four—"old" to most Millennials, but still too young to die.

The nurses sang the birthday song, and my husband and kids brought me pad thai and cake with the best buttercream frosting I'd ever tasted. That night, I looked around the room at the beautiful flowers celebrating my life. And I was still alive to enjoy them. I closed my eyes and inhaled. There was nowhere to go and nothing to do but get well. In that moment, my entire world smelled like lilies and roses.

༄

MEERA BOWMAN-JOHNSON entered the publishing world as a magazine art director at the age of twenty-three. She has contributed art direction and graphic design to magazines including *Essence, Honey* and *Code* and essays to the

Root, the *Washington Post* and *Time Out New York Kids.* A Philadelphia-born graduate of Spelman College, she has lived, worked and played on the East and West Coasts of the United States. She now splits the difference, living with her husband, Mat Johnson, and their three children in Houston, Texas. She is currently training for her first 5k.

A Kid Like Mine

KRISTIN LEAVY MILLER

Night after night, my fifteen-month-old son could not stop scratching the rashes, hives and scales covering his body—a complete eczema exterior—until he was bloody, broken, exhausted and routinely pained with unbearable discomfort.

After months of pediatrician and hospital visits, which included a slew of painful testing, retesting and rigorous examinations, an allergist confirmed his diagnosis: life-threatening food allergies. In essence, I learned that simply feeding my son *could potentially kill him.*

Life-threatening food allergies can spiral into awful skin reactions, infections or anaphylactic shock—an allergic reaction resulting in swelling, lowered blood pressure and dilated blood vessels. His food allergies could deny access to his air supply. Nearly fifteen million Americans have food allergies, according to Food Allergy Research & Education organization, and my child was now one of those fifteen million.

But instead of having one life-threatening food allergy, my son had six. He was allergic to six of the top eight most common allergens identified by the Food and Drug Administration, including milk, eggs, peanuts, tree nuts, fish and shellfish. I was devastated and overwhelmed and lived with the daily fear that he could die at any moment. I felt hopeless: A mere sip of the wrong formula, or bite of the wrong food, could be his absolute last.

The pain of it all—both emotional and physical—wore on us. I began to wonder how my child could still love me as I helplessly watched him suffer. At only one year old, he was no doubt stronger than I, yet we were both exhausted, physically and mentally.

I remember standing in a grocery aisle, sobbing—trying to understand food labels and whether what I was about to select was something safe for my child to eat. I didn't know whether I would unintentionally kill him if I fed him, or end up starving him out of fear of feeding him something that *could* kill him. I was depressed and afraid. I felt like the worst mother in the world and found myself finishing entire bottles of wine, hoping my overloaded brain would temporarily shut off during a rare and quiet nap time.

But I wanted better. I wanted to learn how to care for my son so he could be happy and healthy. I wanted him to smile big during the day, and rest peacefully at night. I wanted him to feel good from the inside out.

I wanted what every mother wants for her child, and I knew that for this to happen I had to begin a dedicated and meticulous journey toward food safety and wellness, a journey that could sustain only minimal mistakes to keep him out of harm's way. I vowed to do just that. I researched, consulted with doctors and allergists and nutritionists, sought medical advice and read every label forward and backward what had to be a minimum of ten times over.

I focused on safe foods that he *could* have instead of what he *couldn't* have. We maintained a required medication regimen prescribed by his allergist. We packed food from home every time we left the house, knowing that finding safe food on the go was rarely an option. Yet caring for him at home would never be enough to keep him safe. If I wanted him to have any sort of life, that meant I'd have to teach those around him about food allergies, even as I had just begun deepening my knowledge about them.

Many were resistant, and a friend might say, "Just give it (food in question) to him. I think he'll be okay," or "Won't he just grow out of it?" And, my personal favorite: "Your son can *never* come to my house!" I understood the confusion due to lack of awareness, but that did not make it less frustrating.

Food often bonds family and communities together. Yet most "traditionally American" dishes include one, if not more, of the top eight allergens sure to cause a frightening reaction in those with food allergies. As such, our entire lives revolve around food. I'm always crestfallen to see the look on my son's face when I say, "No, that's not safe for you to have; it could make you sick," and live for the moments when his face lights up over the perfect dessert, free of any foods that could harm him. I will tear up at the most unexpected of moments, for instance when he knows to choose a safe snack from his lunchbox, as opposed to an unsafe one in a social setting.

Over time, friends and family began to accept and understand the magnitude of our problem, and see that my fears and concerns were valid. They became more willing to learn about allergens and how to help or accommodate my son, and for that, I'm forever grateful.

⌣

Chicago native **KRISTIN LEAVY MILLER** is a freelance writer and blogger, currently based in Baltimore. She devotes her time to writing about her firsthand experience in managing a food-allergic family—complete with stories, allergy-safety tips, recipes and the daily life of her food-allergic preschooler. When not writing, Kristin's busy in her kitchen experimenting with allergy-safe ingredients, making delicious treats for all to enjoy. You can find *Jet* magazine articles written by Kristin at JetMag.com or Kristin's blog at http://www.carsonskitchen. tumblr.com/.

Learning to Thrive

KIRA LYNNE ALLEN

I can't stop the lingerie shows for my husband and fourteen of his closest friends, with silent tears running down my face, because it means actually valuing myself, never mind that my three-year-old daughter sees her whole world through my eyes, never mind that she is about to become me, the three-year-old passing joints so no one has to get up.

Before I marry this man who actually thinks it's okay to use my body as a party favor, eight football players take turns moving from mouth to ass and back again, raping me for hours with the express intent of making me feel worthless. A man drives me up a mountain in a snowstorm to smoke a joint and says, "Don't cry, sweetheart, all I wanna do is fuck you. If not, you can walk home." My high school "friend" drives me home from a party. I'm tipsy; he carries me to my room, soils my unconscious body and pays for the abortion six weeks later. No one has ever valued me enough to protect me before; why should I expect my husband to?

One of the many reasons it takes so long to leave is that I use pot like a gag, to maintain the silence involved in being buried above ground; besides, I lack both an education and an income of my own. When I finally file for divorce, my baby girl is already four years old and the seeds of my "work" are planted.

∾

The year I turned nine, a trifecta of events occurred that shape the woman I am today:

One: Eight and a half years of grand mal seizures finally subside; my mother defies all the doctors' orders and weans me off my epilepsy medication to stop the drool, lack of concentration, tripping over my own feet, wetting the bed every night, profound insomnia and all the teasing that goes with it.

Two: My mother's brother rips my legs open and crams his grown-up body inside of me, and then makes it my fault by saying, "That's what you get, you little nigger bitch." He's angry because he feels he has lost his white sister to my Black father. I am lost in a seventeen-year spell of shame because I feel responsible for his rage.

Three: My fifth-grade teacher, Mr. Bianchi, teaches me to write haiku. His lesson plan becomes my salvation; my invitation to a world of words where I am more than anyone can see, even me. I know now that having a place to silently express the secrets eating me up inside kept me alive. I dropped out of high school at fifteen with everyone—including me—thinking I'd be dead before age twenty, because my silence was killing me.

❧

My life preserver for twenty-one years was writing poems into dark drawers, where their existence kept me alive, but people could never, ever read them. The poems spelled out my confusion, cauterized my tears and contained my fear. In them I felt alive; in the rest of my life I felt numb. They kept me from going crazy when my mother didn't come home at night, when my father died, when my sister told me that she'd been raped, too.

My parents were hippies, which meant I was the three-year-old passing joints so no one had to get up, five the first time

I rolled my own joint and eleven the first time I bought my own bag, instead of going into their stash. Smoking pot in our house was like brushing our teeth or turning on the light when you enter a room at night: No one questioned it. The urgency changed, without me realizing it, after my uncle raped me. It was as if I was turning the light switch on over and over to make sure no one was waiting for me in the dark and also the reason I needed my own bag: so my mom wouldn't realize how much more I was smoking, how afraid I was of my own shadow.

∽

I spent many nights lying awake, preparing for all contingencies of this new adventure called motherhood. I would lie awake, scared to death of failing, even though by the age of twenty-one I'd spent much of the time caring for other people's children and watching over my little sisters. Forty days after my twenty-second birthday, I was holding my newborn for the first time, being mystical about things I couldn't possibly understand. I transitioned from newlywed to new mom seamlessly enough (sort of). But I wasn't quite prepared for nursing a newborn while recovering from an episiotomy—all while my impacted wisdom teeth were also emerging. Nevertheless, one month into becoming a mother, I had to have all four wisdom teeth pulled. I had anesthesia for the actual procedure, but no painkillers afterward, because any medication I ingested might hurt the baby. I cried in constant agony for a month, but I made sure she didn't cry, and I was grateful every day for her perfection.

Poetry's real transformation in my life began with Janice Mirikitani and UC Berkeley Professor June Jordan. During their three years of spiritual and intellectual collaboration at

Glide Memorial Church, Jordan's Poetry for the People (P4P) ran six different six-week workshops. When the first workshop started, my daughters were my only reasons for living. I had a little over three years clean and sober, but no job or savings or ideas about how to make things better except to keep showing up. I went to twelve-step meetings six days a week and church on Sundays and I wrote poetry every single day.

Through Glide's P4P, I found an encouraging environment to manifest vivid, truth-telling poetry meant to be heard and to be published. Finally, my experiences as a woman of color surviving generational racism, incest, rape, addiction, silence and domestic violence mattered. As a direct result of Janice and June, Glide and P4P, I studied for and passed my GED, started my first semester at Mills College on academic probation and finished it on the Dean's List. Within six and a half years I went from being a John F. Kennedy High dropout to earning a master's degree in transformative arts from John F. Kennedy University.

∽

I decided my own redemption was wrapped up in advocating for my daughters in a way that no one had advocated for me. When I found out my fiancé was molesting my oldest daughter, I made sure she never had to see him again by actually sending him to jail. My youngest daughter was born the day I made three years clean and sober. She is the first girl child in five generations to never see her mama loaded; to grow up without a man's hands or tongue or penis inside her prepubescent body. I went back to school so I could give them more. I made sure they ended up at the best schools I could and met with the teachers to ensure their progress. We were all students at the same time, so we sat at the table and did homework together. I listened hard for what they said and what they didn't say. I talked to them about everything I'd been through so that they would see trouble coming. Most importantly, I believed they were capable of anything and encouraged them to follow their dreams. I helped with college and scholarship applications.

I watched my oldest graduate from Oberlin College and a teaching credential program with honors. She's in the Peace Corps now, teaching other teachers to be more effective. My youngest went to Oakland School for the Arts for seven years studying vocal technique, and spent a year and a half out on tour as a backup singer for Zendaya. Then she decided to start community college, where she was both Black Student Union president and associated student body president; now she's poised to start UCLA in the fall as a junior, debt free. I am grateful to know that I played a part in their many accomplishments.

Nurturing their growth and acknowledging my own evolution gave me the courage to engage my community in transformative work as well. Since entering recovery, I've worked as a caretaker for adults with autism and spent fifteen years nurturing writers of color as the workshop participant coordinator for Voices of Our Nations Arts Foundation (VONA); taken side jobs as an independent contractor teaching poetry as empowerment in K-12 schools, homeless shelters, juvenile detention facilities and recovery homes; and earned a living as an outreach consultant, a student services coordinator and an associate director of diversity (ADD). The one unifying action through all these roles, including being a mom, is advocacy for women and children of color. Ensuring my students graduate, teaching women in recovery to write the poems that bear witness to their lives and inspire them to take their own healing journeys, talking through a resume process that illuminates the right job; this is me cultivating a self-acceptance revolution.

∽

After my youngest daughter graduated from high school, I quit my job as an ADD at a university to write a book, a memoir told in poems, twenty years in the making—it's titled *Write This Second*. In this book, I share my journey from desecration to divinity with urgent, truth-telling poems to teach others that standing in our truth is also standing in our power. This book is my true legacy. Many times I wished I could have written it sooner, but I needed every moment of perspective I've gained to tell my story without getting lost in any one particular event or experience. As a survivor of racism, incest, rape, addiction, domestic violence, silence and PTSD, I was doing more than just surviving—I was learning to thrive.

I believe that by teaching people to speak up, we become living, breathing examples to one another that healing is possible. When I had less than sixty days clean and sober, I listened to a woman with twenty-three years of recovery share her story about choosing her best self, one second at a time. She told us all, "Five minutes or five days or five years from now, I can use if I want to, but right this second, I think I won't." Think about it: choosing to claim each moment as the moment to love ourselves enough to say no to our own self-destruction.

Write This Second is more than a book: It is a movement, a call to action, a place for all of us to learn to thrive.

∽

KIRA LYNNE ALLEN is an Oakland-based author, a four-time Voices of Our Nations Arts Foundation (VONA) Fellow, a Poetry for the People alumna, and a phenomenal workshop facilitator. Her literary debut, *Write This Second,* charts her journey from desecration to divinity; from addict and high school dropout to master's degree recipient, poet, performer, collage artist, activist, and community leader. Ms. Allen's story is meant to inspire readers to transform their lives by finding and proclaiming their authentic selves. She has a B.A. in creative writing from Mills College and an M.A. in transformative arts from John F. Kennedy University. Check out www.writethissec.com for more information.

The Black Sickness

Jordan Johnson

Ever since I was young, I've known I was different from my family and peers. I was raised in a Black household and taught that mental issues were issues that only white people with money had. It was a strong Christian home, where I was constantly told having faith in God would fix all of my problems. It didn't help that I had a hard time controlling my emotions. I cried at every movie I saw, I always felt bad for others and I was told I was too dramatic when describing my own feelings. In the end, the more I expressed these emotions, the more I was teased and criticized by those around me: "Only white people worry for animals like that," or "Stop crying for no reason, child."

Eventually, over time, I learned to control my emotions (or at least find a way to better hide them from my family). I learned early to become reserved and have a blank face. It was simply easier that way. It was better to keep it all to myself than to be told I wasn't Black enough or grateful enough.

In middle school, my control started to waver as I inevitably started to compare myself with others. I found myself competing with my peers in everything from grades to beauty. My first crush rejected me because I looked too "masculine and Black." My grades and inspiration suffered because I couldn't express any of my feelings out loud; I didn't want to be accused of not being in control.

In seventh grade, my relationship with my parents started to wane, which some would just chalk up to me being a teenager. Even though I was able to surround myself with friends, that was not enough to comfort me at the end of the day. They had their own lives and I always felt I was outside looking in. Every day, I felt lonelier and lonelier, until eventually I couldn't help but feel my alienation was my fault.

The cutting didn't start until eighth grade. Quite honestly, I don't remember why I started, but the feelings still pulsate in my brain every time I look at a razor.

My tools of the trade were scissors. They didn't leave obvious markings like the blades others use, but they still gave me the sensation I was seeking: the sensation of a cooling pain of ice against the skin with the brush of a warm breeze to lull me to sleep after a night of heavy crying.

I was a cutter from eighth grade to my senior year of high school. At first it was a session a month, something to hold me over whenever an issue blew up in my face. Most times the issues came from arguments with my parents. Arguments I couldn't win. I always walked away from those encounters feeling empty. It was a recurring feeling of watching from the outside, and whenever I watched, I always saw that same ominous shadow. The shadow would blame me for my feelings, for not being the perfect student or talented enough. For not being a perfect girlfriend or a perfect daughter.

By my senior year, I was cutting around three times a week for the first half of the school year. Anything would set me off. I was losing control. It would be something as small as getting a B in class, to arguments with anyone and everyone. I was no longer myself; I was addicted to self-punishment. My regret was that I was not strong enough to end it all. I believed I was no longer worthy of anything good and only deserved my pain.

But, even with the growing depression, I continued thinking I did this to myself; I was to blame for everything.

In time, with a lot of patience and the friendly ear of close friends, I was able to wean myself from self-harming. Though the urge to fulfill those desires has stayed with me to this very day, I have had experiences to distract myself in the past six years—going to college, working and trying to understand what I want to do. But even with all of my good fortune of getting an education and having loving and supportive family and friends, I couldn't shake the feeling that something was wrong. I quit self-harming, but every step I made in adulthood left me feeling like I was sinking lower into despair with no explanation why.

In 2015, I was faced with an unexpected move across the country. Away from friends, working a job I despised and alone because my parents' travel schedule took them away, I was truly as lonely as I had ever felt. I found myself at the same place I'd been many years ago: alone with thoughts and murmurs in the shadows taunting me. I would spend days just lying in bed, with only enough strength to eat sometime in the day and to make my way to work. But I rarely spoke to anyone; I was almost always in tears and nothing could alleviate the feeling. Not even when I found a new job or a group of people to befriend.

I don't know what pushed me to finally seek medical advice. For years I was told I had no need for it if I put faith in God. Maybe I was just angry at my feelings being pushed aside for all these years. Maybe I was tired of feeling empty. I always chalked up the way I felt to me just being overly emotional or even faking it for attention from anyone willing to give it. Maybe I just wanted to know if I was crazy or not. All I knew is that I needed validation.

In early 2016, I was diagnosed with depression and anxiety. I remember the day vividly even if I don't remember the exact date. I remember sitting across from the woman who would be my therapist for the rest of the year. I remember her asking me questions about how I felt when panic hit or what brought me into a darkened mood.

I remember her telling me that I wasn't crazy.

I left that first appointment with a feeling I hadn't felt in a long time. Relief. I felt free for the first time in years. I've had a true feeling of freedom since the day I told myself I would never press blades on my skin again. And while I was admittedly terrified about what this revelation would lead to, I knew it was a road I needed to take.

At that point I didn't care about the potential judgment from family or peers. I didn't mind the new struggles that would emerge, or worry about how to cope with them. I wasn't thinking about medication. All I cared about at that point was discovering my truth and developing a new drive to be better than I have ever been.

∽

JORDAN JOHNSON is a twenty-four-year-old graduate of Ball State University with a bachelor's degree in creative writing. Writing has been her passion since she learned to read. Now that she is out of college, she has time to focus on developing her writing and putting herself out in the world. Her essay explores her experience with self-harming and depression: how it started, her struggle to overcome and, in the end, her journey to learn more about her self worth.

Facing Fear, Finding Light

LISA A. JONES

It was a Friday and my son Nicholas was leaving kindergarten early for his doctor's appointment. He'd picked Michael Jackson's "Bad" to listen to while I drove, so now "MJ" was blaring from our Volvo's stereo: "You know I'm bad, I'm bad, come on, you know/And the whole world has to/Answer right now/Just to tell you once again/Who's bad?" Nicholas sang along, imitating Michael Jackson's falsetto. He was so upbeat, no one would likely guess that our thirty-minute trip was Nicholas's second visit to the Dana-Farber Cancer clinic that week.

When he was only eighteen months old, Nicholas suddenly became very sick. His life had hung in the balance when I brought him into the emergency room at the Queen of the Valley Medical Center in Napa Valley, California, during a family vacation. Days before, we had been seated on a sprawling lawn at a performance by Stevie Wonder in Santa Barbara. On this night, my husband and I were joining a couple from the West Coast for a five-course meal with wine pairings, while our children reunited with their four-year-old daughter for movies with a babysitter. It took many years and the death of a middle-aged friend whose tests confirmed her leukemia diagnosis after she was sent home from the doctor's office for me to realize and internalize that the intake nurse was not being hyperbolic when he told me in September 2007 that Nicholas could have died if we had not brought him directly to the emergency room that night.

Nicholas's spleen was enlarged and his white blood cell counts were off the charts at 750,000, compared with what would be a normal count of 5,000–10,000. He could have easily had a stroke. He could have died. While childhood leukemia has an 85 percent cure rate in many cases, Nicholas's diagnosis was deemed "high risk." Back then, in 2007, cancer was not only in his blood, but also in his spinal column, and he had needed many medical interventions to rid his body of it.

But thankfully that was a long time ago, and by the time of this visit, Nicholas had been in remission for more than four years and had been off cancer treatment for two whole years. He'd already survived the two years of treatment with cranial radiation and daily chemotherapy and multiple hospital stays and sadness and sickness and sheer parental terror that his diagnosis of T cell acute lymphoblastic leukemia had wrought. But that was all in the past.

In the Volvo, listening to Michael Jackson, we were returning to the clinic for a follow-up to his routine quarterly visit. Nicholas was now a happy, inquisitive kindergartner, and we had just experienced another one of our many family trips, this most recent one to San Francisco and Palo Alto, California. Life had resumed a normal cadence of school, work, friends/family and travel, and his cancer was in our rearview mirror.

But three days prior, his oncologist had reported to me that he did not like what he was seeing in the lab results of Nicholas's blood work. Just hearing the words set my heart racing; the panic of the unknown and the dread of death coursed through my being. Unfortunately, the worry and dread of hearing bad news in hospital rooms was all too familiar to me.

"This is *not* leukemia," our world-renowned oncologist had told me with great confidence. As I stared into his wide, icy-blue eyes, I believed him. His words were reassuring. As one of the leading children's leukemia oncologists, this doctor had followed hundreds of thousands of patients through research studies and his clinical work. For the past four years, I had entrusted this doctor with my son's remission, his treatment, his health and his life, and we had come so far.

The hope—the oncologist said—was that his slightly elevated white blood cell count was an indication of strep throat or mononucleosis or some other small nuisance of an illness. He had sent us home earlier that week with the instructions to return in three days for a repeat blood test, so Nicholas and I arrived at the clinic that Friday as planned.

After waiting for an hour for the results of his blood work that day, the nurse quietly brought me back to the office to tell me that these labs now showed that Nicholas had leukemia again. This was unbelievable. Not just because the diagnosis was the worst news ever, but also because I'd left from there just days ago thinking everything would be fine. I wanted to scream! I was screaming—inside myself I was screaming my head off. Could anyone hear me? I had to go back to my son, and when I rushed back into the waiting room of the clinic, I found Nicholas crying.

I had been away too long.

He was with a nurse, but he had been waiting too long without his mom, his mom who had sung him to sleep as a baby, read him book after favorite book and who had held his hand through two years of hospital stays and visits. Without me, he had become scared. I came to him, but I had been motioned to bring him back to the nurses' station. He needed an IV.

At that point, all hell broke loose. Instead of expressing my rage and my sadness, I had no choice but to bring Nicholas into the "infusion area" and hold him on my lap, my legs curled around his legs to force them down like a wrestler as he resisted mightily, each time, yet another assault on his little body, as he shook, pushed, his body wracked by pain; it took multiple nurses to insert his IV so that Nicholas could be admitted.

A leukemia relapse meant he had to stay overnight and get chemotherapy immediately, no waiting around. The plan was for him to be hospitalized for several weeks. Nicholas became a fearful, squirming, fitful child all over again, sitting on my lap, unwilling to get up, holding onto me the way he did those years ago. I wanted to be the anchor of solace, comfort and reason, yet instead I was a frantic wreck. There was a commotion of nurses creating admittance paperwork for me to sign and deciding the bed to which my frustrated and crying child would be assigned. I helplessly tried to reach Ken, my husband, Nicholas's dad. I called his cellphone twice. I could not reach him. As usual, he was working hard and unfortunately unable to be located, so the timing caused the burden of this horrific moment to fall squarely on my shoulders to confront and to navigate. Emotionally, I held my son and myself together as the bottom dropped out from under us.

The nurses then transferred the outwardly healthy Nicholas onto a bed and wheeled him toward ward 6 North while I followed beside him holding onto the gurney. The rest was a blur. By the time Nicholas settled into his room, Ken had called back and I told him the terrible news. When Ken arrived at the hospital distraught, I recounted to him more details about what would come next.

This time, Nicholas would also need a bone marrow transplant in order to get rid of the cancer forever. Unfortunately, the protocol that he had endured as a toddler for two years and one month did not work. This time around the hospital needed to identify a bone marrow donor for him, but that was not even the first priority. They first needed us to focus on the coming four weeks of medicine and procedures to get him into remission.

Our friends, family and acquaintances near and far soon heard the awful news. Love and deep concern for our innocent child and for our family pulled them toward us. *How can we help?*, they all wanted to know.

By fully opening up to them about the pain and the worry, we were held in an embrace and had a new dance of care and sharing with a large and growing community of support. Adults and children flew in from near and far to be there for us and with us. They listened, they visited, they bore witness and they sympathized. Nicholas's young friends cuddled in his hospital bed and played games to distract him from the world of medicine and needles and his missing out on childhood playgrounds and school. While we lived in agony, whenever we could, we tried to find joy in the spaces of time that appeared void of obvious stress. Our friends and family helped beyond measure, and their positive energy and effort filled us with hope and joy.

By December 2, 2011, the results of Nicholas's spinal tap showed that he was in remission. This meant that his leukemia was undetectable by modern science. Upon hearing this great news, we were immediately sent into a room to meet with a new specialist to prepare us for the bone marrow transplant, thus marking a positive plateau and the next step in our son's treatment. Once and for all, his blood production system would be replaced by someone else's, and he would be cured.

Unfortunately, the news from the specialist was not that

simple. She didn't blink an eye and told us the damning fact that was most shocking: Bone marrow transplants have the HIGHEST RATE OF INFANT MORTALITY. My notes in capital letters began to reflect my fear. They have the LONGEST HOSPITAL STAY FOR CHILDREN. Your child WILL NOT BE NORMAL FOR A YEAR. A PARENT will need to be WITH THE PATIENT in the hospital 24/7. Nicholas will not be able to eat due to mouth and throat sores and will therefore need to be fed intravenously, yet will vomit three to thirty times a day.

She told us that we would not have to concern ourselves with the exorbitant cost of the bone marrow transplant, because it is a "rare, rare experience" and insurance companies know we are too terrified to fully understand: This is the last chance to save a life. The specialist uncaringly went on to explain how excruciating the process would be while Ken and I doubled over in psychic pain. Nicholas would need to have whole-body radiation and high doses of chemotherapy in order to empty him of his own marrow and blood cells, which would leave his body weak and vulnerable. He would then need to be in an isolation room in the hospital for six weeks.

"How would this compare with his prior two years of treatment?" I asked, wishing for any silver lining.

"That will feel like a walk in the park," the specialist said matter-of-factly. Internally, I was wailing, my insides were being torn apart. If we consented to the bone marrow transplant, they would next look for a donor. We signed on the dotted line. We were signing Nicholas up for a highly uncertain outcome and a surely harsh treatment ahead. But we had no choice. No matter the predicted survival rate, we were in.

Two weeks later, we learned a new fact. The doctor called to say that "a match just popped up. A real donor. And the date for Nicholas's transplant will be January 20, 2012." The "real donor," we later learned, was a thirty-nine-year-old African American man. There is only one person in the database of sixteen million who matches my son at all. This person is further tested and he turns out to be a perfect 10-out-of-10 match.

We were finally certain that the bone marrow transplant was going to happen, and hope that it will save Nicholas's life. This prayer has been answered, but we know that we will need more prayers, continued optimism and a positive outlook to bring our family across this mighty threshold. One day we will even meet this donor, and this stranger will become part of our extended family.

∾

LISA A. JONES is a former network news producer and award-winning television documentarian who is writing a memoir about her decade-long journey successfully tackling her young son's life-threatening illness, including his bone marrow transplant. Her forthcoming book poignantly tells her family's unique story and draws on her personal journals and her years as a storyteller and a producer for *FRONTLINE* and ABC News. Jones is also a graduate of Yale and Harvard's Kennedy School.

After her family's journey through cancer, Jones served in the Obama Administration as the assistant administrator for communications for the Federal Aviation Administration from 2016 to 2017. She lives with her husband, daughter and son in the Boston area.

A Woman's Journey
Is Never Done

Traveling Far, Wide, and Deep

African in America

UGOCHI EGONU

This is for the girl who asked me if I speak African.
As if every country and tribe speaks the same language
As if a whole continent shared the same history and traditions
As if we don't each deserve our own cultures.
This is for the girl who tells me she wants to go on a service trip
to help the Africans.
She does not know whom she wants to help, or in what country
But she seems to think that showing up with her whiteness will cure
all diseases in Africa
and fill every empty belly.
This is for the posters starring hungry African children
perpetuating the mindset that perpetuates the ads that make Americans think
starving children are the only children Africa has to offer.
No, we do not all need to be held in the arms of an angel.
I will hold myself.

This is for the people who say
"You've never even been to Nigeria, why do you care so much?"
Igbo is not my mother tongue but it is

my mother's tongue
so when I tell her, Ezinne
a hụrụ m gị n'anya I say it
with pride.
This is for all the silent moments spent with my grandmother
moments I wished
I could continue our conversation past *ibola chi* grandma,
kedụ ka ịmere? But I know no other words
in her tongue. I wish I could do more than greet her
wish Igbo would roll off my tongue like
ignorance rolls off of yours
when you ask me if my family had to hunt for our dinner
with spears.

This is for the people who say they don't understand
my mother even when she is speaking clear English.
Know that she is not slowing down
so that you can comprehend her.
Know that she is slowing down so that you can enjoy
the melodious tune of her accent.
Know that she is slowing down
so that you have time to hear
Nigeria in her voice.

This is for the grown men who call me
ewu America when I dare to speak up.
And to the middle school boys who yelled
"ay yo Kunta Kinte!" when I tried to ignore them.
This was a message from a girl
who is tired of your ignorance
stereotypes and impatience.
A girl who has never left California

but knows the Nigerian national anthem
by heart.

Part Two
We have all done this before,
Looked in the mirror and wondered where the woman went,
Wondered how a society can reduce the diamond that you
were to the pebble that you have become.
But this time will be different.
This time you will not be defined by your body,
Not by the parts you were born with or what has been done
to them.
This time you will not be the delicate doll that they expect
you to be,
You will inhale fury,
And exhale power.
This time you might cry,
Not because women are overly sensitive or fragile,
But because you are human and that is what humans do.
This time you will bask in your own glory and the glory of
your sisters around you,
Because you know that they too have become pebbles,
They too have become victims of a culture that treats them
like objects.
This time you will be a woman,
This time you will be a revolution,
This time your story will be told,
And this time,
Yes this time,
You will be the one to tell it.

UGOCHI EGONU is a poet and playwright from Santa Clara, California. Egonu was a finalist in the 2015 Bay Area Teen Poetry Slam and leads spoken word workshops for young women. Her poetry has been featured in BBC's *Africa's Out* radio program and Creative Communication's quarterly student anthology.

What's Left in La Quebrada

Yessenia Funes

My mother grew up in central El Salvador. It's a Latin American country no bigger than New Jersey with a spectrum of nature's personas dotting its landscape. Brilliant rainforests. Bubbling hot springs. Basaltic mountain fields.

My mom's village is just a forty-five-minute drive away from the country's second highest volcano: San Vicente or *Chichontepec*, which translates to "the mountain of two breasts" in the Nahuatl indigenous language. My mother lived a poor life there, hustling to sell *pupusas* on the bus. She left behind an education to help my *abuelita* get by. In other ways, however, her life was rich.

She grew up surrounded by shrubs, vines and all types of flora. In the middle of the brush flowed *la quebrada*, or the ravine. My mother had to cross *la quebrada* to get to certain parts of her *pueblito*. It was nothing special, but it was special to my mom.

There, she, along with my grandma and my four aunts and uncle, would wash their clothes, bathe and play. My mom recounts stories of when fish swam between the rocks, scurrying to their unknown destinations, perhaps to spawn their little ones.

"Now, you don't see that happening anymore," she's told me. "That was way back then."

333

I've been only twice to El Salvador, and the last time was around ten years ago when I was fourteen. I had to cross that ravine to reach my *abuelita's* little house. I would jump on *la quebrada's* rocks to arrive to the other side and head to the convenience store, which sat on the main road about a five-minute walk away. Hopping my way to my grandmother's house, it became evident that my mother was right.

I saw no fish swimming through the rocks. No families washing their clothes in the water. The *quebrada* did feel wild, but I grew up in the urban suburbs of Long Island, so I had nothing to compare it to. Well, except goopy beach coasts full of volleyballs and sandcastles. Those felt artificial. Man-made.

La quebrada grossed me out, really. Garbage was piled along its shores. It looked like the neighborhood dump. In the throw-away age of cheap disposables and wrappers, trash has to go somewhere. It was odd, though, that El Salvador's somewhere was everywhere.

And garbage wasn't the only waste floating through the ravine.

You see, when I first visited my grandmother's home, my family still used outhouses. They had only a couple of cement cylinders to piss in. I was horrified to realize flying cockroaches hid within their crevices. I was relieved to see toilets had been installed the second time I visited. These toilets weren't like the ones at home, though. At home, I had no clue where my business went. With a flush, it was all gone. In El Salvador, a flush sent my waste on a journey I could follow. The pipe's twists and turns ended above *la quebrada*. My sister and I sometimes raced to the edge of the ravine, which sat right outside the outhouses, to catch sight of the foul trip.

We were kids; we had a crude sense of humor. Now? We

wouldn't find that funny at all. What we failed to realize then was how my grandmother's home—the same one my mother grew up in—is a part of a greater issue in the developing world.

El Salvador, like many developing countries, suffers from poor waste management. Cities in developing countries may spend 20 to 50 percent of their budgets on solid waste management but have 30 to 60 percent of solid waste go uncollected—all while serving less than half their cities' populations. As the World Bank notes, open dumping with open burning is still the norm in most developing countries.

These practices translate into environmental hazards. Dirty stenches attract cockroaches, flies and mosquitoes. Mosquitoes are a particular concern for expectant Latin American mothers. Research has linked the blood-sucking pests to the Zika virus outbreak, which has disrupted countless pregnancies, leaving newborns with brain abnormalities.

And waste isn't the only culprit. Climate change is leaving entire ecosystems vulnerable, too. Scientists have speculated that such dramatic warming of environments allowed mosquitoes to flourish. Temperatures will only increase for the global south—Latin America, Africa, Asia. Climate change will hit them the hardest.

The irony is that the Global South didn't contribute much to climate change. The industrial boom of the United States did. We'll likely see the least of it.

But countries like El Salvador? They're going to see increased drought and more severe weather. The country doesn't have proper infrastructure in place to respond appropriately. Even on the federal level. On the individual level, families are too preoccupied with putting food on the table to busy themselves with climate change or environmental pollution.

They barely have time to explore the nature that surrounds their immediate vicinity. Take my family, for example. My *abuelita* and *tias* rarely explore outside their *pueblito* and nearby cities. Even if they wanted to venture into the jungle, those trips require transportation. They require money.

The last time I visited, my family, motivated by my mom's travel budget, was determined to take my siblings and me to these far-off destinations. The trip I remember most led us up a winding mountain road. The drive was steep. Sitting in the back of the pickup, the sun on my shoulders, I looked at where we had started, feeling slightly paranoid about our increasing altitude. As we drove closer to the clouds, the wind bit my face, a surprise in a tropical country.

But we were heading to *La Puerta del Diablo,* or the Devil's Door. You can't expect warmth from a place with that name.

The peak was a striking sight: lush canopies lining the center of two boulders. I felt a sense of disbelief. How could a place be so green? How could rocks form so perfectly?

Now, I ask myself different questions. How long until deforestation turns the green to gray? How long until environmental degradation replaces streams with trash? Better yet, how will *Salvadoreños* fare once climate change scorches their country—my country—to ashes?

Life in paradise isn't all palm trees and coconuts. It's not all treks through the tropics or strolls near the stream. It's hardship. It's strife. It's beauty and it's pain.

In the Land of Volcanoes, an ember glows—within the depths of its mountains and its people's souls. Whether it roars and grows or dims and dies? Only the citizens of the earth can decide.

～

YESSENIA FUNES is a Latina journalist based in New York. She's currently the climate justice reporter at Colorlines, but she covers immigration, race and environmental policy. Growing up in a troubled Long Island suburb, far from the stereotypical Hamptons image, Yessenia reports from a place of experience and understanding. Her parents are Salvadoran immigrants who fled to the United States during the brutal Salvadoran Civil War of the '80s, shaping her lens on international issues.

From the Middle Room to the Mountains: The Artist Within

Nashormeh Lindo

I've perpetually sought out art ever since I was a very small child; when I couldn't find what I was looking for, I had to create it myself. My cousin Ronnie was my first art teacher. He taught me to draw faces. One of my earliest memories of getting in trouble with my parents was because of drawing. I'd added a new, decorative element to my home in Philadelphia: a nightscape of hand-drawn stars on my mama's newly papered living room wall and lampshades.

Even then, I was influenced by and drawn to depictions of the natural landscape; however, this early work was not well-received. Luckily, my parents were encouraging and redirected my creative efforts to what we called "The Little Room," a small room whose ancient, crumbling wallpaper became my new canvas. I was allowed to draw on its walls, and I remember hours spent composing colorful tableaus and murals in crayons and paint. My father worked as an industrial papermaker, and he would bring home stacks of recycled "paperboard," which I would also fill with color and manipulate into collages.

I eventually graduated from "The Little Room" to an actual studio at Penn State University, where my enthusiasm to study art led me to ask, "Where are the Black artists?" None of my professors seemed to have an answer.

I knew—or sensed—that there was a burgeoning Black Arts Movement, but my enthusiasm was somewhat frustrated; I would have to find my own path toward those artists and thinkers. Pattee Library at Penn State became a significant source of guidance; it became my refuge and my gold mine, where I began to introduce myself to minds and talents missing from the standard arts curriculum offered at PSU. Artists such as Romare Bearden, Hale Woodruff, Elizabeth Catlett, Norma Morgan and Henry O. Tanner came into my consciousness, inspired me and informed my work.

Several years after I graduated, Richard Mayhew organized a conference and concurrent exhibition of Black artists called *Since the Harlem Renaissance*. This was exactly what I had been looking for. I traveled to State College with just enough money for a one-way fare, figuring that I'd find a way to get back to Philly later.

The figures that I had previously only read about at the library were suddenly standing in front of me, and I could meet and speak with them. It was as if they'd come to life from the pages of the books to stand as a testament to my longing.

This personal connection with a community of artists might be seen as the beginning of my lifelong work in the arts outside of my studio practice. I am fed spiritually, intellectually and creatively by the wonderful artists and thinkers with whom I interact professionally and personally, whether in positions such as my current capacity as a member of the California Arts Council or simply as an educator, longtime friend, peer or protégé. In turn, I'm proud to know I have provided them some sustenance—whether by teaching, networking, making introductions and facilitating relationships, or by feeding them more literally: Sometimes, artists just need a good glass of wine, a meal and a sympathetic ear.

Besides the library, the other aspect of Penn State that fed me creatively was the curriculum's strong emphasis on landscape: looking closely at the environment and using the natural world as subject matter. My most influential painting and drawing teachers, George Zoretich and Stuart Frost, said things like, "Can you draw a hand? No? All right, fine—go get an anatomy book and learn to draw a hand. But first, go outside and draw five trees and their corresponding leaves..."

They both insisted on spending hours outside, scrutinizing the landscape. This was perfect for me. I relished *plein air* painting, but eventually found it useful to take photographs as a reference to work from, as the natural light was prone to dramatic changes. As a result, in a sort of classical twist, painting actually taught me to compose photographs.

At the Baltimore Museum of Art I was surrounded by a treasure trove of masterworks by artists such as Matisse, Gauguin, Cézanne, Kensett, Stella, Rauschenberg and other European artists—but also a collection of African, Native American and pre-Columbian art. The museum specialized in modern art, which meant sculpture and photography were just as emphasized as painting, so I began to see photography as an art form as well as a device for documentation. The works of James Van Der Zee, Aaron Siskind, Gordon Parks, Cindy Sherman, Roland Freeman, Cary Beth Cryor and others all expanded my consciousness and knowledge of photography as an art.

And it was while at the museum when I began to travel more widely for the sake of art, making my first trip to Africa, where I painted every chance I got and began to seriously take photographs.

The world of human activity is unpredictable and can make a person feel crazy; in creating artworks that depict the landscape, I try to catalyze a moment of reflection. I am able to breathe, relax and encounter an overwhelming visual beauty while creating these works, and I hope that the same meditative breath is transferred to the viewer. At the same time, there is a subtly political dimension to depicting the landscape: I hope that thoughts of naturalism, the environment and conservation are not far from the viewers' minds as they consider the extraordinary wellspring of inspiration that surrounds us both at home and the world over.

∽

NASHORMEH LINDO, artist/educator, is a native of Philadelphia, Pennsylvania. She earned an M.S. in education from the Bank Street College Graduate School of Education, and a B.A. in art from Pennsylvania State University. Ms. Lindo's work in the arts is multidimensional. She works as a practicing visual artist/designer and as an educator/curator. Her professional background includes teaching, program planning, curriculum development and educational training at such institutions as the Schomburg Center for Research in Black Culture, the Pennsylvania Academy of the Fine Arts, the Baltimore Museum of Art, the Fine Arts Museums of San Francisco, the San Francisco Museum of Modern Art and the Oakland Museum of California. Lindo was appointed to the California Arts Council by Governor Jerry Brown. She serves as vice chair of the Council. She lives and works in the Bay Area and New Jersey.

When Life Is
a Crystal Stair

RITA ROBERTS-TURNER

Neither of my grandmothers graduated from high school. They were certainly smart enough, but life's necessities made formal education a luxury secondary to work. Faced with the daily Southern indignities of being referred to as gals, girls, niggers and negras, they didn't just struggle to be seen as women; they struggled to be seen as human. It would be decades before they could walk through certain front doors, be served with dignity in restaurants, drink from any public water fountain or even consider life beyond the confines of a "Black neighborhood."

Their sons, husbands, brothers and fathers could be stripped away and lynched under the cover of darkness with no recourse from the Department of Justice or the FBI. Life for my grandmothers was in many ways the rough side of the mountain. By comparison, my life has been a crystal stair.

In elementary school, I was the lone Black girl among our group of friends. I was good enough for birthday cake and ice cream at a classmate's house, but not quite good enough to join the weekend sleepover. "Sorry, there's not enough room," my friend said.

My college years weren't much better. At the predominantly white university I attended, a professor once boldly asked me how I was going to end starvation and excessive birth rates in Africa. "When you solve all of white America's problems, I'll tackle the problems of an entire continent that I've never visited," I retorted.

There was the rescinded invitation to a country club pool party; there was being bypassed by a restaurant hostess while waiting in line with a white college boyfriend. And there was my suffering an unusually embarrassing chastisement from a federal judge during a trial at which he refused to even acknowledge my objections to evidence for the record.

"Do you think the judge has a problem with women or Black female attorneys?" I asked a mentor.

My mentor responded, "Probably both."

I could describe the pain I felt as I fought tearful anger in trying to explain to my beautiful and intelligent young Black sons the judicial decisions around the murders of Trayvon Martin and Michael Brown. I don't define my life by those moments that reflect someone else's insanity or insecurities. I define it by how far I rise above it.

Pushed by my grandmothers' hopes and dreams, I rose above the stereotypes and obstacles created by a culture still grappling with its history and treatment of African Americans. I excelled in school, received a scholarship to college and graduated with honors. As is the irony of life, the white grandmother who had instructed her granddaughter to politely disinvite me to her sleepover as a child saw me years later and pleaded with me to come to their house and convince my friend to stay in college.

I became a successful litigator, winning multiple cases, including one before the same judge who had dismissed my very existence.

A few years ago, I was the speaker at a very exclusive club in Nashville, Tennessee—the kind that fifty years earlier my ancestors would have only been allowed to enter through the back door to make deliveries or perform kitchen duty. Everyone was welcoming and engaged in entertaining conversation. As I surveyed the room, I noticed I was one of only three brown faces. After the event, I drove home wondering what my grandmother, "Granny," must be thinking in heaven. I was tickled by the thought that she might be sitting up there with Jesus, head thrown back with laughter, proudly telling all the angels, "That's my granddaughter."

Just a few days later, I was a lunch guest at an even more exclusive women's organization. About a dozen of us ate in a private room, separated from the general guests. This time there were no other brown faces except the server's. I thought she was trying to mask her surprise at seeing me when she entered the dining room. Her smile was genuine as she asked, "Would you like more tea?" I smiled back.

This time, when I left, I sat in my car holding back tears. Could Granny have imagined? *Yes, she could*, the Lord whispered.

Recently, I was reflecting on my life from childhood to the present and became overwhelmed with emotion, knowing that God and some very godly women must have seen something in me the moment I was born. My grandmothers in particular saw much more than a little Black girl descended from slaves, sharecroppers and domestics. They saw the birth of a new generation of African American womanhood. They saw a generation filled with endless possibilities.

When life for you has been a crystal stair, you don't tap-dance your way farther to the top. Instead, you work to help others build their own staircase of dreams. And as you stand regally looking at how far you've come and at even greater things ahead, clasp hands with others and give them an opportunity to climb a few rungs of the staircase with you.

At a time when popular culture has once again misrepresented, maligned and marginalized African American females as violent, promiscuous and irresponsible subjects pitted against equally violent, promiscuous and irresponsible African American males, I have a good and gainfully employed husband.

My family is thriving. Our sons are honor roll students who believe and know that they can be president of the United States one day. We have good health and are privileged to have access to good health care. God blessed us with our dream home, and I have had a career that I could not have planned or imagined. Yes, life for me has been a crystal stair.

∽

RITA ROBERTS-TURNER is a former trial lawyer and served as the first African American female chief of staff for the Nashville and Davidson County Mayor's Office. She currently serves in executive leadership in the public transit industry and recently published her first novel, *God's Daughters and Their Almost Happily Ever Afters.*

In a World Obsessed with Passport Tiers

ROBTEL NEAJAI PAILEY

The miniature red suitcase I had packed lay abandoned on my wooden floor. I caressed my dark green Liberian passport as if to reassure this inanimate marker of identity that my citizenship was not on trial here.

The specter of Ebola had simply triumphed over reason. Like other countries across the globe, the United Arab Emirates halted travel for those with Guinean, Liberian and Sierra Leonean passports during the height of the Ebola outbreak in West Africa. It had not lifted these restrictions when, in June 2015, I was informed that I would not be able to travel to Dubai for an important meeting scheduled months earlier.

This was punishment for simply being born in Africa with a particular African passport. Even the organizers of the meeting were shocked, disbelief sprinkled in their conciliatory emails and phone calls. All diplomatic channels had proved futile. The verdict was irreversible. I would not be getting on that plush Emirates flight.

Never mind that Liberia had been declared Ebola-free for the first time on May 9, 2015, exactly one month before my scheduled UAE trip. Never mind that I had not been to my homeland ten months prior. I was not even asked about recent travel there.

Never mind that my country and its people were slowly

trying to recover from an invisible foe that killed nearly 5,000 and infected about 11,000.

☙

During Ebola, I'd seen my passport scrutinized more intently than ever before, but the UAE blanket bias felt like adding salt to a fresh wound.

At first, I experienced blinding rage with a touch of indignation, the kind that gurgles in the pit of your gut, and then explodes.

Then I was amused by the absurdity of it all. If I were traveling directly from Guinea, Liberia or Sierra Leone and had a passport from a country on UAE's list of exemptions, I would have gotten a visa on arrival with ease. No questions asked.

Mild acceptance slowly seeped in, reminding me that we maintain immigration hierarchies as a form of erasure and silencing. In our obsession with citizenship tiers, West is best. North trumps South. And white is inevitably right.

☙

I had shied away from returning home, fearing the kind of immobility that arises from seeing people not as complex beings but as nameless, faceless "threats" to national security. A sedentarist kind of metaphysic that keeps certain people in their place. People like me.

For all the rhetoric about globalization's free flow of ideas, capital and technology, the world remains obsessed with restricting the movement of people who don't fit into neat boxes of what is tolerable or even desirable. The UAE saga was a microcosm of a larger debate about the need for immigration reforms worldwide.

The scapegoating of migrants across the globe deflects attention from the fact that most countries have failed to improve the quality of life of their domestic citizens. Afrophobic attacks in South Africa, Australia's Pacific Solution and the plight of Rohingya Muslims off the coast of Indonesia are extreme examples.

Immigration is framed as a zero-sum game, with finite rights and resources available to a select few. I watch migrants who look like me risk their lives on sardine-packed, rickety boats to cross the Mediterranean, and I know intuitively that they wouldn't flee if they had a choice. With each desperate attempt to cross over, what they are effectively saying is that Europe must make amends for waging unjustifiable wars and supporting authoritarian regimes in some of their countries of origin.

∽

Centuries ago, Africans were so desperate to escape lives of bondage, some dove to sudden death in the Atlantic. They were the first forced migrants I can recall. Now, many of us travel across these same waters—not because of some deep, abiding love for life abroad, but because it gives us a measure of flexibility and keeps us physically connected to the rest of the world. And for someone like me, with chronic wanderlust, the ability to travel unencumbered is almost as necessary as oxygen itself. I used to be suspicious of Liberians who changed their nationality out of convenience. But after interviewing more than two hundred of us across five urban centers in West Africa, North America and Europe for my doctoral thesis on citizenship construction and practice, I have become more empathetic. Many of us make the switch because of the access so easily denied me by the UAE.

But we shouldn't have to.

∽

ROBTEL NEAJAI PAILEY is a Liberian academic, activist and author with fifteen years of combined professional experience in Africa, Europe and North America. Her scholarly research and popular writing have been published in academic journals, edited book volumes, newspapers and magazines. Robtel is the author of *Gbagba*, an anti-corruption children's book published in 2013 to critical acclaim and subsequently placed on the list of supplemental readers for third- to fifth-graders in Liberia and for Primary 3 in Ghana. A sequel of the book is forthcoming in 2018.

Small Places

Roshila Nair

1

I was small—seven or eight—when I entered a small place, a whites-only toilet on the Durban beachfront. There, in a strange way, I became instantly smaller.

2

"Coolie! Out!"

3

Addressed as a beast to which neither age nor need for care applied, it was in that jail-sized space where I first heard that so different was I that any sense of normality I had about myself withered on the spot.

The bullet left the plump white woman's mouth and the world shrank into a foul-smelling toilet.

4

Or: The bullet left the plump white woman's mouth and my world ebbed away, leaving me stranded in a shit-hole so lonely, it drained me. Looking down, I saw my small feet in a pool of stench on the white tiles. I had peed myself in the small toilet on the whites-only beach.

5

I was a dreamy child living in a two-bedroom house with four siblings and given to bouts of brooding on the wardrobe top in my parents' bedroom. In my small place up there, behind the jumble of my mother's sari boxes, my nose in a book and close to the ceiling, I glimpsed on occasion the void, that sensation of separateness and separation that is an intrinsic part of human existence.

The void is a sense of the vastness of space and time, of life, one is born into. It arrived with the child's intuition that at some point in the future it would require a meaning to be made solely by me. There was, too, an inkling that this immensity is shaped by borders that stretch inside or outside one's self, or both ways, or no ways at all even. The mystery I would roam in one day, nevertheless, felt at a safe enough distance so that after a while I could climb down the wardrobe and join again with the others.

6

But in that small toilet I came abruptly face to face with your shriek that I was disagreeably different, not at all who I had known myself to be—a little girl with a family and friends. Your certainty evoked my terror, your disgust at my body shattered the aura of belonging I carried on my back, the carapace of love I had begun growing to compensate for the womb left at the moment of birth. Your white face flung me into the void where I stood paralyzed for eons staring into its eye that stared unflinchingly back at me.

7

There it was, the Black child's task of finding the way back from hell after the first death, a journey that comes with no map but which *must* be made.

And not back to the small places, the ghettoes and killing spaces of Blackness made by the white hand, nor to the white world, adorned with its illusion of grandeur. And never back to the small trap in the mind that under the death gaze folds away your little body, life itself, like a touch-me-not.

But hear the echoes ringing in the void, of prophets and poets who travelled through and emerged from the darkness singing—Du Bois, Viktor Frankl, Audre Lorde, Jamaica Kincaid, Fanon, Biko, Khayyam…!

8

I sit in my first class at the white university, for knowledge. It is in Durban, ten years later in February 1987, my first time in their world since that day on the beach. The classroom threatens to swallow me whole into the solid eternity that is their world. If I do not speak, lob a word at the poem they're celebrating, the vastness I have been attempting to reach in me from the centre of the void will vanish forever. And forever is too much of a long time.

I unclasp my jaw, move tongue muscle against teeth bone; a voice emerges, too loud even for my ear. And which poet was it that day—Chaucer, Shakespeare, Marais—who bore with precious grace the spear of my "NO!"?

The lecturer squints from the blueness of his eyes; he has seen me. Finally, I am taking a step out of the toilet at the end of the world.

9

Botha wags his finger from the television, warning he has crossed the Rubicon. But it is too late; you have joined your first protest march on the streets. You lunge, surge forward with the throng that is seeking life—*toyi-toyi!*

10

Making love for the first time, you reach the body inside the body that throbs with life. Giving, receiving joy, you learn when nobody robs you the body does move the earth!

11

Truth, justice, peace alight at your doorstep; from deep within your own immensity—life—poetry and paradox arrive. Love embraces you.

> The Moving Finger writes; and, having writ,
> Moves on: nor all thy Piety nor Wit,
> Shall lure it back to cancel half a Line,
> Nor all thy Tears wash out a Word of it.
>
> ...
>
> I sent my Soul through the Invisible,
> Some letter of that After-life to spell:
> And by and by my Soul return'd to me,
> And answer'd: "I Myself am Heav'n and Hell."

12

And now I make my body with ink. The ink seeks and finds its hold on the paper, the paper that is my skin. The ink escapes the small places; the page, a wide sea with new sightings of my body, floats me out the void. Written by my own handwriting, I step clear into the sunlight.

13

These days I still look for you in crowds. You will be withered
by time now or perhaps swollen beyond memory. Perhaps
you still wear your hair in a golden permanent. Perhaps you
still wear the same orange on the lips you aimed at me that for
years after riveted my eyes to the faces of white women sport-
ing that shade. I look for you in the sunlight, hoping you too
have opened the door to the vastness in you, that you too have
stepped out and left behind forever the toilet at the end of the
world, for nobody should live in that small a place.

$\sim$

ROSHILA NAIR was born and grew up in KwaZulu-Natal,
South Africa. She is a descendent of Hindu Indian indentured
laborers on the Natal sugar plantations and Malay slaves in the
Cape, also Khoikhoi, San and Irish. She self-identifies as Black,
as accorded by Black Consciousness anti-apartheid struggle politics. Ms. Nair is a feminist and social activist. After
twenty-one years working as a professional editor and public
educationist in civil society, she has taken up studying for a
master's degree in creative writing at the University of Cape
Town's Centre for Creative Writing.

This is an abridged version of a longer essay by the author
that is forthcoming.

The Road to El Camino

Denise Diaab

When my marriage ended after twenty-three years, I took Dr. Laura's advice seriously: I planned to wait two years, not just her recommended one year, before getting back in the pool again. I spent time rediscovering Denise. I bought season tickets to the Geffen Playhouse. I hiked with the Sierra Club and climbed Half Dome in Yosemite. I took morning walks at the beach and bike rides along the riverbed. I even finally enrolled in a creative writing class. My life was good. I do have to admit, though: By the end of my seventh year in the singles lane, my heart yearned to meet someone special. That spring I met Karl. He'd driven down from Berkeley for the birthday celebration of a mutual friend. Karl was a welcome rain after the drought.

By summer we had abandoned our initial shyness, the cautious testing of the water with one toe. I was sixty-five and Karl was seventy; we both agreed we didn't have a lot of time to waste. We jumped in with boldness; we embraced the hope of new beginnings with openness and vulnerability. He called me "My Honey," and it touched a place in my heart that plain "Honey" never could. I called him "MDD," short for "My Dearest Darling." I wrote a poem and mailed letters on perfumed stationery to Karl in Berkeley. He, more comfortable with music than words, put together a playlist for me—songs that spoke for him: "The Closer I Get to You," by Luther

Vandross; "Share My Life," by Kem; "Ready to Love Again,"
by Lady Antebellum; and so many more (he had to burn three
CDs to fit them all).

My cellphone rang one afternoon as I was having lunch with
my friend, Helen.

"That had to be Karl," she said as I laid the phone on the table.

"Why do you say that?"

"Because you're all lit up like a Christmas tree," she laughed.

I had to laugh myself.

I enjoyed the surprise "Thinking of you" texts and calls
during the day. The evening calls helped make the distance
between L.A. and Berkeley bearable—long talks where we
continued to discover each other and build our relationship.
One evening toward the end of summer we talked about our
travels. Karl's photo safari in Tanzania was his favorite trip.
I couldn't decide between horseback riding in the surf in
Jamaica or climbing to the bell tower of the famed *Hunchback
of Notre-Dame* in Paris.

"Where would you like to go for your next vacation?" he
asked casually.

"Greece." I responded without missing a beat. "It's at the top
of my list." I drifted off thinking about the Greek hiking tour I
had been planning for almost a decade.

"...go there with you," caught my attention.

"I'm sorry, my mind must have wandered and I didn't hear
you."

There was an audible sigh before he spoke. "I said, 'Greece
wasn't on my radar, but, it would be cool to go there with you.'"

"Really!"

"Yeah, really. Would you like...to take a vacation...together?"

"Really? Well, uh yes, I'd like to do a vacation with you...it's just…I was planning a hiking trip in Greece. I know you have problems with your knees and back and wouldn't be able to hike."

"There must be other things to do in Greece besides hiking," he said.

"Oh, heavens, yes. There's plenty to do and lots to see, not to mention Greek food."

"So…is that a yes?"

"Yes. That's a yes…I'd like that. I'd like that a lot."

Fall found us planning our Greek vacation for October of the following year. On one of my visits to Berkeley, I showed Karl a picture of the Samaria Gorge I'd found in a travel book.

"It's a day hike," I started hesitantly. "Maybe we could go to Crete before going to Santorini. You could do something in town while I hike the gorge. Then we could meet up for dinner…and you know, share our day."

"Let's talk about it later," he said. "I'll check out the book when you're finished."

After the holidays, Karl said, "I've been thinking about our trip. Do you still need to do hiking?"

"I would like to do a day hike if we can work it in—if not, it will be okay." I was making peace with holding off on hiking in Greece since Karl couldn't. I told myself I could hike some other time.

Spring found me not just cleaning but also making plans to paint the entire inside of my house. Taking a break from painting preparations one morning, I was sitting at the computer going over my monthly bills when I found myself drawn to REI's travel website. I looked at the information on the Greek Island Hopper Adventures scheduled for the summer.

REI had completely sold out the first two adventures. That's when it hit me. This was something my soul had yearned to do for a long time. It also hit me that I might never again have the opportunity to hike Samaria Gorge. The saying "tomorrow isn't promised" isn't cliché when you're sixty-five—it's reality. As I sat there I had another epiphany: I would not be able to live with the ache of regret.

I immediately called REI. The staff person explained the full payment was due sixty days prior to the trip start date. She asked if I wanted to pay the deposit then and call back in two days to pay the remaining balance. I said, "I'm all the way in, 100 percent committed! Charge the full amount right now." Although I was acting with boldness, there was a part of me that was afraid that if I didn't fully commit right then, something would come up to prevent me from going.

I didn't know how or what I was going to tell Karl. I expected his feelings would be hurt and I dreaded being the cause. On the other hand, I hoped he would understand and that we'd work through it and still do our vacation together in October. It took me more than a month to tell Karl that I had booked the hiking trip.

"I understand," he said. "I'm happy for you."

As I looked in his eyes, my heart didn't believe either was true.

Three weeks later, Helen drove me to the metro station.

"Denise, I can take you to LAX," she said, eyeing my luggage.

"I know you can. I also know I need to learn to pack lighter. But that's a lesson for another trip. I'm good. No point in you having to drive in all that airport traffic."

"Okay, have it your way. Gimme a hug and get going." We hugged, and as we separated, Helen said, "Denise, I'm so proud of you. You need to do this for you."

"I know," I said, giving her another hug. "Thanks for the ride. See you in two weeks."

Helen was right. I needed to honor the promise I made to myself. As I boarded the plane, I felt a mixture of excitement and nervousness—wondering if I would fit in with the other members of the tour group, keep pace with everyone on the hikes, and hold onto my passport and credit cards. Fifteen and a half hours later, as I deplaned in Athens, I was excited and confident. *You're here, really here,* I told myself. "Girl, if you can do Greece, you can do the Camino. But don't get ahead of yourself. One trip at a time."

The airport in Athens reminded me of LAX except the signs were different. It was all Greek to me! As I hailed a cab I wanted to shout: "Greece, I'm here! Bring it on!"

The cab made its way to the hotel, through the ancient and modern areas of the city. We passed a Roman arch that was built in 131 CE. A short distance later, I saw the remaining colossal columns of the Temple of Olympian Zeus, built between 515 BCE and 132 CE. I was amazed to see the ruins of the Acropolis perched on a hill from almost anywhere in the city. By contrast, my hotel was modern silver and black art deco.

Eager to meet the other people in my tour group, I was the first person to arrive at the REI designated spot in the hotel lobby, followed by our tour guide and newlyweds from Philadelphia. Next to arrive was a tall man dressed in khaki knee-length shorts and a white short-sleeve shirt that highlighted his healthy tan. Lean and fit, he looked like a man comfortable with outdoor adventures.

I'm Rick," he said, extending his hand. "I'm here with my wife, Marissa, and our two daughters. They'll be down shortly."

"I'm Denise, from Los Angeles."

"We're from Denver, and we've been traveling almost a month now. We just finished the last 115 kilometers of the Camino de Santiago."

My heart almost stopped. After confirming Rick was indeed talking about the Camino that I'd been thinking about a few hours earlier, I began to pepper him with questions. He answered my questions and promised we'd talk more during the coming week.

El Camino de Santiago is a 500-mile pilgrimage from St. Jean Pied de Port in France, over the Pyrenees and across northern Spain. I first learned about the Camino two years earlier when I saw the movie *The Way*. I left the theater thinking, "I would like to do that someday!" In talking with Rick, I realized my Internet searches for information about the Camino had not been fruitful because I hadn't used the right search words. As time passed, I got busy with life and just filed it away. I hadn't thought about the Camino again until that morning when I arrived in Athens.

As I was talking with Rick, I knew the Camino would be my next trip. I got chills as I became aware that my hiking trip to Greece wasn't solely about me fulfilling a dream (although that was huge in and of itself). Rather, it was about me going to Greece at that particular time, for that specific REI Adventure, to get the information I needed for the next part of my life journey. I knew I was being guided by a higher power.

Some might say my meeting Rick was a lucky coincidence —you know, what appears to be the accidental merging of related events. The more preposterous the likelihood of those events coming together is perceived to be, the more likely the "coincidence" is considered extraordinary or remarkable. I always smile when I hear people talk about coincidences because I believe there are no coincidences. I believe events happen not by chance, but rather by design and purpose.

The German philosopher Goethe talked about what happens when one fully commits to a decision: "All sorts of things occur to help one that would never otherwise have occurred. A whole stream of events issues from the decision raising in one's favor all manner of unforeseen events, meetings and material assistance which no one could have dreamed would have come their way."

And so it was. My pilgrimage to El Camino de Santiago actually began the spring morning I booked my Greek hiking adventure.

❦

DENISE DIAAB is a writer who is striving to live her life in such a way as to be a channel of God's grace. Ms. Diaab says her primary legacy is her four children and three grandchildren. She is working on her first book, *Buen Camino: Getting to St. Jean Pied de Port,* in which she shares stories of personal growth, transformation and synchronicity in preparing for her 500-mile pilgrimage on El Camino de Santiago. She finished her Camino journey on June 22, 2016 after thirty-three days of walking.

Acknowledgments

Thank you:

Favianna Rodriguez for your stunning *Pleasure is Power* from YBCA's *Take This Hammer* exhibit. It has guided the journey.

Early readers Sarah Ladipo Manyika and Kendall Laidlaw.

Chris Bronstein—for having the idea and gifting it to me.

Essay writers—for bringing truth and light to these pages.

Carl Lumbly—whose love and wisdom nurtured my belief in this book.

Deborah Santana
November 2017

About the Editor

Deborah Santana is an author, seeker and activist for peace and social justice. She is founder of Do A Little, a nonprofit that serves women and girls in the areas of health, education and happiness. In 2005 she published a memoir, *Space Between the Stars: My Journey to an Open Heart.* Santana has produced five short documentary films. She is mother to three beloved adult children: Salvador, a songwriter and instrumental artist; Stella, a singer/songwriter; and Angelica, an archivist and film producer. She is a leadership donor to the Smithsonian National Museum of African American History and Culture and has a master's degree in philosophy and religion, with a concentration in women's spirituality.

CPSIA information can be obtained
at www.ICGtesting.com
Printed in the USA
FSOW01n2337041217
42026FS